500 Free Days Out

Credits

Reprinted 2005, 2006
© Automobile Association
Developments Limited 2005

A CIP catalogue record for this
book is available from the British
Library.

Directory generated by the AA
Establishment Database,
Information Research

All photographs in this guide
come from the AA World Travel
Library and were taken by: Rick
Strange (cover), Michael Busselle
(p1 background), Van Greaves (p1
foreground), Wyn Voysey (p3)
and Caroline Jones (p5)

Design by Jamie Wiltshire.
Typeset/Repro by iCandy Design
Ltd, Basingstoke
Printed by Everbest, China

Published by AA Publishing,
which is a trading name of
Automobile Association
Developments Limited, whose
registered office is Fanum House,
Basing View, Basingstoke,
Hampshire, RG21 4EA.
Registered number 1878835.

ISBN 07495 42705
A03096

500 Free Days Out

Welcome to the Guide

The AA's 500 Free Days Out provides information on a comprehensive selection of attractions in England, Scotland, Wales and Ireland, all free of admission charges. These range through factory tours, standing stones, castles, parks and gardens to town, city and national museums and art galleries. Through these pages, you can discover many of the country's most beautiful open spaces, ancient monuments, evocations of our cultural, industrial and social heritage and some of our finest collections of art. The entries give a short description for each attraction, along with contact details, opening times, how to get there, and specific facilities for parking, refreshments and accessibility.

How to Use this Guide

Sample Entry

1 — **NEWTOWN**

Museum & Art Gallery

Queen's Road BXX 1XX

3 — ☎ 01234 567890 📠 01234 567890

e museum@gov.uk

2 — **Dir:** Follow signs to City Centre, then follow tourist signs to Museum & Art Gallery

The Museum and Art Gallery is the largest in the region, with collections of local, national and international importance. It is located in an Edwardian building close to the university and offers a regularly changing temporary exhibition programme in addition to its large and diverse permanent collection. Free events and activities are a regular feature, please telephone for further details.

4 — **Times:** Open all year, daily 10-5. (Closed 25-26 Dec).

5 — **Facilities:** Ⓟ (NCP 400yds) ✕ (licenced) ♿ (lift) toilets for disabled 🐕 (ex guide dogs) 🚌 (pre-booked only)

1 THE DIRECTORY is arranged in countries, counties, then in alphabetical order by location within each county. County names appear down the side of each page.

2 DIRECTIONS may be given after the address of each attraction and where shown have been provided by the places of interest themselves. Please telephone for directions where these are not supplied.

3 TELEPHONE NUMBERS have the STD code shown before the telephone number. (If dialling Northern Ireland from England, Scotland or Wales, use the STD code, but for the Republic of Ireland you need to prefix the number with 00353, and drop the first zero from the Irish area code).

④ OPENING TIMES quoted in the guide are inclusive – for instance, where you see Apr-Oct, that place will be open from the beginning of April to the end of October.

⑤ FACILITIES This section includes information on parking, refreshments, accessibility and whether dogs are allowed admission. Visitors with mobility disabilities should look for the wheelchair symbol showing where all or most of the attraction is accessible to wheelchair users. We strongly recommend that you telephone in advance of your visit to check the exact details, particularly regarding access to toilets and refreshment facilities. Assistance dogs are usually accepted where the attractions show the 'No Dogs' symbol unless otherwise stated.

See page 6 for a key to the Symbols and Abbreviations used in this guide.

PLEASE NOTE Opening times and free admission policies are subject to change. There may be charges made for parking, toilets or audio equipment etc.

Please check with the attraction before making your journey.

Key to Symbols and Abbreviations

☎ Telephone number

📄 Fax number

♿ Suitable for visitors in wheelchairs plus further information for disabled visitors

🅿 Parking at Establishments

🅿 Parking nearby

🅿 Parking nearby

✗ Restaurant

🐕 No Dogs

🚌 Info on coaches

* Opening dates & times are for 2004. Please telephone to confirm.

💳 Credit cards. Attractions that accept credit cards in their shop or for special exhibitions.

✥ Cadw (Welsh Historic Monuments)

❖ English Heritage

❦ National Trust

❦ National Trust for Scotland

🔖 Historic Scotland

BH Bank Holidays

PH Public Holidays

Etr Easter

ex except

6

AMPTHILL

Houghton House

Dir: 1m NE off A421

Now a ruin, Houghton House was built for Mary Countess of Pembroke, the sister of Sir Philip Sidney, in 1621. Sadly, she didn't have long to enjoy the property as she died three years later. A grand frieze on the western front of the house, incorporating heraldic devices of the Sidney and Dudley families, is thought to be the work of Inigo Jones. The pine panelling from the Haynes Grange Room is now exhibited in the Victoria & Albert Museum, and the staircase, attributed to Christopher Wren, is now in the Swan Hotel, Bedford. The mansion is believed to have been the inspiration for the 'House Beautiful' in Bunyan's 'Pilgrim's Progress'.

Times: *Open all reasonable times.
Facilities: 🅿 ♿ Ground floor, Garden & Grounds accessible 🚌 ⌗

LUTON

John Dony Field Centre

Hancock Drive Bushmead LU2 7SF
☎ 01582 486983
📧 donyj@luton.gov.uk

Dir: Signed from rdbt on A6, at Barnfield College on New Bedford Rd

This is a purpose-built study centre for exploring the landscapes, plants and animals of the Luton area. Featuring permanent displays on local archaeology, natural history and the management of the local nature reserve, it explains how ancient grasslands and hedgerows are conserved and follows 4,000 years of history from the Bronze Age to modern times. Sessions at the Field Centre, combined with fieldwork on a number of sites in the borough, cover a range of study areas, including rivers, hedgerows, minibeasts, habitats, ecosystems, dinosaurs, settlements, and land use and conservation.

Times: *Open all year, Mon-Fri 9.30-4.45. Closed BHs.
Facilities: 🅿 🅿 (100mtrs) ♿ all parts accessible toilets for disabled ✖ (ex assist dogs) 🚌 (prior booking required)

LUTON

Stockwood Park Museum

Stockwood Country Park Farley Hill LU1 4BH
☎ 01582 738714 🖹 01582 546763
✆ museum.gallery@luton.gov.uk

Dir: Signed from M1 J10 and from Hitchin, Dunstable, Bedford and from Luton town centre

This museum of rural crafts and trades is set in parkland, two miles south of Luton town centre, where Stockwood House once stood. The Period Gardens reflect nine centuries of gardening history, including an Elizabethan knot garden and Victorian cottage gardens, while the classical-style Improvement Garden features sculptures by Scottish artist Ian Hamilton Finlay. The Mossman collection of over 50 horse-drawn vehicles traces the history of transport from Roman times to the 1940s. Craft demonstrations, events and activities are held throughout the year, please telephone for details.

Times: *Open all year; Mar-Oct, Tue-Sun 10-5; Nov-Mar, wknds 10-4. (closed Xmas & 1 Jan) Facilities: 🅿 Ⓟ (200mtrs) (coach parking by appointment) 🍽 ♿ all parts accessible (stair lift, parking, induction loop, automatic door) toilets for disabled ✻ (ex guide & hearing dogs) 🚌 (advance bookings)

LUTON

Wardown Park Museum

Wardown Park Old Bedford Road LU2 7HA
☎ 01582 546722 🖹 01582 546763
✆ museum.gallery@luton.gov.uk

Dir: Follow brown signs N from town centre. Turn off A6 towards Bedford

The museum is housed in a Victorian mansion, with displays illustrating the natural and cultural history, archaeology and industries of the area. These include the development of Luton's hat industry and the Bedfordshire and Hertfordshire Regimental Collections. More recent additions are the 'Luton Life' displays, which tell the story of the town and its residents over the past 200 years. Please telephone for details of exhibitions and events held throughout the year.

Times: Open all year, Tue-Sat 10-5, Sun 1-5 (Closed Xmas, 1 Jan & Mon ex BH Mons). Facilities: 🅿 Ⓟ (500mtrs) 🍽 ♿ all parts accessible (parking adjacent to entrance, lift to 1st floor) toilets for disabled ✻ (ex guide dogs & hearing dogs) 🚌 (advance bookings only)

NEWBURY

West Berkshire Museum

The Wharf RG14 5AS
☎ 01635 30511 📠 01635 38535
✉ heritage@westberks.gov.uk

Dir: From London take M4 J13, then S on A34, follow signs for town centre

Two of Newbury's most historic buildings on the town's wharf house the West Berkshire Museum: the Cloth Hall built 1626-1627, and the Granary in 1723. The latter dates from the opening of the River Kennet Navigation, when Newbury became a thriving inland port. The two buildings were linked when new galleries were built in 1934, and the Granary Tea Rooms and Desmoulin Gallery are located on part of the ground floor. Apart from local history and archaeology, birds and fossils, the museum displays costume and other decorative art.

Times: *Open all year: Apr-Sep, Mon-Fri (Wed during school hols only) 10-5, Sat 10-4.30. Oct-Mar, Mon-Sat (Wed during school hols only) 10-4. (Closed Sun & BHs).
Facilities: ℗ (15yds) ♿ Ground floor only accessible ✝ (ex guide dogs) 🚌 (advance booking, max 50)

BRISTOL

Blaise Castle House Museum

Henbury Road Henbury BS10 7QS
☎ 0117 903 9818 📠 0117 959 3475
✉ general_museum@bristol-city.gov.uk

Dir: 4m NW of city, off B4057

Blaise Castle is a folly built in 1766 by Thomas Farr and used as a summer house by the Harford family, who later built Blaise Castle House, which since 1949 has been a branch of the Bristol City Museum and Art Gallery. The mansion, designed by Thomas Paty, is set in lovely parkland designed by Humphrey Repton, including wooded areas, rocks and pathways down to where the River Trym flows through a gorge. Interesting buildings are dotted about the grounds, including a watermill rescued in the 1960s and cottages for pensioned-off staff. Inside the museum you'll find a Victorian school room, kitchens, laundry, toys, model trains, costume displays and a Victorian Picture Room hung with paintings.

Times: Open all year, Sat-Wed, 10-5.
Facilities: 🅿 ℗ (200yds) ♿ Ground floor, Garden & Grounds accessible ✝ (ex guide dogs) 🚌 (pre-booked)

Bristol City Museum & Art Gallery

Queen's Road Clifton BS8 1RL
☎ 0117 922 3571 ▯ 0117 922 2047
✉ general_museum@bristol-city.gov.uk

Dir: Follow signs to City Centre, then follow tourist signs to City Museum & Art Gallery

Awarded Designated status by the Government, the City Museum and Art Gallery is the largest in the region, with collections of local, national and international importance. It is located in an Edwardian Baroque building close to the university and offers a regularly changing temporary exhibition programme in addition to its large and diverse permanent collection. Art galleries upstairs include Old Masters, French School, British Collection, Modern Art and Bristol School. Museum galleries offer sections on archaeology, Egyptology, world wildlife, the natural history of the Southwest (with a freshwater aquarium), costume and pottery. Free events and activities are a regular feature, please telephone for further details.

Times: Open all year, daily 10-5. (Closed 25-26 Dec).
Facilities: ▯ (NCP 400yds) ▯ (licenced) ᙐ (lift) toilets for disabled ✘ (ex guide dogs) ▭ (pre-booking)

Bristol Industrial Museum

Prince's Wharf
Prince St City Docks BS1 4RN
☎ 0117 925 1470 ▯ 0117 729 7318
✉ general_museum@bristol-city.gov.uk

Dir: Within walking distance of the city centre

The museum is housed in a converted dockside transit shed. Motor and horse-drawn vehicles from the Bristol area are shown, with locally built aircraft and aero-engines. Railway exhibits include the industrial locomotive 'Henbury'. At weekends from April to October there are trips around the harbour in the tug 'John King', the steam tug 'Mayflower', or the fire boat 'Pyronant'. Alternatively, there are trips around the dockside on the Bristol Harbour Railway. On certain weekends visitors can watch the steam crane and electric crane at work.

Times: Open all year Sat-Wed 10-5
Facilities: ▯ charged ᙐ all parts accessible toilets for disabled ✘ (ex guide dogs) ▭ (pre-book)

Red Lodge

Park Row BS1 5LJ
☎ 0117 921 1360 🖷 0117 922 2047
✉ general_museum@bristol-city.gov.uk

Dir: 5 mins walk from Bristol City Centre

Built in 1590 as the lodge to a Great House where Queen Elizabeth once stayed, the Red Lodge has a magnificent Great Oak Room, accessed by a winding staircase, with oak panelling, a carved stone fireplace and plasterwork ceiling - all original. The house was extended in the Georgian era and there are some interesting rooms from the period. In 1854 the house was opened as a Reform School for girls by Mary Carpenter, and one room is dedicated to her. The garden has now been laid out in Elizabethan knot garden style, walled and south-facing. Living history days are themed around life in the 17th and 18th centuries. Please telephone for details.

Times: Open Sat-Wed 10-5.
Facilities: 🅿 (NCP, adjacent) 🐕 (ex guide dogs) 🚌 (pre-booking)

The Georgian House

7 Great George St off Park Street BS1 5RR
☎ 0117 921 1362 🖷 0117 922 2047
✉ general_museum@bristol-city.gov.uk

Dir: 5 mins walk from Bristol City Centre

The Georgian House is a carefully preserved example of a late 18th-century merchant's town house, with many original features. Four of the six storeys are open to visitors and the rooms have been furnished to illustrate life both above and below stairs. These include two drawing rooms, a bedroom, library, an authentically equipped kitchen and cold-water plunge bath in the basement. A small display recounts Bristol's involvement in the slave trade.

Times: Open Sat-Wed, 10-5.
Facilities: 🅿 (pay & display street parking) 🐕 (ex guide dogs) 🚌 (pre-booking)

BRISTOL

HIGH WYCOMBE

Wycombe Museum

Castle Hill House Priory Avenue HP13 6PX
☎ 01494 421895 📠 01494 421897
✉ museum@wycombe.gov.uk

Dir: Brown tourist sign from A404 (Amersham Hill) N of High Wycombe town centre just past railway station

Local history museum for the Wycombe area with a particular focus on the furniture industry, including the the notable Windsor chair collection and displays of regional Thames Valley chairs and Wycombe-made Ercol and G-Plan furniture. Buckinghamshire lace displays are another attraction. The museum is situated in an 18th-century house set in attractive grounds. Temporary exhibitions and hands-on children's activities feature.

Times: *Open all year, Mon-Sat 10-5, Sun 2-5. Closed on BHs except special events - ring for details. **Facilities:** 🅿 🅟 (on road outside) (town centre multi-storey 5mins walk) 🍴 ♿ Ground floor, Garden & Grounds accessible (special parking & drop off point) toilets for disabled ✖ (ex guide dogs) 🚌 (pre-booking) 🚭

CAMBRIDGE

Fitzwilliam Museum

Trumpington Street CB2 1RB
☎ 01223 332900 📠 01223 332923
✉ fitzmuseum-enquiries@lists.cam.ac.uk

Dir: M11 J11, 12 or 13. Near city centre

The Fitzwilliam is the art museum of the University of Cambridge and one of the oldest public museums in Britain, founded by bequest of Richard, the 7th Viscount Fitzwilliam of Merrion, in 1816. He left his works of art and his library to the university, along with the money to house them. Over the years the collections have grown, through gift, bequest and purchase, and now contain some half a million items of national and international importance spanning centuries and civilisations, including antiquities from Ancient Egypt, Greece and Rome; sculpture, furniture, armour, ceramics; manuscripts, coins and medals, paintings, drawings and prints.

Times: *Open all year Tue-Sat 10-5, Sun 12-5. (Closed Mon ex BH, & 24-26, 31 Dec & 1 Jan). **Facilities:** 🅟 (400yds) (2hr max, metered) 🍴 ♿ all parts accessible (induction loop) toilets for disabled ✖ (ex guide dogs) 🚌 (pre-booking essential)

CAMBRIDGE

Scott Polar Research Institute Museum

Lensfield Road CB2 1ER
☎ 01223 336540 🖷 01223 336549
✉ rkh10@cam.ac.uk

Dir: 1km S of City Centre

An international centre for polar studies, including a museum featuring displays of Arctic and Antarctic expeditions, with special emphasis on those of Captain Scott. Other exhibits include Eskimo work and various arts of the polar regions, as well as displays on current scientific exploration. Public lectures run from October to December and February to April. Special exhibitions are a regular feature.

Times: Open all year, Tue-Sat 2.30-4. Closed some public & university hols.
Facilities: ℗ (400mtrs) ₺ all parts accessible ✗ (ex guide dogs) 🚌 (pre-booking essential)

CAMBRIDGE

University Museum of Archaeology & Anthropology

Downing Street CB2 3DZ
☎ 01223 333516 🖷 01223 333517
✉ cumaa@hermes.cam.ac.uk

Dir: Located opp Crowne Plaza Hotel

The museum is part of the Faculty of Archaeology and Anthropology of the University of Cambridge. It was established in 1884 and is still housed in its 1916 building on the Downing Site in the city centre. It has three floors displaying renowned archaeological and anthropological collections from around the world. The ground floor is devoted to world pre-history and local archaeology; the first floor, social anthropology (historical and geographical), while on the third floor special exhibitions are shown reflecting current research.

Times: Open all year Tue-Sat 2-4.30. (Closed 1wk Etr & 1wk Xmas). Telephone for extended summer hours.
Facilities: ℗ (100yds) ₺ all parts accessible (lift available) ✗ (ex guide dogs) 🚌 (pre-booking essential)

CHESTER

Chester Visitor Centre

Vicars Lane CH1 1QX
☎ 01244 351609 📠 01244 403188
✉ tis@chestercc.gov.uk

Dir: Opp St Johns Church Roman Amphitheatre on Vicars Lane

Among the attractions at this large visitor information centre are guided walks of Chester; brass rubbing; candle-making; World of Names, which explores the history of family and first names; displays on the history of Chester; a café and a gift shop. Chester is the most complete walled city in Britain, and was originally settled by the Romans in the first century AD. The city also played its part in battles with the Vikings, the Norman invasion, and the Civil War.

Times: Open all year,
Mon-Sat 10-5, Sun 10-4
Facilities: ℗ (200mtrs) (short stay visitor parking) 🍽 ♿ Ground floor, Garden & Grounds accessible (ramped access from Vicars Lane) toilets for disabled
🐕 (ex guide dogs) 🚌

FOWEY

St Catherine's Castle

Dir: 0.75m SW of Fowey along footpath off A3082

St Catherine's Castle is a small fort built by Henry VIII to defend Fowey Harbour. It has two storeys with gun ports at ground level. Below the 16th-century fort is a two-gun battery built in 1855. The fort recalls a time when Fowey was the chief port in Cornwall, rather than the fishing village and seaside resort we see today.

Times: *Open all year,
any reasonable time.
Facilities: ℗ (0.5m) 🐕 (ex dogs on leads)
🚌 ♿

SANCREED

Carn Euny Ancient Village

Dir: 1.25m SW of Sancreed, off A30

The remains of an Iron-Age settlement, occupation of which seems to have ended around the end of the last century. The surviving features of the village, once inhabited by hill farmers, include the foundations of stone huts and an intriguing curved underground passage or 'fogou' at the centre. This comprises a 20-metre long passage, which a grown man can stand upright in, with a circular side chamber with a small opening in the roof where light floods in. One can only speculate on the function of the fougou, which remains a mystery to modern man.

Times: *Open any reasonable time.
Facilities: P (600mtrs)

BROUGH

Brough Castle

CA17 4EJ

☎ 191 261 1585 **Dir:** 8m SE of Appleby, S of A66

Brough Castle, now a ruin, was originally built around 1100 on the site of the Roman camp of Verteris. It was in an area much disputed by the Scots and the English, and the Scots destroyed the castle in 1174. In 1203 Robert de Vieuxpont was given the castle by King John, and he added a gatehouse and hall, but over time the castle fell into disrepair. In the 14th century Roger Clifford replaced the hall and the castle became a family home until 1521 when it was rendered uninhabitable by fire. Lady Anne Clifford restored the castle in the 17th century and you can still see the outline of her kitchen gardens.

Times: *Open any reasonable time.
Facilities: P (ex dogs on leads)

CARLISLE

The Guildhall Museum

Green Market CA3 8JE
☎ 01228 534781 📠 01228 810249
✉ barbaral@carlisle-city.gov.uk

Dir: Town centre, opposite
The Crown & Mitre Hotel

*One of Carlisle's oldest buildings, dating
from around 1405 and Grade I listed. The
Guildhall was once the meeting place of
Carlisle's eight trade guilds, few of which
still meet today. Experience the cabin-like
atmosphere of the shoemaker's room and
the 'modernised' butcher's room with its
Victorian features. There are amazing
objects such as the medieval town chest,
dating from around 1400, two small silver
balls (one dated 1599), reputed to be the
earliest surviving horse racing prizes in the
country.*

Times: Open Apr-Oct, 12-4.30
Facilities: Ⓟ (500yds) (disc parking on
street, 1 hr limit) ✘ (ex guide dogs) � (no
disabled access, steep stairs)

HARDKNOTT CASTLE ROMAN FORT

Hardknott Castle Roman Fort

Dir: 9m NE of Ravenglass, at W end
of Hardknott Pass

*Hardknott Roman Fort, called
Mediobogdum by the Romans, is one of
the most dramatic Roman sites in Britain,
with stunning views over the Lakeland
fells. Built between AD 120 and AD 138,
the fort controlled the road from
Ravenglass to Ambleside and 500
infantrymen were stationed here. The
remains include the headquarters building,
commandant's house and granaries, with a
bath house and parade ground outside the
walls.*

Times: *Open any reasonable time. Access
may be hazardous in winter.
Facilities: ✘ (ex dogs on leads) 🦌

PENRITH

Wetheriggs Country Pottery

Clifton Dykes CA10 2DH
☎ 01768 892733
🖶 01768 892733 ext 231
✉ info@wetheriggs-pottery.co.uk

Dir: Approx 2m off A6, S from Penrith, signed

The only steam-powered pottery in Britain, Wetheriggs is a 19th-century industrial monument. The pottery was founded in the 1860s by John Schofield and Margaret Thorburn and restored in the mid 1990s. Guided tours are available all through the year and you can see designer-makers at work. There are 7.5 acres of things to do, including the Pots of Fun Studio, where you can throw or paint a pot, the pottery museum, play areas, newt pond, café, bistro and shops.

Times: Open daily, Winter 10-5, Summer 10-5.30
Facilities: 🅿 🍴 ✗ (licenced) ♿ Ground floor, Garden & Grounds accessible toilets for disabled ✖ (ex guide dogs) 🚌 (pre-booking essential) 🍴

SEDBERGH

National Park Centre

72 Main Street LA10 5AS
☎ 015396 20125 🖶 015396 21732
✉ sedbergh@yorkshiredales.org.uk

Dir: On Sedburgh main street at end of one way system

At the north-western corner of the Yorkshire Dales National Park, Sedbergh is set below the Howgill Fells. The rich natural history of the area and the beautiful scenery created a need for this visitor centre - the park's only visitor centre in the county of Cumbria - located in the centre of the town. Maps, walks, guides, local information and interpretative displays can be found here, and there is a full tourist information service.

Times: *Open Apr-Oct, daily 10-4; Nov-Mar Fri-Sun.
Facilities: 🅿 charged 🅿 ♿ all parts accessible (accessible with help Radar key scheme) 🚌

SHAP

Shap Abbey

CA10 3NB

Dir: 1.5m W of Shap on bank of River Lowther

In an isolated spot in the wilds of Cumbria the Premonstratensian order founded this abbey, dedicated to St Mary Magdalene, in 1199. Most of the ruins you see today date from 13th-century date but the most impressive feature is the 15th-century west tower of the church, built by Richard Redman, abbot of Shap for 50 years until his death in 1505. The abbey escaped the first phase of the Dissolution in 1536 but was suppressed in 1540. The church was demolished and the stone quarried, and the monastic buildings were incorporated into farm buildings.

Times: *Open any reasonable time.
Facilities: ◘ & all parts accessible ✖ (ex dogs on leads) ▭

DENBY

Denby Pottery Visitor Centre

Derby Road DE5 8NX
☎ 01773 740799 ▤ 01773 740749
✉ visitor.centre@denby.co.uk

Dir: 8m N of Derby off A38, on B6179, 2m S of Ripley

The visitor centre is situated around a cobbled courtyard including shops and a restaurant. Pottery tours are available daily and offer hands on activities such as painting a plate and making a clay souvenir. The extensive cookshop runs free half-hour demonstrations daily. There is a factory shop selling Denby seconds, hand-made blown glass from the Glass Studio, a Dartington Crystal Shop, local artists' gallery and hand painted Denby.

Times: Open all year. Factory tours, Mon-Thu 10.30 & 1. Craftroom tour, daily 11-3. Visitor Centre Mon-Sat 9.30-5, Sun 10-5. Closed 25-26 Dec.
Facilities: ◘ ◕ ✖ (licenced) & all parts accessible (lift) toilets for disabled ✖ (outside only, ex guide dogs) ▭ (pre-book for tour visit) ◀

DERBY

Derby Museum & Art Gallery

The Strand DE1 1BS
☎ 01332 716659 ▤ 01332 716670
✉ david.fraser@derby.gov.uk

Dir: Follow directions to city centre

The museum has a wide range of displays, most notably the collection of Derby porcelain, made in the city since 1750, and the largest collection in the world of paintings by local artist Joseph Wright (1734-97). There are also archaeology and militaria galleries, a Bonnie Prince Charlie Room commemorating Derby's role in the Jacobite uprising, and a Derbyshire geology and wildlife feature. The museum also has a temporary exhibition programme and school holiday activities.

Times: Open all year, Mon 11-5, Tue-Sat 10-5, Sun & BHs 2-5. Closed Xmas & New Year, telephone for details.
Facilities: ℗ (50yds) & all parts accessible (lift to all floors, portable mini-loop, large print labels) toilets for disabled
✖ (ex guide dogs) ⊟

DERBY

Industrial Museum

The Silk Mill Silk Mill Lane off Full Street DE1 3AR
☎ 01332 255308 ▤ 01332 716670
✉ david.fraser@derby.gov.uk

Dir: From Derby inner ring road, head for Cathedral & Assembly Rooms car park. 5 mins walk from here

The museum is set in an early 18th-century silk mill and adjacent flour mill. Displays cover local mining, quarrying and castings from local foundries, and a major collection of Rolls Royce aero-engines from 1915 to the present day. There is also a section on the history of the Midland Railway network, with memorabilia, technology and a life-size engine driver's cab that you can step up into and imagine driving the train.

Times: Open all year, Mon 11-5, Tue-Sat 10-5, Sun & BHs 2-5. (Closed Xmas & New Year, telephone for details.
Facilities: ℗ ℗ (museum parking restricted to disabled) & all parts accessible (lift to all floors) toilets for disabled
✖ (ex guide dogs) ⊟

DERBY

Pickford's House Museum of Georgian Life & Costume

41 Friar Gate DE1 1DA
☎ 01332 255363 🖹 01332 255527
✉ ellen.malin@derby.gov.uk

Dir: From A38 into Derby, follow signs to city centre

The house was built in 1770 by the architect Joseph Pickford as a combined workplace and family home. It now shows domestic life at different periods, with Georgian reception rooms and service areas and a 1930's bathroom. Other galleries are devoted to temporary exhibitions. There is also a display on the growth of Georgian Derby, and on Pickford's contribution to Midlands' architecture.

Times: Open all year, Mon 11-5, Tue-Sat 10-5, Sun & BHs 2-5. (Closed Xmas & New Year, telephone for details).
Facilities: 🅿 🅿 (500metres) ♿ Ground floor, Garden & Grounds accessible (tape guides, video with sign language subtitles) ✖ (ex guide dogs) 🚌 (no parking facilities for coaches)

OLD WHITTINGTON

Revolution House

High Street S41 9LA
☎ 01246 345727 🖹 01246 345720
✉ museum@chesterfieldbc.gov.uk

Dir: 3m N of Chesterfield town centre, on B6052 off A61, signed

The Revolution House is located in the village of Old Whittington, three miles north of Chesterfield. Originally the Cock and Pynot alehouse, it was the scene of a meeting between three local noblemen - the Earl of Devonshire, the Earl of Danby and Mr John D'Arcy - to plan their part in the Revolution of 1688. The house is now furnished in 17th-century style. A video relates the story of the Revolution and there is a small temporary exhibition room.

Times: Open Good Fri-Sep, daily 11-4 (ex Tue). Contact museum for Xmas opening hours.
Facilities: 🅿 (100yds) ♿ Ground floor, Garden & Grounds accessible (signing available by prior arrangement) ✖ (ex guide dogs) 🚌 (by prior arrangement)

BUCKFASTLEIGH

Buckfast Abbey

TQ11 0EE
☎ 01364 645500 📠 01364 643891
✉ enquiries@buckfast.org.uk

> **Dir:** 0.5m from A38, midway between Exeter and Plymouth. Turn off at 'Dart Bridge' junct and follow brown tourist signs

The Abbey, founded in 1018, was dissolved by Henry VIII in the 16th century. Restoration began in 1907, when four monks with little building experience began the work. The church was built on the old foundations, using local blue limestone and Ham Hill stone. The precinct contains several medieval monastic buildings, including the 14th-century guest hall where there is an exhibition of the history of the Abbey.

Times: *Open all year daily. Closed Good Fri, 24-26 Dec.
Facilities: 🅿 ❖ (licensed) ♿ all parts accessible (Braile & audio information) toilets for disabled
✈ (ex guide dogs) 🚌 🛒

DARTMOUTH

Bayard's Cove Fort

TQ6 9AT

> **Dir:** In Dartmouth on riverfront

This single-storey Tudor artillery fort was built by the townspeople to protect the harbour from hostile vessels that might have managed to slip past the castles at Kingswear and Dartmouth. The remains of the circular stronghold still stand at the southern end of the harbour and it looks particularly impressive from the river.

Times: *Open at all reasonable times.
Facilities: 🚌 ❖

Guildhall

High Street EX4 3EB
☎ 01392 665500
✉ guildhall@exeter.gov.uk

Dir: In city centre

Exeter Guildhall is one of the oldest municipal buildings still in use. It was built in 1330 and then altered in 1446, and the arches and façade were added in 1592-5. The roof timbers rest on bosses of bears holding staves, and there are portraits of Exeter dignitaries, guild crests, civic silver and regalia. Exeter has a roll of mayors going back even longer than London.

Times: *Open when there are no mayoral functions. Times are posted outside weekly. Special opening by arrangement.
Facilities: P (200yds) & Ground floor only accessible toilets for disabled ✗ (ex guide dogs) ⊟

Royal Albert Memorial Museum

Queen St EX4 3RX
☎ 01392 265858 🖷 01392 421252

Dir: In city centre

Situated in the heart of Exeter, the Royal Albert Memorial Museum is home to 16 galleries of displays and a lively programme of events and exhibitions. Its World Cultures collection has received Designated status as a mark of its importance. Exhibits allow you to travel in time form pre-history to the present day and take a voyage of discovery from Exeter all around the world. The museum is also home to the city's largest gallery and exhibition space.

Times: *Open Mon-Sat 10-5.
Facilities: P (200yds) ● & All parts accessible (parking, ramp) toilets for disabled ✗ (ex guide dogs) ⊟

DEVON

LYDFORD

Lydford Castle and Saxon Town

EX20 4BH

Dir: In Lydford off A386

The tower of Lydford Castle stands above the gorge of the River Lyd, it dates from the 12th century and was once notorious as a prison. The earthworks of the earlier Norman fort lie to the south. Lydford is the site of the Anglo-Saxon town Hlidan, built in about AD 890 by King Alfred the Great to defend Wessex from the Vikings. Anglo-Saxon defensive earthworks can still be seen.

Times: *Open all reasonable times.
Facilities: 🅿 🚍 ♿

OTTERTON

Otterton Mill

EX9 7HG
☎ 01392 568521
✉ escape@ottertonmill.com

Dir: On the B3178 between Budleigh Salterton and Newton Poppleford

Set beside the River Otter in one of Devon's loveliest valleys, Otterton Mill is a centuries-old working watermill, incorporating a renowned bakery and shop full of local produce. The mill fell into disrepair in the mid 20th-century but was restored in 1977 and regularly mills organic corn on alternate Mondays. There is also a restaurant on site, artists' studios, and a gallery exhibiting artwork and crafts by local artists and craftspeople. Live music is a feature on Thursday nights.

Times: Open every day from 10.
Facilities: 🅿 🅿 (100yds) ✗ (licenced) ♿ Ground floor, Garden & Grounds accessible (free entry to ground floor)
🚍 (pre-booked) 🍴

DEVON

PLYMOUTH

City Museum & Art Gallery

Drake Circus PL4 8AJ
☎ 01752 304774 📠 01752 304775
✉ museum@plymouth.gov.uk

Dir: Off A38 onto A374, museum NW of city centre, opp university

The City Museum and Art Gallery is home to a Fine and Decorative Art Collection of paintings, prints and Reynolds family portraits, silver and Plymouth China, and the Cottonian Collection of drawings, sculpture and books. There is a lively programme of art exhibitions, as well as archaeology, local and natural history displays, and the Discovery Centre with a 'hands-on' section for children.

Times: *Open all year, Tue-Fri 10-5.30, Sat 10-5, BH Mon 10-5.
Closed Good Fri & 25-26 Dec.
Facilities: ℗ (200yds) ♿ all parts accessible (wheelchair available) toilets for disabled ✖ (ex guide dogs) 🚾

YELVERTON

Yelverton Paperweight Centre

4 Buckland Terrace Leg O'Mutton Corner PL20 6AD
☎ 01822 854250 📠 01822 854250
✉ paperweightcentre@btinternet.com

Dir: At Yelverton off A386, Plymouth to Tavistock road

This unusual centre is the home of the Broughton Collection - a glittering permanent collection of glass paperweights of all sizes and designs. Bernard Broughton collected paperweights over many years, inspired by the legacy of a rare French paperweight to his wife. The centre also has an extensive range of modern glass paperweights for sale. Prices range from a few pounds to over £1,000. There is also a series of oil and watercolour paintings by talented local artists.

Times: *Open Apr-Oct, daily 10.30-5; 10-24 Dec, daily; Nov & Jan-Mar wknds only or by appointment.
Facilities: ℗ (100yds) ♿ Ground floor only accessible (ramp on request) 🚾 (advance booking requested) 🍴

CHRISTCHURCH

Christchurch Castle & Norman House

Dir: Near Christchurch Priory

Although ruined, the 12th-century Constable's House on the river bank has one of only five Norman chimneys left in Britain and one of the earliest lavatories. Just behind the Norman Constable's House are the ruins of Christchurch Castle keep and motte. If you climb to the top of the mound you'll be rewarded with a fine view.

Times: *Open any reasonable time.
Facilities: 🚌 ⚏

CORFE CASTLE

Corfe Castle Museum

West Street BH20 5HE
☎ 01929 480974 🖨 01929 480974
✉ kenwollaston@tesco.net

Dir: To side of church on L of West St upon leaving village square

Corfe Castle Museum is housed in the smallest town hall building in England, a tiny rectangular property, partly rebuilt in brick after a fire in 1780. A council chamber on the first floor is reached by a staircase at one end. The Ancient Order of Marblers meets here each Shrove Tuesday. Museum exhibits include old village relics, and dinosaur footprints 130 million years old.

Times: *Open all year, Apr-Oct, daily 9.30-6; Nov-Mar, wknds and Xmas holidays 10-5.
Facilities: 🅿 (200yds) & Ground floor only accessible 🚌

DORCHESTER

Maiden Castle

DT1 9PR

Dir: 2m S of Dorchester, access off A354, N of bypass

Maiden Castle Iron Age fort ranks among the finest in Britain. It covers 47 acres, and has daunting earthworks with a complicated defensive system around the entrances. One of its main purposes may well have been to protect grain from marauding bands. The first single-rampart fort dates from around 700BC, and by 100BC the earthworks covered the whole plateau. It was finally overrun by Roman troops in AD 43.

Times: *Open any reasonable time.
Facilities: 🅿 🚌 🛱

POOLE

Waterfront Museum

4 High St BH15 1BW
☎ 01202 262600 📄 01202 262622
✉ museums@poole.gov.uk

Dir: Off Poole Quay

The museum tells the story of Poole's seafaring past. Learn of the Roman occupation and see material raised from the Studland Bay wreck. Scaplen's Court, just a few yards from the museum, is a beautifully restored domestic building dating from the medieval period. Although it is only open to the public in August, Scaplen's Court is not to be missed, with a Victorian school room, a kitchen and scullery.

Times: *Museum: open Apr-Oct, Mon-Sat 10-5, Sun noon-5; Nov-Mar, Mon-Sat 10-3, Sun noon-3. Scaplen's Court: Aug, Mon-Sat 10-5, Sun noon-5.
Facilities: 🅿 (250mtrs) ♿ all parts accessible (Scaplen's Court not accessible) toilets for disabled
🐕 (ex guide dogs) 🚌 🍴

TOLPUDDLE

Tolpuddle Martyrs Museum

DT2 7EH
☎ 01305 848237 📄 01305 848237
📧 jpickering@tuc.org.uk

Dir: Off A35 from Dorchester, Tolpuddle is signed at Troytown turn off. On old A35, Museum has brown sign giving clear directions

One dawn, in the bitter February of 1834, six Tolpuddle farm labourers were arrested after forming a trade union. A frightened squire's trumped up charge triggered one of the most celebrated stories in the history of human rights. That early morning arrest created the Tolpuddle Martyrs, who were punished with transportation as convicts to Australia. Packed with illustrative displays, this state-of-the-art, interactive exhibition tells the Tolpuddle Martyrs story. Every summer, the weekend of the third Sunday in July, the museum holds the Tolpuddle Martyrs Festival. The weekend combines celebration with traditional, offering both traditional and contemporary music as well as many other attractions.

Times: Open all year, Apr-Oct, Tue-Sat 10-5.30, Sun 11-5.30; Nov-Mar, Tue-Sat 10-4, Sun 11-4. Open BH Mon. Closed 20 Dec-2 Jan. **Facilities:** 🅿 (outside museum) ♿ all parts accessible (interactive computers at wheelchair height & parking) toilets for disabled 🐕 (ex guide dogs) 🚌 (prior booking required)

BARNARD CASTLE

Egglestone Abbey

DL12 8QN

Dir: 1m S of Barnard Castle on minor road off B6277

The picturesque ruins of Egglestone are located above a bend in the River Tees, and while the remains of the medieval monastery are scant they are nonetheless charming. The monastery was dissolved in 1540 and it is believed that the church tower was demolished shortly after. Stone from the site was taken for building elsewhere up until the early 20th century, but a large part of the church can still be seen, as can remnants of monastic buildings.

Times: *Open any reasonable time.
Facilities: 🅿 ♿ all parts accessible 🚌 🚻

BOWES

Bowes Castle

DL12 9LD

Dir: In Bowes village, just off A66

Bowes Castle is a Norman earthwork fortress believed to have been built by Alan, Earl of Richmond within the Roman fort of Lavatrae. Its job was to guard the Stainmore pass. In the 12th century King Henry II added the massive three-storey hall keep and fore-building. It's the ruin of this that still stands proud, overlooking the valley of the River Greta.

Times: *Open any reasonable time.
Facilities: & Ground floor, Garden & Grounds accessible ✿

SHILDON

Locomotion: The National Railway Museum at Shildon

DL4 1PQ
☎ 01388 777999 📄 01388 777999
✉ gill@hamer-loco.fsnet.co.uk

Dir: A1(M) J68, take A68 & A6072 to Shildon, museum is 0.25m SE of town centre

Timothy Hackwood (1786-1850) was an important figure in the development of steam travel. He constructed 'Puffing Billy' for William Hedley, ran Stephenson's Newcastle Works, and also became the first superintendent of the Stockton & Darlington Railway. The museum and house detail Hackwood's life and the steam transport revolution, as well as displaying working models and locomotives from various periods. Steam train rides are available throughout the year.

Times: Open 3 Nov-18 Mar, Wed-Sun 10-4. Closed 13 Dec-5 Jan. 19 Mar-30 Oct daily 10-5 **Facilities:** 🅿 🅿 ☕ & All parts accessible (bus available to transport guests, please contact) toilets for disabled ✗ (ex guide dogs) 🚍

HADLEIGH

Hadleigh Castle

☎ 01760 755161

Dir: 0.75m S of A13

The subject of paintings by both Constable and Turner, the castle has fine views of the Thames estuary and Essex marshes. Though ruined, the castle's northeast and southeast towers are still impressive. The castle dates from 1230 and was built for Hubert de Burgh, Chief Justiciar to King John and regent for the young King Henry II. The relationship soured and Henry confiscated the castle but continued with the building work. Further additions were made by Edward III in the 14th century and it is these that we still see today.

Times: *Open any reasonable time.
Facilities: (limited access due to hilly surroundings) 🚌 ✿

WALTHAM ABBEY

Waltham Abbey Gatehouse, Bridge & Entrance to Cloisters

☎ 01992 702200

Dir: In Waltham Abbey off A112

Beside the great Norman church at Waltham are the slight remains of the abbey buildings - bridge, gatehouse and part of the north cloister. The bridge is named after King Harold, the last Saxon king of England, who founded the abbey in 1060, and the gatehouse is a massive isolated tower.

Times: *Open any reasonable time.
Facilities: ♿ all parts accessible (sensory trail guide) 🚌 ✿

CHELTENHAM

Cheltenham Art Gallery & Museum

Clarence St GL50 3JT
☎ 01242 237431 📄 01242 262334
✉ artgallery@cheltenham.gov.uk

Dir: Close to town centre and bus station, 2 min walk from promenade

The museum has an outstanding collection relating to the Arts and Crafts Movement, including fine furniture and exquisite metalwork. The Art Gallery contains Dutch and British paintings from the 17th century to the present day. The Oriental Gallery features pottery, costumes and treasures from the Ming Dynasty to the reign of the last Chinese Emperor. There is also a display about Edward Wilson who journeyed with Captain Scott in 1911-12, together with the history of Britain's most complete Regency town and archaeological treasures from the neighbouring Cotswolds. Special exhibitions are held throughout the year.

Times: Open all year, Mon-Sat 10-5.20 (first Thu in month, 11-5.20). Closed BHs.
Facilities: 🅿 (500 mtrs) disabled parking on site ♥ ♿ all parts accessible (handling tables; speech reinforcement system) toilets for disabled 🐕 (ex guide dogs) 🚗 (prior notice preferred) 🍴

DEERHURST

Odda's Chapel

Dir: Off B4213 near River Severn at Abbots Court SW of parish church

This rare Saxon chapel was built by Earl Odda and dedicated in 1056. When it was discovered it had been incorporated into a medieval timber-framed farmhouse. It has now been carefully restored and retains its original chancel arch and Saxon windows. Odda was Earl of Hwicce, captain of the Royal Fleet and a kinsman of King Edward the Confessor.

Times: *Open Apr-Oct, daily 10-6; Nov-Mar, daily 10-4. Closed 24-26 Dec & 1 Jan.
Facilities: 🅿 charged 🚗

Gloucester City Museum & Art Gallery

Brunswick Road GL1 1HP
☎ 01452 396131 🖷 01452 410898
✉ city.museum@gloucester.gov.uk

Dir: Centre of Gloucester

There is something for everyone at this city museum and art gallery: an impressive range of Roman artefacts including the Rufus Sita tombstone; the Iron Age Birdlip Mirror; one of the earliest backgammon sets in the world; dinosaur fossils; and paintings by Turner and Gainsborough. You can also see full-sized dinosaurs; Gloucestershire wildlife; and beautiful antique furniture, glass, ceramics and silver. Hands-on displays, computer quizzes and activity workstations add to the fun, and there's an exciting programme of temporary exhibitions. Look out for children's holiday activities and special events.

Times: *Open all year, Tue-Sat 10-5.
Facilities: ℙ (500yds) ♿ all parts accessible toilets for disabled ✖ (ex guide dogs) 🚌 (advance booking) ▰

Gloucester Folk Museum

99-103 Westgate Street GL1 2PG
☎ 01452 396467 🖷 01452 330495
✉ folk.museum@gloucester.gov.uk

Dir: A40 and A48 from the W, A38 and M5 from the N, A40 & B4073 from the E and A4173 & A38 from the S

Three floors of splendid Tudor and Jacobean timber-framed buildings dating from the 16th and 17th centuries, along with new buildings housing the dairy, ironmonger's, wheelwright and carpenters' workshops. Local history, domestic life, crafts, trades and industries from 1500 to the present are reflected in the exhibits, including a childhood, the Siege of Gloucester, a Victorian classroom, Victorian kitchen and laundry equipment. Special exhibitions, hands-on activities, events, demonstrations and role play sessions are held throughout the year, and there's a cottage garden and courtyard for events, often with live animals and games.

Times: *Tue-Sat, 10-5 (For ten weeks only during half terms and holidays)
Facilities: ℙ (500yds) ♿ Ground floor, Garden & Grounds accessible (hands-on displays, virtual tour of Protal gallery) ✖ (ex guide dogs) 🚌 (book in advance) ▰

ASHTON-UNDER-LYNE

Central Art Gallery

Central Library Building Old Street OL6 7SG
☎ 0161 342 2650 🖶 0161 342 2650
📧 central.artgallery@tameside.gov.uk

Set in a fine Victorian Gothic building, the Central Art Gallery has three areas, each of which offers a varied programme of temporary exhibitions. A range of tastes and styles are covered, with group and solo shows of work by artists from the region including paintings, sculpture, installation and textiles.

Times: *Open all year, Tue, Wed & Fri 10-12.30 & 1-5; Thu 1-7.30 & Sat 9-12.30 & 1-4. **Facilities:** 🅿 (100mtrs) (pay and display) & all parts accessible (induction loop) toilets for disabled ✖ (ex guide dogs) 🚍

ASHTON-UNDER-LYNE

Museum of The Manchester Regiment

The Town Hall Market Place OL6 6DL
☎ 0161 342 3078 🖶 0161 343 2869
📧 portland.basin@tameside.gov.uk

Dir: In town centre, on market square, follow signs for museum

The Museum of the Manchester Regiment has reopened following refurbishment with new features including an extended World War 1 trench, a medals room, inter-active exhibits and items not previously on display. The regiment fought in both World Wars, the Boer War, and the Crimea War, and the museum explores the social and regimental history of the Manchesters, tracing the story back to its origins in the 18th century.

Times: Open all year, Mon-Sat, 10-4. (Closed Sun).
Facilities: 🅿 (50yds) (pay & display) & All parts accessible toilets for disabled ✖ (ex guide dogs) 🚍 (must pre-book, max 50 people)

ASHTON-UNDER-LYNE

Portland Basin Museum

Portland Place OL7 0QA
☎ 0161 343 2878 📠 0161 343 2869
✉ portland.basin@tameside.gov.uk

Dir: M60 J23 into Ashton town centre. Museum is near Cross Hill Street & car park

Exploring the social and industrial history of Tameside, this museum is part of the recently rebuilt Ashton Canal Warehouse, built in 1834. Visitors can walk around a 1920s street, dress up in old hats and gloves, steer a virtual canal boat, and see the original canal powered waterwheel that once drove the warehouse machinery. Portland Basin Museum also features changing exhibitions and event programme - so there's always something new to see!

Times: Open all year, Tue-Sun 10-5. (Closed Mon, ex BHs)
Facilities: 🅿 🅿 (100yds) 🍽 ♿ All parts accessible (wheelchair, lift, loop system) toilets for disabled
✖ (ex guide dogs) 🚌 🚄

MANCHESTER

Gallery of Costume

Platt Hall Rusholme M14 5LL
☎ 0161 224 5217 📠 0161 256 3278
✉ a.jarvis@notes.manchester.gov.uk

Dir: Situated in Platt Fields Park, Rusholme, access from Wilmslow Rd. 2m S of city centre

With one of the most comprehensive costume collections in Great Britain, this gallery makes captivating viewing. Housed in a fine Georgian mansion, the displays focus on the changing styles of everyday fashion and accessories over the last 400 years. Contemporary fashion is also illustrated. Because of the vast amount of material in the collection, no one period is permanently illustrated.

Times: Open to public on last Sat of month. Mon-Fri by appointment, please ring; 0161 224 5217
Facilities: 🅿 ♿ Ground floor only accessible ✖ (ex guide dogs) 🚌

GREATER MANCHESTER

MANCHESTER

Imperial War Museum North

The Quays Trafford Wharf Road Trafford Park M17 1TZ
☎ 0161 836 4000 📠 0161 836 4012
📧 info@iwmnorth.org.uk

Dir: M60 J9, join Parkway (A5081) towards Trafford Park. At 1st island take 3rd exit onto Village Way. At next island take 2nd exit onto Warren Bruce Rd. R at T-jct onto Trafford Wharf Rd. Or leave M602 J2 and follow signs

This recently-opened war museum is built to resemble three shards of a shattered globe, representing conflict on land, sea and in the air. The fabulous building on The Quays was designed by Daniel Libeskind. Inside are thousands of exhibits, interactive sessions, performances, and recreations that explore the way that 20th-century conflict has shaped our lives. Exhibitions of war-inspired art are a regular feature.

Times: Open daily Mar-Oct 10-6, Nov-Feb 10-5. Closed 24-26 Dec.
Facilities: 🅿 charged 🅿 (15 min walk) (£3 for 3hrs) ✕ (licenced) ♿ all parts accessible (lifts, parking, manual wheelchairs) toilets for disabled 🐕 (ex guide dogs) 🚌 (Pre-booked preferred)

MANCHESTER

John Rylands Library

150 Deansgate M3 3EH
☎ 0161 834 5343 📠 0161 834 5574
📧 spcoll72@fs1.li.man.ac.uk

Dir: On Deangate, a main thoroughfare in city centre, A56. Situated next to the Manchester Evening News Building

Founded as a memorial to Manchester cotton magnate and millionaire John Rylands, this is both a public library and the Special Collections Division of the John Rylands University Library of Manchester. Internationally renowned, it extends to two million books, manuscripts and archival items representing some 50 cultures and ranging in date from the third millennium BC to the present day.

Times: *Open all year, Mon-Fri 10-5.30, Sat 10-1. (Closed Sun, BH & Xmas-New Year).* **Facilities:** 🅿 (400yds) (pay and display) 🐕 (ex guide dogs by arrangement) 🚌 (prior notice required)

Manchester Museum

The University Oxford Road M13 9PL
☎ 0161 275 2634 🖷 0161 275 2676
✉ anna.j.davey@man.ac.uk

Dir: S of city centre on B5117

The Manchester Museum has recently undergone major refurbishment and rebuilding. It has leading research facilities and collections in archaeology, botany, Egyptology, ethnology, mineralogy, numismatics and zoology, among others, including some six million items from all over the world. There are large galleries devoted to most of these departments, but the Egyptology collection is particularly impressive, featuring mummies excavated by Sir William Flinders Petrie.

Times: Open all year, Mon-Sat 10-5, Sun & BHs 11-4.
Facilities: 🅿 charged Ⓟ 🍵 占 all parts accessible (lift access, hearing loop, accessible parking) toilets for disabled 🐕 (ex guide dogs)
🚌 (pre-booking required) 🔲

The Museum of Science and Industry in Manchester

Liverpool Road Castlefield M3 4FP
☎ 0161 832 2244 & 🖷 0161 833 1471
✉ marketing@msim.org.uk

Dir: Follow brown tourist signs from city centre

This museum is housed in the buildings of the world's oldest passenger railway station. Colourful galleries packed full of fascinating facts and amazing artefacts bring the past to life. Walk away from your own shadow in Xperiment!, the mind bending science centre, see wheels of industry turning in the Power Hall, and the planes that made flying history in the Air and Space Hall. There is also a programme of regularly changing exhibitions.

Times: *Open all year, daily 10-5. Last admission 4.30. Closed 24-26 Dec.
Facilities: 🅿 charged Ⓟ (10 mins walk) 🍵 ✗ (licenced) 占 all parts accessible (lifts, wheelchair loan service) toilets for disabled 🐕 (ex guide dogs)
🚌 (no coach parking) 🔲

MANCHESTER

The Whitworth Art Gallery

The University of Manchester Oxford Road M15 6ER
☎ 0161 275 7450 📄 0161 275 7451
✉ whitworth@man.ac.uk

Dir: Follow brown tourist signs, on Oxford road on B5117 to S of Manchester City Centre. Gallery in Whitworth Park, opp Manchester Royal Infirmary

The Whitworth Art Gallery houses an impressive range of modern and historic drawings, prints, paintings and sculpture. It has the largest collection of textiles and wallpapers outside London, and an internationally famous collection of British watercolours. The gallery hosts an innovative programme of touring exhibitions. A selection of tour lectures, workshops and concerts complement the exhibition programme.

Times: Open Mon-Sat 10-5, Sun 2-5. Closed Good Fri & Xmas-New Year.
Facilities: 🅿 🅿 (on road) (car park full at peak times) 🍽 ♿ all parts accessible (wheelchair available, induction loop, Braille lift buttons) toilets for disabled ✖ (ex guide dogs) 🚌 (with prior notice)

MANCHESTER

Urbis

Cathedral Gardens M4 3BG
☎ 0161 907 9099 📄 0161 605 8201
✉ info@urbis.org.uk

Dir: Next to Victoria Railway Station

Urbis is a unique institution dedicated to the exploration of contemporary urban culture. The Level One Gallery offers a programme of large-scale international exhibitions, while Project Space on the ground floor shows the best of Manchester's creativity. Levels two, three and four feature interactive exhibits exploring cities around the world from Tokyo to Paris, revealing how different cities work, how they change and how they affect others.

Times: Open all year daily 10-6
Facilities: 🅿 (200yds) 🍽 ✖ (licenced) ♿ all parts accessible toilets for disabled ✖ (ex guide dogs) 🚌 (Advance booking required) 🚌

PRESTWICH

Heaton Hall

Heaton Park M25 2SW
☎ 0161 773 1231 or 0161
🖹 0161 236 2880

Designed by James Wyatt for Sir Thomas Egerton in 1772, the house has magnificent period interiors decorated with fine plasterwork, paintings and furniture. Other attractions include a unique circular room with Pompeian-style paintings, and the original Samuel Green organ still in working order.

Times: *Open Etr-end Oct, but phone for time details on 0161-234 1456.
Facilities: 🅿 charged 🅿 (100m) (parking charged wknds only) ♿ Ground floor, Garden & Grounds accessible (occasional 'touch tours'. Phone for details) toilets for disabled ✱ (ex guide dogs) 🚻

SALFORD

Salford Museum & Art Gallery

Peel Park Crescent M5 4WU
☎ 0161 736 2649 🖹 0161 745 9490
✉ salford.museum@salford.gov.uk

Dir: M60 J13, A666. From S follow signs from end of M602. Museum on A6

The museum features a reconstruction of a 19th-20th century northern street with original shop fronts. Upstairs in the galleries there are temporary exhibitions and a gallery displaying paintings, sculptures and ceramics. Recent additions include the lifetimes gallery, featuring audio presentations, IT zones, temporary exhibitions, a spectacular Pilkington's display and lots of hands-on activities and dressing up areas.

Times: *Open all year Mon-Fri 10-4.45, Sat & Sun 1-5. Closed Good Fri, Etr Sat, 25 & 26 Dec, 1 Jan.
Facilities: 🅿 🅿 (0.25m) 🍴 ♿ All parts accessible (Braille & large print labels & visitor packs, hearing loop) toilets for disabled ✱ (ex guide dogs) 🚻 (must pre-book) 🚻

SALFORD

The Lowry

Pier Eight Salford Quays M50 3AZ
☎ 870 787 5774 🖹 0161 876 2001
✉ info@thelowry.com

Dir: M60 J12 for M602. Salford Quays is 0.25m from J3 of M602, follow brown Lowry signs

The Lowry is a stunning waterside complex at Salford Quays, taking in galleries, shops, cafés and a restaurant, plus two theatres showing everything from West End plays and musicals to comedians, ballet and live bands. In addition to the L S Lowry gallery, a tribute to the celebrated local artist, contemporary art exhibitions are also a feature. With regular family activities, too, you can make a whole day of your visit.

Times: *Open daily from 10. Galleries, Sun-Fri from 11, Sat from 10. Closed 25 Dec. **Facilities:** 🅿 charged 🅿 (150 mtrs) 🍴 ✗ (licenced) ♿ Ground floor only accessible (Sennheiser System) toilets for disabled ✗ (ex guide dogs) 🚌 (pre-booking advised) 🚆

STALYBRIDGE

Astley Cheetham Art Gallery

Trinity Street GK15 2BN
☎ 0161 338 6767
✉ astley.cheetham@tameside.gov.uk

Built as a gift to the town in 1901 by mill owner John Frederick Cheetham, this one-time lecture hall has been an art gallery since 1932 when Cheetham left his collection to the town. Among the works are Italian paintings from the Renaissance, British masters such as Cox and Burne-Jones, and more recent gifts such as works by Turner and local artist Harry Rutherford. The gallery hosts a programme of temporary exhibitions of the collection and regional artists, and a variety of workshops are run for families throughout the year.

Times: *Open all year, Mon-Wed & Fri 10-12.30, 1-5; Sat 9-12.30, 1-4.
Facilities: 🅿 (2hrs on street parking) (induction loop) ✗ (ex guide dogs) 🚌

FAREHAM

Royal Armouries Fort Nelson

Downend Road PO17 6AN
☎ 01329 233734 🖹 01329 822092
✉ fnenquiries@armouries.org.uk

Dir: From M27 J11, follow brown tourist signs for Royal Armouries

Superbly restored 19-acre Victorian fort overlooking Portsmouth Harbour providing visitors with spectacular views. It was built in the 1860s to deter a threatened French invasion, and there are secret tunnels, underground chambers and grass ramparts to explore. Fort Nelson is home to the Royal Armouries' collection of artillery, part of the National Museum of Arms and Armour, with over 350 pieces from the Roman era to the infamous Iraqi supergun.

Times: Open all year, daily. Closed 25-26 Dec. Facilities: 🅿 🅿 (disabled parking on same side as fort) 🍽 (licenced) ♿ Ground floor, Garden & Grounds accessible (access & audio guide, ramps, induction loop, wheelchair) toilets for disabled 🐕 (ex guide & hearing dogs) 🚌 (pre-booking advised for catering) 🍴

NETLEY

Netley Abbey

SO31 5FB

☎ 2392 581059 **Dir:** 4m SE of Southampton, facing Southampton Water

A romantic ruin, set among green lawns and trees, this 13th-century abbey was founded by Peter des Roches, tutor to Henry III. A group from the Cistercian Order crossed Southampton Water from Beaulieu to establish a new religious house here in 1239. Following the Dissolution, Henry VIII gave the site to William Paulet who made it into a private dwelling. In 1700 the 2nd Earl of Hertford sold off much of the stone fabric of the abbey, leaving the ruin we see today. Nearby is the 19th-century Gothic Netley Castle.

Times: *Open any reasonable time. Facilities: 🅿 ♿ all parts accessible 🚌 ⚙

HAMPSHIRE

PORTSMOUTH

City Museum & Records Office

Museum Rd PO1 2LJ
☎ 23 9282 7261 📄 023 9287 5276
✉ Christopher.Spendlove@portsmouthcc.gov.uk

Dir: M27/M275 into Portsmouth, follow museum symbol signs

Dedicated to local history, fine and decorative art, 'The Story of Portsmouth' displays room settings showing life here from the 17th century to the 1950s. The 'Portsmouth at Play' exhibition features leisure pursuits from the Victorian period to the 1970s. The museum has a fine and decorative art gallery, plus a temporary exhibition gallery with regularly changing exhibitions. The Record Office contains the official records of the City of Portsmouth from the 14th century.

Times: *Open all year, Apr-Oct daily 10-5.30; Nov-Mar daily 10-5. Closed 24-26 Dec and Record Office closed on public holidays. **Facilities:** 🅿 🅿 (200mtrs) 🍽 ⅋ all parts accessible (induction loops, lift & wheelchairs available, parking) toilets for disabled ✈ (ex guide & helper dogs) 🚌 (pre-booking)

PORTSMOUTH

Eastney Beam Engine House

Henderson Rd Eastney PO4 9JF
☎ 23 9282 7261 📄 023 9287 5276
✉ christopher.spendlove@portsmouthcc.gov.uk

Dir: Accessible from A3(M), A27 & A2030, at Bransbury Park traffic lights

The main attraction here is a magnificent pair of James Watt Beam Engines still housed in their original High-Victorian engine house opened in 1887. One of these engines is in steam when the museum is open. A variety of other pumping engines, many in running order, are also on display.

Times: *Open last wknd of month, 1-5 (last admission 30 minutes before closing). (Closed Aug & Dec).
Facilities: 🅿 (300mtrs) ✈ (ex guide & helper dogs) 🚌 (telephone in advance)

SILCHESTER

Calleva Museum

Bramley Road RG7 2LU

Dir: Between Basingstoke & Reading. Reached from A340, follow brown tourist signs

Little remains of the Roman town of Calleva Atrebatum except the 1.5 miles of city wall, still an impressive sight, and the ampitheatre. This small museum shows what life may have been like in a Roman town, while the main artefacts from the site can be seen in the Silchester Gallery at Reading Museum.

Times: *Open daily 9.30-sunset. Closed 25 Dec. **Facilities:** 🅿 🅟 (0.25m) (very limited parking at museum) ♿ Garden & Grounds only accessible 🚍 (pre-book, ring 01962 846735)

SOUTHAMPTON

Museum of Archaeology

God's House Tower Winkle Street SO14 2NY
☎ 23 8063 5904 📄 023 8033 9601
✉ historic.sites@southampton.gov.uk

Dir: Near the waterfront close to Queen's Park and the Town Quay

The museum is housed in an early fortified building, which dates from the 1400s and takes its name, God's House Tower, from the nearby medieval hospital, founded in 1196. Exhibits on the Roman, Saxon and medieval towns of Southampton are displayed in the three main galleries. The collection is Designated in recognition of its national and international importance. There are resources for children and families, plus special events.

Times: Open Nov-Mar: Tue-Fri 10-4; Sat 10-12 & 1-4; Sun 1-4. Apr-Oct: Tue-Fri 10-12 & 1-5; Sat 10-12 & 1-4; Sun 2-5. Also open BH Mon.
Facilities: 🅟 (400 yds) (designated areas only, parking charges) ♿ Ground floor only accessible 🐕 (ex guide dogs) 🚍 (pre-booking)

SOUTHAMPTON

Southampton City Art Gallery

Civic Centre Commercial Rd SO14 7LP
☎ 23 8083 2277 📄 023 8083 2153
🌐 art.gallery@southampton.gov.uk

Dir: Situated on the Watts Park side of the Civic Centre, a short walk from the station, on Commercial Rd

The largest gallery in the south of England, with the finest collection of contemporary art in the country outside London. A diverse range of media is represented, including sculpture, photography, installation and video work among its 3,500 pieces. A notable collection of studio pottery is also shown. Varied displays of landscapes, portrait paintings or recent British art are always available, as well as a special display, selected by members of the public.

Times: *Open all year, Tue-Sat 10-5, Sun 1-4. Closed 25-27 & 31 Dec.
Facilities: 🅿 (50yds) (nearby street parking is 1hr only) 🍽 ✕ (licenced) ♿ all parts accessible (free BSL signed tours by arrangement, 'touch tour') toilets for disabled ✖ (ex guide dogs) 🚌 (over 50 people, call ahead of visit)

SOUTHAMPTON

Southampton Maritime Museum

The Wool House Town Quay SO14 2AR
☎ 23 8022 3941 & 📄 023 8033 9601
🌐 historic.sites@southampton.gov.uk

Dir: On the waterfront, near to the Town Quay

The Wool House was built in the 14th century as a warehouse for storing wool that was due to be exported to Flanders and Italy. In the early 19th century it was used as a prison, and the names of French prisoners can still be seen carved into the wooden beams. It now houses the Southampton Maritime Museum, with models and displays telling the history of the Victorian and modern port of Southampton. Features include exhibitions themed around the 'Titanic' and the 'Queen Mary', and there is an interactive area for children.

Times: Open Nov-Mar: Tue-Fri 10-4; Sat 10-1 & 2-4; Sun 1-4. Apr-Oct: Tue-Fri 10-1 & 2-5; Sat 10-1 & 2-4; Sun 2-5.
Also open BH Mon.
Facilities: 🅿 (400yds) (metered parking adjacent) ♿ Ground floor only accessible (hearing loop on Titanic presentation) ✖ (ex guide dogs) 🚌 (pre-booking)

TITCHFIELD

Titchfield Abbey

Place House Studio Mill Lane PO15 5RA
☎ 1329 842133

Dir: 0.5m N off Titchfield, off A27

Also known as 'Place House', in Tudor times this was the seat of the Earl of Southampton, built on the site of the abbey founded in 1232. He incorporated the gatehouse and the nave of the church into his house. It has been claimed that some of Shakespeare's plays including 'Romeo and Juliet' and a 'A Midsummer Night's Dream' were first performed here.

Times: *Open Apr-Sep, daily 10-6; Oct, daily 10-5; Nov-Mar, daily 10-4. Closed 25 Dec. **Facilities:** 🅿 ♿ all parts accessible 🚌 (no coaches on site)

WINCHESTER

Royal Hampshire Regiment Museum & Memorial Garden

Serle's House Southgate Street SO23 9EG
☎ 01962 863658
✉ mail@royalhampshireregiment.org.uk

Dir: Museum near city centre, 150mtrs from traffic lights in High St

The Regimental Museum of the Royal Hampshire Regiment, 1702-1992, is located in Serle's House, an impressive residence built for William Sheldon in 1730. His son Peter was a Lieutenant Colonel commanding the South Hants Militia. His interest in amateur soldiering ate away at his personal fortune, and having always used his house as his HQ, he sold it to the government, and it has been in military use ever since. The museum tells the history of the regiment, its regulars, militia, volunteers and territorials, and the large garden at the front is dedicated to the memory of the regiment's members who died in service.

Times: *Normally open all year (ex 2 wks Xmas & New Year), Mon-Fri 11-3.30; Apr-Oct wknds & BH 12-4.
Facilities: 🅿 (800mtrs) ♿ Ground floor, Garden & Grounds accessible 🐕 (ex guide dogs) 🚌 (by appointment only)

WINCHESTER

The Great Hall

Castle Avenue SO23 8PJ
☎ 01962 846476 🖷 01962 841326

Dir: Situated at top of High St. Park & Ride recommended

The only surviving part of Winchester Castle, once home to the Domesday Book, this 13th-century hall was at the centre of court and government life. Built between 1222 and 1235, during the reign of Henry III, it is one of the largest and finest five bay halls in England to have survived to the present day. The Round Table based on the Arthurian Legend and built between 1230 and 1280 hangs in the hall. Queen Eleanor's Garden, a re-creation of a late 13th-century ornamental garden, was opened in 1986 by the Queen Mother.

Times: *Open all year, Mar-Oct daily 10-5; Nov-Feb, daily 10-5, wknds 10-4. Closed 25-26 Dec. **Facilities:** 🅿 (200yds) & All parts accessible toilets for disabled 🐕 (ex guide/hearing dogs) 🚌 (no parking for coaches) 🔳

WINCHESTER

The King's Royal Hussars Regimental Museum

Peninsula Barracks Romsey Road SO23 8TS
☎ 01962 828539 & 🖷 01962 828538
✉ beresford@krhmuseum.freeserve.co.uk

Dir: M3 J9/10 follow signs for city centre, then hospital A&E red signs to Romsey road. Vehicle access is from Romsey road

The Royal Hussars were formed by the amalgamation of two regiments raised at the time of the Jacobite Rebellion in 1715, the 10th Royal Hussars and the 11th Hussars. This museum tells their story. 'Hussar' is a 15th-century Hungarian word meaning one in 20, relating to the one in 20 men from each village to be conscripted.

Times: Open 5 Jan-18 Dec, Tue-Fri 10-4, wknds, BHs & half term Mon, 12-4. (Closed daily between 12.45-1.15). (Closed 1 Nov 2005-Spring 2006 for refurbishment) **Facilities:** 🅿 🅿 (400mtrs) (limited spaces on wkdays) & all parts accessible (lift to first floor) toilets for disabled 🐕 (ex guide dogs) 🚌 (appointment only)

HEREFORD

Old House

High Town HR1 2AA
☎ 01432 260694

Dir: Located in the centre of the High Town

The Old House is a fine half-timbered Jacobean building dating from around 1621, and was once part of a row of similar houses. It became a museum in 1929, and its rooms are furnished in 17th-century style giving visitors the chance to learn what life was like in Cromwell's time. A virtual tour is offered on the ground floor for those unable to access the upper floors.

Times: *Open all year, 10-5. Apr-Sep, Tue-Sat 10-5, Sun & BH Mon 10-4.
Facilities: P & Ground floor only accessible ✱ (ex guide dogs) 🚌 (prior notice)

BERKHAMSTED

Berkhamsted Castle

HP4 1HF

Dir: By Berkhamsted station

Roads and a railway have cut into the castle site, but its huge banks and ditches remain impressive. The original motte-and-bailey was built after the Norman Conquest, and there is a later stone keep, owned by the Black Prince, eldest son of King Edward III, where King John of France was imprisoned.

Times: *Open all year, daily, summer 10-6; winter 10-4. Closed 25 Dec & 1 Jan.
Facilities: 🚌 ❄

LETCHWORTH

Museum & Art Gallery

Broadway SG6 3PF
☎ 01462 685647 ▤ 01462 481879
✉ letchworth.museum@north-herts.gov.uk

Dir: Situated next door to Public Library, in town centre, near Broadway Cinema

Opened in 1914 to house the collections of the Letchworth Naturalists' Society, this friendly town-centre museum has exhibits on local wildlife, geology, arts and crafts, and archaeology. Monthly changing exhibitions of paintings, photography and crafts are shown in the art gallery and mezzanine gallery, and many items are available for sale. There is also a museum shop.

Times: *Open all year Mon-Tue, Thu-Sat (Closed BHs), 10-5.
Facilities: P (100yds) & Ground floor only accessible (special provisions on request) ✶ (ex guide dogs) 🚌 (coach parking is limited)

ST ALBANS

Museum of St Albans

Hatfield Road AL1 3RR
☎ 01727 819340 ▤ 01727 837472
✉ museum@stalbans.gov.uk

Dir: City centre on A1057 Hatfield road

Exhibits at the Museum of St Albans include the Salaman collection of craft tools, and reconstructed workshops. The history of St Albans is traced from the departure of the Romans up to the present day. There is a special exhibition gallery with a wide variety of exhibitions and a wildlife garden with a picnic area.

Times: Open all year, daily 10-5, Sun 2-5. Closed 25-26 Dec.
Facilities: P P (0.5m) & Ground floor only accessible toilets for disabled ✶ (ex guide dogs) 🚌 (no coach parking on site, pre-book) 🚻

TRING

The Walter Rothschild Zoological Museum

Akeman Street HP23 6AP
☎ 20 7942 6171 🖷 020 7942 6150
✉ tring-enquiries@nhm.ac.uk

Dir: Signed from A41

This unusual museum was founded in the 1890s by Lionel Walter, 2nd Baron Rothschild, a scientist, eccentric and natural history enthusiast. Now part of the Natural History Museum, it houses more than 4,000 specimens from whales to fleas, and humming birds to tigers. Themed activity trails and innovative exhibitions are a regular feature.

Times: Open all year, Mon-Sat 10-5, Sun 2-5. Closed 24-26 Dec.
Facilities: 🅿 🅿 (on street) 🍵 ♿ Ground floor, Garden & Grounds accessible (ramps to shop & cafe, disabled parking space) toilets for disabled ✖ (ex guide dogs) 🚌 (no parking at site, must park in town)

WARE

Scott's Grotto

Scott's Road SG12 9JQ
☎ 01920 464131 🖷 0870 120 6902
✉ jg@ware-herts.org.uk

Dir: Off A119

Scott's Grotto, built in the 1760s by the Quaker poet John Scott, has been described by English Heritage as 'one of the finest in England'. Recently restored by the Ware Society, it consists of underground passages and chambers decorated with flints, shells, minerals and stones, and extends 67 feet into the side of the hill. Please wear flat shoes and bring a torch.

Times: Open Apr-Sep, Sat & BH Mon 2-4.30. Other times by appointment only.
Facilities: 🅿 (on street)

AYLESFORD

Aylesford Priory

The Friars ME20 7BX
☎ 01622 717272 📠 01622 715575
✉ friarsevents@hotmail.com

Dir: M20 J6 onto A229, M2 J3 onto
A229, signposted

*Built in the 13th and 14th centuries, the
Priory has been restored by the Carmelite
community and is now used as a house of
prayer, a guesthouse, a conference centre
and a place of pilgrimage and retreat. It
has fine cloisters, and displays sculpture
and ceramics by modern artists. It is also
home to the shrine of the Glorious
Assumption and St Simon Stock.*

Times: *Open all year, daily 9-dusk. Gift &
book shop May-Sep, 10-5; Oct-Apr, 10-4
(Sun 11am). Guided tours of the priory by
arrangement.
Facilities: 🅿 🍽 ♿ Ground floor, Garden &
Grounds accessible (wheelchairs available,
ramps) toilets for disabled 🐕 (ex guide &
hearing dogs) 🚐 (prior booking preferred)

BIDDENDEN

Biddenden Vineyards & Cider Works

Little Whatmans Gribble Bridge Lane
TN27 8DF
☎ 01580 291726 📠 01580 291933
✉ info@biddendenvineyards.co.uk

Dir: 0.5m S off A262, 0.5m from
Biddenden Village. Bear R at Woolpack
Corner

*The present vineyard was established in
1969 and now covers 22 acres. Visitors are
welcome to stroll around the vineyard,
enjoy views of the surrounding countryside
and see the presses and bottling line in the
winery. In the tasting room you get to
sample the wines, ciders and apple juices,
which are available to buy at the shop. A
coffee shop is also provided on site.*

Times: *Open all year, Shop: Mon-Fri 10-5,
Sat 10-5, Sun & BH 11-5. Closed noon 24
Dec-2 Jan & Sun in Jan & Feb.
Facilities: 🅿 🍽 (licenced) ♿ Ground floor,
Garden & Grounds accessible 🚐 🍴

CANTERBURY

Royal Museum & Art Gallery with Buffs Museum

High Street CT1 2RA
☎ 01227 452747 📠 01227 455047
📧 museums@canterbury.gov.uk

Dir: In Beaney Institute (1st floor) in High St

A splendid Victorian building, houses decorative arts and the city's picture collections - including a gallery for T S Cooper, England finest cattle painter. The art gallery is the major space in the area for the visual arts with a varied exhibition programme. Here too is the Buffs Museum, which tells the story of one of England's oldest infantry regiments and its worldwide service.

Times: *Open all year, Mon-Sat 10-5. Closed Good Fri and Xmas period. (Last admission 4.45)
Facilities: P (500mtrs) ✈ (ex guide dogs) 🚌 (pre-booked preferred)

EYNSFORD

Eynsford Castle

Dir: In Eynsford, off A225

The pretty village of Eynsford provides the setting for the romantic ruins of one of the earliest stone castles to be built in England. Work began on the castle in 1088 on a man-made site dating from the Saxon era. The moat and remains of the curtain wall and hall can still be seen, the wall standing at 30 feet in places.

Times: *Open all year, Apr-Sep, daily 10-6; Oct-Feb, daily 10-4. Opening times relate to 2004, for further details phone or log onto www.english-heritage.org.uk/visits
Facilities: P & all parts accessible 🚌 ⌗

KENT

MAIDSTONE

Maidstone Museum & Bentlif Art Gallery

Saint Faith's Street ME14 1LH
☎ 01622 602838 📠 01622 685022
✉ alexgurr@maidstone.gov.uk

Dir: Close to County Hall & Maidstone East train stn

Set in an Elizabethan manor house, which has been much extended over the years, this museum houses an outstanding collection of fine and applied arts, including watercolours, furniture, ceramics, and a collection of Japanese art and artefacts. The museum of the Queen's Own Royal West Kent Regiment is also accommodated here. Please apply for details of temporary exhibitions, workshops and events.

Times: *Open all year, Mon-Sat 10-5.15, Sun & BH Mon 11-4. Closed 25-26 Dec.
Facilities: Ⓟ (150 mtrs) 🍽 ♿ Ground floor, Garden & Grounds accessible ✖ (ex guide dogs) 🚗 🍴

MAIDSTONE

Tyrwhitt Drake Museum of Carriages

The Archbishop's Stables Mill Street ME15 6YE
☎ 01622 602838 📠 01622 685022
✉ museuminfo@maidstone.gov.uk

Dir: Close to River Medway & Archbishops Palace, just off A229 in town centre

The museum is home to a unique collection of horse-drawn vehicles and transport curiosities, probably the largest collection of its kind in the country. More than 60 vehicles are on display, from grand carriages and ornate sleighs to antique sedan chairs and Victorian cabs, there is even an original ice-cream cart. The museum is housed in the 14th-century Archbishop's stables.

Times: Open Jun-mid Sep, 10.30-4.30
Facilities: Ⓟ (50 yds) ♿ Ground floor only accessible ✖ (ex guide dogs) 🚗

RECULVER

Reculver Towers & Roman Fort

CT6 6SU

☎ 1227 740676 **Dir:** 3m E of Herne Bay

Most of the Roman fort at Reculver has been lost to the sea, though when it was built in about AD210 it was a mile from the coast. The original building is believed to have been around 600 feet long, but all that remains is the southern wall foundations. The twin towers, known as the 'Two Sisters' are the remains of the 12th century church of St Mary's, and are now relied upon as a useful landmark for ships out at sea.

Times: *Open any reasonable time.
Facilities: 🅿 ♿ Ground floor only accessible (long slope from car park to fort) 🚌 ✿

ROYAL TUNBRIDGE WELLS

Tunbridge Wells Museum and Art Gallery

Civic Centre Mount Pleasant TN1 1JN
☎ 01892 554171 🖻 01892 534227

Dir: Adjacent to Town Hall, off A264

A local history museum showing Tunbridge ware, archaeology, toys and dolls, and domestic and agricultural bygones. There is also a natural history room with displays of British birds, local butterflies, live insects, geology, minerals and fossils. The art gallery has regularly changing art and craft exhibitions and touring displays from British and European museums. Educational workshops and special events are featured.

Times: Open all year, daily 9.30-5. Sun 10-4. Closed BHs & Etr Sat.
Facilities: 🅿 (200 yds) ♿ all parts accessible (parking adjacent to building) 🛪 (ex guide dogs) 🚌 (pre-booking)

WEST MALLING

St Leonard's Tower

ME19 6PE

☎ 1732 870872 **Dir:** On unclass road W of A228

A early example of a Norman tower keep, St Leonard's Tower was built around 1080 by Gundulf, Bishop of Rochester, who also built Rochester Cathedral and the White Tower of London. The tower stands almost to its original height and takes its name from a chapel dedicated to St Leonard that once stood nearby.

Times: *Open any reasonable time for exterior viewing. Contact West Malling Parish Council for interior viewing - 01732 870872.
Facilities: ♿ Garden & Grounds only accessible ➔ ✤

CHORLEY

Astley Hall Museum & Art Gallery

Astley Park PR7 1NP
☎ 01257 515555 ▤ 01257 515556
✉ astleyhall@lineone.net

Dir: 2m W of Chorley off A581 Southport road

A charming building, the earliest part of which dates from the late 1500s, Astley Hall is set amid beautiful parkland. While it is impressive to look at, it retains a comfortable lived-in atmosphere. There are pictures and pottery to see, as well as fine furniture and rare plasterwork ceilings, plus the first ever Rugby League Cup and the contents of a clog-maker's workshop. The gallery shows an interesting programme of exhibitions.

Times: Open Apr-Sep, Sat-Sun 12-5; By appointment only during the week
Facilities: 🅿 🅿 (200 yds) ♿ Ground floor, Garden & Grounds accessible (video of upper floors, print/Braille guide, CD audio guide) ✘ (ex guide dogs) ➔ (pre booked) ➔

PRESTON

Harris Museum & Art Gallery

Market Square PR1 2PP
☎ 01772 258248 📠 01772 886764
✉ harris.museum@preston.gov.uk

Dir: M6 J31, follow signs for city centre, park at bus stn car park

An impressive Grade I listed Greek Revival building containing extensive collections of fine and decorative art including a gallery of clothes and fashion. The Story of Preston covers the city's history and the lively exhibition programmes of contemporary art and social history are accompanied by events and activities throughout the year.

Times: *Open all year, Mon-Sat 10-5, Sun 11-4. Closed BHs.
Facilities: 🅿 (5 mins walk) (blue badge disabled parking only) 🍽 & all parts accessible (wheelchair available, chair lift to mezzanine galleries) toilets for disabled 🐕 (ex guide & assistance dogs) 💷 (contact prior to visit) 🍴

PRESTON

The National Football Museum

Sir Tom Finney Way Deepdale PR1 6RY
☎ 01772 908442 📠 01772 908433
✉ enquiries@nationalfootballmuseum.com

Dir: 2m from M6 J31, 31A or 32. Follow brown tourist signs

What location could be more fitting for a National Football Museum than Deepdale Stadium, the home of Preston North End, first winners of the professional football league in 1888-9? This fascinating trip through football past and present includes the FIFA Museum Collection, a fine display of memorabilia and artefacts; interactive displays that allow visitors to commentate on matches, and take virtual trips to every league ground in the country; and an art gallery dedicated to the Beautiful Game.

Times: *Open Tue-Sat 10-5, Sun 11-5. Closed Mon ex BHs. Contact for opening times on match days.
Facilities: 🅿 🅿 (50mtrs) 🍽 (licenced) & all parts accessible (lifts, multi-sensory exhibitions) toilets for disabled 🐕 (ex guide dogs) 💷 🍴

ROSSENDALE

Rossendale Museum

Whitaker Park Haslingden Road
Rawtenstall BB4 6RE
☎ 01706 244682 🖷 01706 250037
✉ rossendalemuseum@btconnect.com

Dir: Off A681, 0.25m W of Rawtenstall centre

Rossendale Museum is located in a former mill owner's house, built in 1840 and set in the delightful Whitaker Park. Displays include fine and decorative arts, a Victorian drawing room, natural history, costume, local and social history, plus items of historic taxidermy - a tiger, python and young African elephant. There is also a programme of regular temporary exhibitions. Access to the museum has recently been improved through lottery funding.

Times: Closed for refurbishment until mid-Feb 2005. From then open Sun/Wed/Thu 1-4.30, phone to verify
Facilities: 🅿 🅿 250yds (limited parking) ♿ all parts accessible (large print, audio guides, induction loop, lift) toilets for disabled ✖ (ex guide dogs) 🚌 (by arrangement)

DONINGTON LE HEATH

Donington le Heath Manor House

Manor Road LE67 2FW
☎ 01530 831259 🖷 01530 831259
✉ museum@leics.gov.uk

Dir: S of Coalville

This is a rare example of a medieval manor house, tracing its history back to about 1280. It has now been restored as a period house, with fine oak furnishings. The surrounding grounds include period gardens, and the adjoining stone barn houses a restaurant. A monthly programme of events includes crafts, demonstrations, re-enactments and hands-on activities.

Times: *Open Apr-Sep, 11-5; Oct, Nov & Mar 11-3. Dec-Feb wknds only
Facilities: 🅿 🍴 ✖ ♿ Ground floor, Garden & Grounds accessible toilets for disabled ✖ (ex guide dogs) 🚌 (max 50)

LEICESTER

Abbey Pumping Station

Corporation Road Abbey Lane LE4 5PX
☎ 0116 299 5111 ▤ 0116 299 5125

Dir: Off A6, 1m N from city centre

Built as a sewage pumping station in 1891, this fascinating museum features some of the largest steam beam engines in the country, and an exhibition on the history and technology of toilets, water and hygiene. The famous interactive loo is quite a talking point, and there is a steam shovel and a passenger carrying narrow gauge railway. The historic vehicle collection also on site stars a coal-fired fish and chip van.

Times: *Open Apr-Sep, Mon-Sat 10-5, Sun 1-5; Oct-Mar, Mon-Sat 10-4, Sun 1-4. Closed 24-26 & 31 Dec-1 Jan.
Facilities: ▣ ℙ (on road parking) ♿ Ground floor, Garden & Grounds accessible (loan of wheelchairs, wheelchair lift) toilets for disabled ✖ (ex guide dogs) ☞ (large coaches drop off at entrance) ☞

LEICESTER

Belgrave Hall & Gardens

Church Road off Thurcaston Rd Belgrave LE4 5PE
☎ 0116 266 6590 ▤ 0116 261 3063

Dir: Off Belgrave/Loughborough road, 1m from city centre

A delightful three-storey Queen Anne house dating from 1709 with beautiful period and botanic gardens. Authentic room settings contrast Georgian elegance with Victorian cosiness and include the kitchen, drawing room, music room and nursery. The Belgrave Story exhibition is themed around the history of the house, the village and the local people. The Community Gallery provides space for contemporary work by local artists. The Hall is reputedly haunted, causing quite a stir in 1998 when two ghostlike apparitions were captured by security cameras.

Times: *Open all year, Apr-Sep, Mon-Sat 10-5, Sun 1-5; Oct-Mar, Mon-Sat 10-4, Sun 1-4. Closed 24-26 Dec & 31 Dec-1 Jan.
Facilities: ▣ ℙ ♿ Ground floor, Garden & Grounds accessible (loan of wheelchair) toilets for disabled ✖ (ex guide dogs) ☞

LEICESTER

Jewry Wall Museum & Site

St Nicholas Circle LE1 4LB
☎ 0116 225 4971 🖷 0116 225 4966

Dir: Opposite The Holiday Inn

The museum is set behind the massive fragment of the Roman Jewry Wall, one of Leicester's best known landmarks, and a Roman Baths site of the 2nd century AD. It is a museum of Leicestershire archaeology, which covers finds from the earliest times to the Middle Ages. A multi-media exhibition, 'The Making of Leicester' focuses on the people behind the city's history, demonstrating how archaeology reveals their secrets. Children have the opportunity to dress up in historical costumes and to become 'archaeological detectives'. Portraits of Leicester through the ages are another feature.

Times: *Open Apr-Sep, Mon-Sat 10-5, Sun 1-5; Oct-Mar, Mon-Sat 10-4, Sun 1-4. Closed 24-26 & 31 Dec & 1 Jan.
Facilities: P (300yds) (limited on-street parking) & Ground floor only accessible toilets for disabled ✱ (ex guide dogs) ▦ (by arrangement)

LEICESTER

New Walk Museum & Art Gallery

53 New Walk LE1 7EA
☎ 0116 225 4900 🖷 0116 225 4927

Dir: Situated on New Walk. Access by car from A6 onto Waterloo Way at Railway Stn. R into Regent Rd, R onto West St, R onto Princess Rd which leads to car park

Leicester's oldest museum is a major regional venue housing local and national collections. Major exhibits include 'Wild Space' a hands-on exhibition interpreting biodiversity and the widely varying habitats of the world, along with the self-explanatory 'Mighty Dinosaurs', 'Leicestershire's Rocks' and 'Ancient Egyptians'. The first floor art galleries are newly refurbished to include a new 'World Arts' gallery, while 'Gallery Nine' reflects the city's diversity by providing space for communities to show their own exhibitions. Specifically for children is 'Discover', a gallery where two to eight-year-olds are encouraged to play and interact with objects. There is also a programme of special exhibitions.

Times: *Open all year, Apr-Sep, Mon-Sat 10-5, Sun 1-5. Oct-Mar, Mon-Sat 10-4, Sun 1-4. Closed 24-26 & 31 Dec & 1 Jan)
Facilities: P P (1km) ▰ & all parts accessible (wheelchairs for loan, minicom, induction loop) toilets for disabled ✱ (ex guide dogs) ▦ ▰

LEICESTER

Newarke Houses

The Newarke LE2 7BY
☎ 0116 225 4980 📠 0116 225 4982

Dir: Opposite De Montfort University

Newarke Houses Museum comprises two houses, Wygston's Chantry House dating from around 1511, and Skeffington House built by Sir Thomas Skeffington between 1560 and 1583, both set in lovely gardens. William Wygston built the Chantry House to accommodate two chantry priests to sing masses for his soul in a nearby church, long since demolished. Reopening in Autumn 2005 after a period of refurbishment, the new emphasis of the museum will be on the daily life of the 'everyman' in Leicester in the 20th century, with exhibits on immigration, leisure and shopping.

Times: *Open Apr-Sep, Mon-Sat 10-5, Sun 1-5; Oct-Mar, Mon-Sat 10-4, Sun 1-4. Closed 24-26 & 31 Dec & 1 Jan.
Facilities: ℙ (200yds) ♿ Ground floor only accessible (car parking can be arranged) ✈ (ex guide dogs) 🚻

LEICESTER

The Guildhall

Guildhall Lane LE1 5FQ
☎ 0116 253 2569 📠 0116 253 9626

Dir: Next to Leicester Cathedral

A preserved medieval building dating back to the 14th century, The Guildhall is the city's oldest building still in use. Over the centuries it has served as the Hall of the Guild of Corpus Christi, the Civic Centre and Town Hall, a judicial centre for court sessions and home to Leicester's first police force. The Guildhall now houses one of the oldest libraries in the country, as well as hosting events, activities and performances.

Times: *Open all year: Apr-Sep, Mon-Sat 10-5, Sun 1-5; Oct-Mar, Mon-Sat 10-4, Sun 1-4. Closed 24-26 Dec & 1 Jan.
Facilities: ℙ (100yds) ♿ Ground floor only accessible (wheelchair loan, induction loop, voice minicom) toilets for disabled ✈ (ex guide dogs) 🚻 🚻

The Record Office for Leicestershire & Rutland

Long Street Wigston Magna LE18 2AH
☎ 0116 257 1080 📠 0116 257 1120
✉ museums@leics.gov.uk

Dir: Old A50, S of Leicester City

Housed in a converted 19th-century school in Wigston, the Record Office provides a centre of research for Leicestershire, Leicester city and Rutland. It holds photographs, electoral registers and archive film, files of local newspapers, history tapes and sound recordings, all of which can be studied. Proof of identity and address is needed before readers' tickets can be issued.

Times: *Open all year, Mon, Tue & Thu 9.15-5, Wed 9.15-7.30, Fri 9.15-4.45, Sat 9.15-12.15. Closed Sun & BH wknds Sat-Tue. Facilities: 🅿 🅿 ᕕ all parts accessible toilets for disabled ✖ (ex guide dogs)

University of Leicester Harold Martin Botanic Garden

Beaumont Hall Stoughton Drive South Oadby LE2 2NA
☎ 116 271 7725

Dir: 3m SE A6, entrance at 'The Knoll', Glebe Rd, Oadby

The grounds of four houses, now used as student residences, which are not open to the public, make up this 16-acre garden. Here you can see a great variety of plants in different settings, in what is a delightful place to walk. There are rock, water and sunken gardens, trees, borders, heathers and glasshouses.

Times: *Open Mon-Fri 10-4, Sat & Sun 10-4 (from 3rd wknd in Mar to 2nd wknd in Nov inclusive). Closed 25-26 Dec & 1 Jan. Facilities: 🅿 (adjacent) ᕕ Garden & Grounds only accessible toilets for disabled ✖ (ex guide dogs) 🚍

HECKINGTON

The Pearoom

Station Yard Station Road NG34 9JJ
☎ 01529 460765 📄 01529 460948

Dir: 4m E of Sleaford, off A17

The Pearoom has a craft shop, galleries and workshops for 10 resident craft workers. Their products include pottery, textiles and calligraphy; and there is also a weaver-feltmaker. An active programme of craft exhibitions runs throughout the year accompanied by a programme of weekend course activities. A commissioning centre shows the work of many local makers willing to work to commission.

Times: Open all year, Mon-Sat & BHs 10-5, Sun 12-5.
Facilities: 🅿 💷 (licenced) ♿ Ground floor only accessible ✖ (ex guide dogs) 🚌

LINCOLN

Greyfriars Exhibition Centre

Danes Terrace LN2 1LP
☎ 01522 530724 📄 01522 552811
✉ thecollection@lincolnshire.gov.uk

Dir: Located in the lower part of Lincoln, between Central Library and St Swithins close to the Waterside Shopping Centre

Greyfriars is a lovely 13th-century building originally constructed as a church for the Franciscans in the lower part of the city. Today it serves as the county's main archaeology museum, showing artefacts from the City and County Museum collections, which number more than two million items. It is also the venue for a variety of special exhibitions, which are accompanied by educational workshops and a programme of events.

Times: *Open all year, Tue-Sat (closed Xmas/New Year).
Facilities: ♿ Ground floor only accessible ✖ (ex guide dogs) 🚌 (must book in advance)

LINCOLN

Usher Gallery

Lindum Road LN2 1NN
☎ 01522 527980 📠 01522 560165
✉ usher.gallery@lincolnshire.gov.uk

Dir: In city centre, signed

Built as the result of a bequest by Lincoln jeweller James Ward Usher, the Gallery houses his magnificent collection of watches, porcelain and miniatures, as well as topographical works, watercolours by Peter de Wint, Tennyson memorabilia and coins. The gallery has a popular and changing display of contemporary visual arts and crafts. There is a lively lecture programme and children's activity diary.

Times: Open all year, Tue-Sat 10-5 (last entry 4.30), Sun 1-5 (last entry 4.30), from 1 Jun daily 10-5. Open BHs. Closed 24-26 Dec & 1 Jan.
Facilities: 🅿 🅿 (150yds) 🍽 & all parts accessible (large print guides, induction loop, parking) toilets for disabled 🐕 (ex guide dogs) 🚼 🍴

SKEGNESS

Church Farm Museum

Church Road South PE25 2HF
☎ 01754 766658 📠 01754 898243
✉ churchfarmmuseum@lincolnshire.gov.uk

Dir: Follow brown museum signs on entering Skegness

Church Farm Museum comprises a farmhouse and outbuildings restored to show the way of life on a Lincolnshire farm at the end of the 19th century. Items on display include farm implements and machinery plus household equipment. Temporary exhibitions are held in the barn with special events throughout the season. A timber framed mud and stud cottage has been restored on site.

Times: *Open Apr-Oct, daily 10-5
Facilities: 🅿 🍽 & Ground floor, Garden & Grounds accessible (wheelchair available, grounds accessible with care) toilets for disabled 🐕 (ex guide dogs) 🚼

STAMFORD

Stamford Museum

Broad Street PE9 1PJ
☎ 01780 766317 ▤ 01780 480363
✉ stamford_museum@lincolnshire.gov.uk

Dir: From A1 follow town centre signs from any Stamford exit

Displays illustrate the history of this fine stone town and include Stamford Ware pottery, the visit of Daniel Lambert and the town's more recent industrial past. The new Stamford Tapestry depicts the history of the town in wool. Holiday activities are provided for children, and there are information sheets on Daniel Lambert, the Stamford Spitfire, Sir Malcolm Sargent, and the filming of 'Middlemarch'.

Times: Open all year, Apr-Sep, Mon-Sat 10-5, Sun 1-4; Oct-Mar Mon-Sat 10-5. Closed 24-26 & 31 Dec & 1 Jan.
Facilities: ℗ (200yds) (on street parking is limited waiting) ♿ All parts accessible (audio loop at reception, Braille leaflets) ✖ (ex guide dogs) ➡ (prior notice prefered)

LONDON E17

William Morris Gallery

Lloyd Park Forest Road E17 4PP
☎ 20 8527 3782 ▤ 020 8527 7070

Dir: Underground - Blackhorse Rd, take bus no. 123 along Forest Rd, get off at the Lloyd Park stop

Victorian artist, craftsman, poet and free thinker William Morris lived here from 1848 to 1856, and the gallery houses displays illustrating his life and work. Exhibits include fabrics, stained glass, wallpaper and furniture, as well as Pre-Raphaelite paintings, ceramics and a collection of pictures by Frank Brangwyn, who worked briefly for Morris.

Times: Open all year, Tue-Sat and 1st Sun in each month 10-1 & 2-5. Closed Mon & BHs. Telephone for Xmas/New Year opening times. **Facilities:** ℗ ℗ (75yds) ♿ Ground floor, Garden & Grounds accessible ✖ (ex guide dogs) ➡ (pre-booking) ➡

LONDON E2

Geffrye Museum

136 Kingsland Road Shoreditch E2 8EA
☎ 20 7739 9893 📠 020 7729 5647
✉ info@geffrye-museum.org.uk

Dir: S end of Kingsland Rd A10 in Shoreditch between Cremer St & Pearson St

The only museum in the UK to specialise in the domestic interiors and furniture of the urban middle classes. Displays span the 400 years from 1600 to the present day, forming a sequence of period rooms which capture the nature of English interior style. The museum is set in elegant, 18th-century buildings, surrounded by delightful grounds, including an award-winning walled herb garden and a series of historical gardens which highlight changes in urban middle-class gardening from the 17th to 20th centuries. One of the museum's historic almshouses has recently been fully restored to its original condition and is open on selected days (ring for details).

Times: Open all year, Tue-Sat 10-5, Sun & BH Mon 12-5. Closed Mon, Good Fri, 24-26 Dec & New Year.
Facilities: 🅿 (150yds) (meter parking, very restricted) ✗ (licenced) ♿ all parts accessible (ramps, lift, wheelchair available) toilets for disabled 🐕 (ex guide dogs) 🚌 (booked in advance)

LONDON E2

Museum of Childhood at Bethnal Green

Cambridge Heath Road E2 9PA
☎ 20 8980 2415 📠 020 8983 5225
✉ bgmc@vam.ac.uk

Dir: Underground - Bethnal Green

The Museum of Childhood houses a multitude of childhood delights. Toys, dolls and dolls' houses, model soldiers, puppets, games, model theatres, children's costume and nursery antiques are all included in its well planned displays. Art activities and soft play are available every weekend throughout the school holidays. There is a permanent under-fives play area and games zone with board games and giant snakes and ladders.

Times: Open all year, Mon-Thu & Sat-Sun 10-5.50. Closed Fri, 24-26 Dec & 1 Jan.
Facilities: 🅿 (metered parking) 🍴 (licenced) ♿ All parts accessible (disabled parking by arrangement) toilets for disabled 🚌 (prior booking)

LONDON EC1

Wesley's Chapel, House & Museum of Methodism

49 City Road EC1Y 1AU
☎ 20 7253 2262 📠 020 7608 3825
✉ museum@wesleychapel.org.uk

Dir: Underground - Old Street - exit number 4

Wesley's Chapel has been the Mother Church of World Methodism since its construction in 1778. The crypt houses a museum which traces the development of Methodism from the 18th century to the present day. Wesley's house - built by him in 1779 - was his home when not touring and preaching. Special events are held on May 24 (the anniversary of Wesley's conversion), and November 1 (the anniversary of the Chapel's opening).

Times: Open all year, Mon-Sat , 10-4, Sun 12-2. Closed Thu 12.45-1.30, Xmas & New Year, BHs, except Good Fri.
Facilities: ℙ (5min) (NCP at Finsbury Square) & Ground floor, Garden & Grounds accessible (lift to the crypt of the chapel) toilets for disabled ✖ (ex guide dogs) 🚌 (max 50 people per party) 🚌

LONDON EC2

Bank of England Museum

Threadneedle Street EC2R 8AH
☎ 20 7601 5545 📠 020 7601 5808
✉ museum@bankofengland.co.uk

Dir: Museum housed in Bank of London, entrance in Bartholomew Lane

The museum tells the story of the Bank of England from its foundation in 1694 to its role in today's economy. Interactive programmes with graphics and video presentations help explain its many and varied roles. Collections, amassed over 300 years, include a unique array of coins and banknotes, books, furniture, pictures, photographs and cartoons. A popular exhibit is a genuine gold bar, which may be handled.

Times: *Open all year, Mon-Fri 10-5. Closed wknds & BHs. Open on day of Lord Major's Show.
Facilities: ℙ (10 mins walk) & all parts accessible (special need presentation, advance notice helpful) toilets for disabled 🚌 (no parking)

LONDON EC2

The Guildhall

Gresham Street EC2V 5AE
☎ 20 7606 3030 📄 020 7260 1119
✉ pro@corpoflondon.gov.uk

Dir: Underground - Bank, St Paul's

The Court of Common Council (presided over by the Lord Mayor) administers the City of London and meets in the Guildhall. Dating from 1411, the building was badly damaged in the Great Fire and again in the Blitz. The great hall, traditionally used for the Lord Mayor's Banquet and other important civic functions, is impressively decorated with the banners and shields of the livery companies, of which there are more than 90. The Clock Museum, which has a collection of 700 exhibits, charts the history of 500 years of time-keeping.

Times: *Open all year, May-Sep, daily 10-5; Oct-Apr, Mon-Sat 10-5. Closed Xmas, New Year, Good Fri, Etr Mon & infrequently for Civic occasions. Please contact 020 7606 3030 ext 1463 before visit to be certain of access. **Facilities:** P (NCP parking nearby) ♿ Ground floor only accessible (lift for east and west crypts) toilets for disabled ▬

LONDON EC4

Middle Temple Hall

The Temple EC4Y 9AT
☎ 20 7427 4800 📄 020 7427 4801
✉ library@middletemple.org.uk

Dir: Underground - Temple, Blackfriars. Turn L at embankment & L into Middle Temple Lane. Hall half way up on L

Between Fleet Street and the Thames are the Middle and Inner Temples, separate Inns of Court, so named after the Knights Templar who occupied the site from about 1160. Middle Temple Hall is a fine example of Tudor architecture and was completed in about 1570. The hall has a double hammerbeam roof and beautiful stained glass. The 29 foot-long high table was made from a single oak tree from Windsor Forest. Sir Francis Drake was a visitor to and friend of the Middle Temple, and a table made from timbers from the 'Golden Hind' is where newly called barristers enter their names in the Inn's books.

Times: *Open all year, Mon-Fri 10-12 & 3-4. Closed BH & legal vacations.
Facilities: ♿ Ground floor only accessible

LONDON NW3

Kenwood House

Hampstead Lane NW3 7JR
☎ 20 8348 1286 ▤ 020 7973 3891

Dir: Underground - Hampstead

In splendid grounds beside Hampstead Heath, this outstanding neo-classical house contains one of the most important collections of paintings ever given to the nation. Works by Rembrandt, Vermeer, Turner, Gainsborough and Reynolds are all set against a backdrop of sumptuous rooms. Scenes from 'Notting Hill' and 'Mansfield Park' were both fimed here. Stroll through the lakeside gardens and woodland and see sculptures by Henry Moore and Barbara Hepworth.

Times: *Open all year, Apr-Oct, daily 10-5; Nov-Mar, daily 10-4 (park stays open later, see notices). On Wed & Fri house opens at 10.30. Closed 24-26 Dec & 1 Jan.
Facilities: 🅿 🅟 (limited) 🍽 ✕ (licensed) ⅋ Ground floor, Garden & Grounds accessible toilets for disabled 🚌 ♿

LONDON NW9

Royal Air Force Museum

Grahame Park Way Hendon NW9 5LL
☎ 20 8205 2266 ▤ 020 8358 4981
🌐 groups@rafmuseum.org

Dir: Within easy reach of the A5, A41, M1 and North Circular A406 roads. Tube on Northern Line to Colindale. Rail to Mill Hill Broadway station. Bus route 303 passes the door

Take off to the Royal Air Force Museum and soar through the history of aviation from the earliest balloon flights to the latest Eurofighter. A recent addition is the dramatic 'Milestones of Flight' hall, with an exciting display of suspended aircraft and touch screen technology. Visitors can experience the bi-plane era in the beautifully restored Grahame-White factory, or have some hands-on fun in the expanded Aeronauts Interactive Centre. All this plus a huge collection of aircraft, simulator rides, uniforms, light and sound show, and much more.

Times: Open daily 10-6. (Last admission 5.30). Closed 24-26 Dec & 1 Jan
Facilities: 🅿 🅟 (0.5m) (only available while museum is open) 🍽 ✕ (licensed) ⅋ all parts accessible (lifts, ramps & wheelchairs available) toilets for disabled ✈ (ex guide dogs) 🚌 (pre-booking preferred) ◀

LONDON SE1

Bankside Gallery

48 Hopton Street SE1 9JH
☎ 20 7928 7521 📄 020 7928 2820
✉ info@banksidegallery.com

Dir: E of Blackfriars Bridge, South Bank of the Thames, adjacent to Tate Modern and the Millennium Bridge

The Bankside Gallery is the home of the Royal Watercolour Society (RWS) and the Royal Society of Painter-Printmakers (RE). A series of regularly changing exhibitions throughout the year displays the work of both societies. Members are elected to the societies by their peers to represent a standard of excellence in their field, upholding a tradition that dates back 200 years.

Times: Opening dates vary according to exhibitions programme - Mon-Fri 10-5, Sat & Sun 11-5
Facilities: P & Ground floor only accessible 🚌 Notice required 🚌

LONDON SE1

Imperial War Museum

Lambeth Rd SE1 6HZ
☎ 20 7416 5000 📄 020 7416 5374
✉ mail@iwm.org.uk

Dir: Underground - Lambeth North, Elephant & Castle or Waterloo

Founded in 1917, this museum illustrates and records all aspects of the two World Wars and other military operations involving Britain and the Commonwealth since 1914. There are always special exhibitions and the programme of events includes film shows and lectures. The museum has a wealth of military reference material, although some reference departments are open to the public by appointment only.

Times: *Open all year, daily 10-6. Closed 24-26 Dec. **Facilities:** P (on street, 100mtrs) (metered Mon-Fri) ● ✗ (licenced) & all parts accessible (parking & wheelchair hire book in advance, study room) toilets for disabled ✗ (ex guide dogs) 🚌 (book in advance) 🚌

LONDON SE1

Museum of Garden History

Lambeth Palace Road SE1 7LB
☎ 20 7401 8865 📄 020 7401 8869
✉ info@museumgardenhistory.org

Dir: Underground - Waterloo/Lambeth North, next to Lambeth Palace opposite Houses of Parliament

Situated in the restored church of St. Mary-At-Lambeth, adjacent to Lambeth Palace, the Museum of Garden History provides an insight into the history and development of gardens and gardening in the UK. It houses a fine public display of tools and artefacts. In addition, there is a replica 17th-century knot garden filled with flowers and shrubs of the period, created around the tombs of the famous plant hunters, the John Tradescants, father and son, and Captain William Bligh of the 'Bounty'.

Times: Daily, 10.30-5.
Facilities: 🅿 (100yds) (metered) 🍽 ♿ all parts accessible toilets for disabled 🐕 (ex guide dogs) 🚐

LONDON SE1

Tate Modern

Bankside SE1 9TG
☎ 20 7887 8008 (info) 📄 020 7401 5052
✉ information@tate.org.uk

Dir: Underground - Southwark, Blackfriars

The Tate Modern, on the bank of the River Thames, is the world's most popular art museum. It is housed in the former Bankside Power Station with a stunning entrance hall in the vast turbine hall. The three levels of galleries are topped with a two-storey glass roof, which affords spectacular views over London. The Tate Modern presents a permanent collection of modern and contemporary art from 1900 to the present day. Admission to the main gallery is free, but there is generally a fee for the special exhibitions.

Times: *Open all year, Sun-Thu 10-6, Fri & Sat 10am-10pm. Closed 24-26 Dec.
Facilities: 🅿 (very limited) 🍽 ✕ (licenced) ♿ all parts accessible (parking & wheelchairs available call 020 7887 8888) toilets for disabled 🐕 (ex guide dogs) 🚐 (pre-booking required) 🍴

LONDON SE10

National Maritime Museum

Romney Rd SE10 9NF
☎ 20 8312 6565 📄 020 8312 6632

Dir: Central Greenwich

Britain's seafaring history is represented in a series of exhibits in this impressive modern museum. Themes include exploration and discovery, Nelson, trade and empire, passenger shipping and luxury liners, maritime London, costume, art and the sea, and the future of the sea. There are interactive displays for children and a diverse programme of special exhibitions.

Times: Open all year, daily 10-5. Closed Xmas/New Year.
Facilities: ℗ (50 yds) (parking in Greenwich limited) ⬤ ✕ (licenced) ♿ Ground floor, Garden & Grounds accessible (wheelchairs, advisory service for hearing/sight impaired) toilets for disabled ✄ (guide dogs) 🚌 🚃

LONDON SE10

Old Royal Naval College

2 Cutty Sark Gardens Greenwich SE10 9LW
☎ 20 8269 4791 📄 020 8269 4757
✉ info@greenwichfoundation.org.uk

Dir: In centre of Greenwich, off the one way system, (college approach), located on the Thames next to the Cutty Sark and Greenwich Pier

The Grade I listed Old Royal Naval College buildings are now in the care of the Greenwich Foundation. They occupy the site of the Tudor palace where Henry VIII and Elizabeth I were born. The former Greenwich Hospital buildings incorporate the magnificent Painted Hall by Thornhill and a chapel by James Stuart. Also open to the public are the beautiful grounds of the estate, and a visitor centre featuring an exhibition on the World Heritage Site of maritime Greenwich and its history.

Times: *Open all year (Painted Hall, Chapel and Visitor Centre), daily 10-5 (last admission 4.15). Chapel closed until 12.30 on Sun.
Facilities: ℗ (200mtrs) (all local streets, yellow line roads) ⬤ ✕ (licenced) ♿ Ground floor, Garden & Grounds accessible (parking, wheelchair, staircrawler, access, all with notice) toilets for disabled ✄ (ex guide dogs) 🚌 (no coach parking available) 🚃

Royal Observatory Greenwich

Greenwich Park Greenwich SE10 9NF
☎ 20 8312 6565 📠 020 8312 6632

Dir: Off A2, Greenwich Park

Charles II founded the Royal Observatory in 1675 with the purpose of 'perfecting navigation and astronomy'. It stands at zero meridian longitude and is the original home of Greenwich Mean Time. It houses an extensive collection of historic timekeeping, astronomical and navigational instruments. There are Planetarium shows throughout the year, and special events are planned for the school holidays.

Times: Open all year, daily 10-5. Closed 24-26 Dec & 1 Jan.
Facilities: 🅿 charged ♿ Ground floor, Garden & Grounds accessible toilets for disabled 🚌 🔊

The Queens House

Romney Road Greenwich SE10 9NF
☎ 20 8312 6565 📠 020 8312 6632

Dir: Central Greenwich

The first Palladian-style villa in England, The Queen's House was designed by Inigo Jones for Anne of Denmark and completed for Queen Henrietta Maria, wife of Charles I. Restoration means that the house can be seen as it appeared when new, with bright silks and furnishings. The Great Hall, the State Rooms and a Loggia overlooking Greenwich Park are notable features.

Times: Please telephone for opening times
Facilities: 🅿 (50 yds) ✕ (licenced) ♿ All parts accessible (blind kit / stairclimber / wheelchairs) toilets for disabled 🚌 🔊

LONDON SE23

The Horniman Museum & Gardens

London Road Forest Hill SE23 3PQ
☎ 20 8699 2339 (rec info)
🖷 020 8291 5506
✉ marketing@horniman.ac.uk.oeuk

Dir: Situated on A205

Founder Frederick Horniman, a tea merchant, gave the museum to the people of London in 1901. The three main collections cover ethnography (80,000 artefacts), natural history (250,000 specimens), and music (over 7,000 musical instruments). The ethnography and music collections both have designated status, reflecting their national importance. There are 16 acres of gardens to explore, and the museum runs a full programme of events and activities for adults and children.

Times: *Open all year, Mon-Sat 10.30-5.30, Sun 2-5.30. Closed 24-26 Dec. Gardens close at sunset.
Facilities: P (opposite museum) ♥ & Ground floor, Garden & Grounds accessible (chair lift to parts of upper floor) toilets for disabled ✖ (ex guide dogs or in gardens) 🚃 (telephone in advance)

LONDON SE5

South London Gallery

65 Peckham Road SE5 8UH
☎ 20 7703 6120 🖷 020 7252 4730
✉ mail@southlondongallery.org

Dir: From Vauxhall take A202 to Camberwell Green. Gallery halfway between Camberwell Green and Peckham.

The gallery presents a programme of up to eight exhibitions a year of cutting-edge contemporary art, and has established itself as South East London's premier venue for contemporary visual arts. The Gallery also aims to bring contemporary art of the highest standards to audiences in South London and to assist in the regeneration of the area by attracting audiences from across Britain and abroad.

Times: Tue-Sun 12-6 & Thu 12-8.30. Closed Mon
Facilities: P (on-street parking) & all parts accessible (disabled access, induction loop) toilets for disabled ✖ (ex guide dogs) 🚃 (telephone in advance)

Tate Britain

Millbank SW1P 4RG
☎ 20 7887 8000 & rec info
✉ information@tate.org.uk

Dir: Underground - Pimlico

Tate Britain is the national gallery of British art from 1500 to the present day, from Tudors to the Turner Prize. Tate holds the greatest collection of British art in the world, including works by Blake, Constable, Epstein, Gainsborough, Gilbert and George, Hatoum, Hirst, Hockney, Hodgkin, Hogarth, Moore, Rossetti, Sickert, Spencer, Stubbs and Turner. The gallery is the world centre for the understanding and enjoyment of British art. The opening of the Tate Centenary provides Tate Britain with ten new and five refurbished galleries used for special exhibitions and the permanent collection.

Times: *Open daily 10-5.50. Closed 24-26 Dec.
Facilities: ℗ (100mtrs) (1hr stay) ▶ ✗ (licenced) ⅙ All parts accessible (wheelchairs on request, parking by prior arrangement) toilets for disabled ✗ (ex guide & hearing dogs) ☎ (contact in advance) ◼

Westminster Cathedral

Victoria Street SW1P 1QW
☎ 20 7798 9055 ▤ 020 7798 9090
✉ barrypalmer@rcdow.org.uk

Dir: 300 yds from Victoria Station

Westminster Cathedral is a fascinating example of Victorian architecture. Designed in the Early Christian Byzantine style by John Francis Bentley, its strongly oriental appearance makes it very distinctive. The foundation stone was laid in 1895 but the interior decorations are not fully completed. The Campanile Bell Tower is 273 feet high and has a four-sided viewing gallery with magnificent views over London. The lift is open daily 9am-5pm Mar-Nov but shut Mon-Wed from Dec-Feb.

Times: Open all year, daily 7am-7pm.
Facilities: ℗ (0.25m) (2hr metered parking) ▶ ⅙ Ground floor only accessible (all parts accessible except side chapels) ✗ (ex guide dogs) ◼

LONDON

National Army Museum

Royal Hospital Road Chelsea SW3 4HT
☎ 20 7730 0717 📄 020 7823 6573
✆ info@national-army-museum.ac.uk

Dir: Underground - Sloane Square

The National Army Museum in Chelsea is the only museum embracing the whole of the British Army, from the 15th-century Battle of Agincourt to the present day. Museum exhibits offer a unique insight into the lives of Britain's soldiers, with displays including paintings, weapons, equipment, medals, and uniforms. Reconstructions and life-size models bring history vividly to life.

Times: *Open all year, daily 10-5.30. Closed Good Fri, May Day, 24-26 Dec & 1 Jan.
Facilities: 🅿 🅿 (meters) (coach parking only if pre booked) ♥ ♿ all parts accessible (wheelchair lift to access lower ground floor) toilets for disabled ✕ (ex guide dogs) 🚌 advance booking for free parking & talk

SW3

Royal Hospital Chelsea

Royal Hospital Road SW3 4SR
☎ 20 7881 5204 📄 020 7881 5463
✆ info@chelsea-pensioners.org.uk

Dir: Near Sloane Square, off A3216 & A3031

The Royal Hospital Chelsea was founded in 1682 by Charles II as a retreat for army veterans who had become unfit for duty, through injury or long service. The hospital was built on the site of a theological college founded by James I in 1610. The buildings were designed by Sir Christopher Wren, and then added to by Robert Adam and Sir John Soane. Some 350 'In-Pensioners' are housed here, some of whom do voluntary work as tour guides, clerical assistants and ground staff. Visitors can stroll around the grounds, gain admission to the chapel and Great Hall and visit the Museum.

Times: Open Mon-Sat 10-12 & 2-4, Sun 2-4. (Museum closed Oct-Mar)
Facilities: 🅿 (limited) ♿ Ground floor, Garden & Grounds accessible toilets for disabled 🚌 Limit of 50 per group

Natural History Museum

Cromwell Road SW7 5BD
☎ 20 7942 5000 🖷 020 7942 5075
marketing@nhm.ac.uk

Dir: Underground - South Kensington

The Natural History Museum - the UK's national museum of natural history - is a vast and elaborate Romanesque-style building covering an area of four acres, its terracotta facing decorated with relief mouldings of animals, birds and fishes. A collection of over 70 million specimens from all over the globe ranges from dinosaurs to diamonds and earthquakes to ants, and the exhibits take you on a journey into Earth's past, present and future. Permanent exhibitions include the Earth Galleries, the Darwin Centre, and the Wildlife Garden, the museum's first living exhibition. There is also a varied programme of special exhibitions and children's activities.

Times: Mon-Sat 10-5.50, Sun 11-5.50 (last admission 5.30). Closed 24-26 Dec.
Facilities: P (180yds) (limited parking, use public transport) ☕ ✕ (licenced) ♿ Ground floor only accessible (top floor/one gallery not accessible, wheelchair hire) toilets for disabled 🐕 (ex guide dogs) 🚌 🎫

Science Museum

Exhibition Road South Kensington
SW7 2DD
☎ 20 7942 4000 🖷 020 7942 4421
sciencemuseum@nmsi.ac.uk

Dir: Underground - South Kensington, signed from tube stn

Ideal for children and adults too, the displays feature many working models with knobs to press, handles to turn and buttons to push to various different effects: exhibits are set in motion, light up, rotate and make noises. The collections cover science, technology, engineering and industry through the ages; there are galleries dealing with printing, chemistry, nuclear physics, navigation, photography, electricity, communications and medicine. The new Wellcome Wing includes an IMAX cinema, six new galleries and a restaurant.

Times: *Open all year, daily 10-6. Closed 24-26 Dec.
Facilities: ☕ ✕ (licenced) ♿ all parts accessible (personal 2hr tour of museum) toilets for disabled
🐕 (ex guide dogs) 🚌 🎫

LONDON SW7

Victoria and Albert Museum

Cromwell Road South Kensington SW7 2RL
☎ 20 7942 2000 ✉ vanda@vam.ac.uk

Dir: Underground - South Kensington, Museum situated on A4, Buses C1,14, 74, 414 stop outside the Cromwell Road entrance

The world's finest museum of art and design has collections spanning 3,000 years, comprising sculpture, furniture, fashion and textiles, paintings, silver, glass, ceramics, jewellery, books, prints, and photographs from Britain and all over the world. Highlights include the national collection of paintings by John Constable, the Dress Court showing fashion from 1500 to the present day, a superb Asian collection, the Jewellery Gallery including the Russian Crown Jewels, and the 20th Century Gallery, devoted to contemporary art and design. The stunning British Galleries 1500-1900 tell the story of British design from the Tudor age to the Victorian era.

Times: Open all year, Mon-Sun 10-5.45. Closed 24-26 Dec. Wed & last Fri of month open late, 10am-10pm.
Facilities: P (500yds) (limited, charged parking) ♥ ✕ (licenced) & All parts accessible (Facilities available. Call for details 020 7942 2211) toilets for disabled ✈ (ex guide dogs) ⛴ (must pre-book) ⛴

LONDON W1

The Wallace Collection

Hertford House Manchester Square
W1U 3BN
☎ 20 7563 9500 🖨 020 7224 2155
✉ enquiries@wallacecollection.org

Dir: Underground - Bond St, Baker St, Oxford Circus

An elegant 18th-century town house is an appropriate gallery for this outstanding collection of art. Founded by the 1st Marquis of Hertford, it was bequeathed to the nation in 1897 and came on public display three years later. As well as an unrivalled representation of 18th-century French art with paintings by Boucher, Watteau and Fragonard, Hertford House is the home of Frans Hals' 'Laughing Cavalier' and paintings by Gainsborough, Rubens, Delacroix and Titian. It also houses the largest collection of arms and armour outside the Tower of London.

Times: *Open all year, Mon-Sat 10-5, Sun 12-5. Closed Good Fri, May BH, 24-26 Dec & 1 Jan. Facilities: P (NCP & meters) (meters free on Sun) ♥ ✕ (licenced) & all parts accessible (lift, ramp, wheelchair available upon request) toilets for disabled ✈ (ex guide dogs) ⛴ ⛴

LONDON W2

Serpentine Gallery

Kensington Gardens W2 3XA
☎ 20 7402 6075 🖷 020 7402 4103
✉ varind@serpentinegallery.org

Dir: Underground - Knightsbridge, Lancaster Gate, South Kensington. Bus 9, 10, 12, 52, 94

The Serpentine Gallery, named after the lake in Hyde Park, is situated in the heart of Kensington Gardens in a 1934 tea pavilion, and was founded in 1970 by the Arts Council of Great Britain. Today the Gallery attracts over 400,000 visitors a year and is one the best places in London for modern and contemporary art and architecture.

Times: *Open daily 10-6.
Facilities: 🅿 charged ♿ all parts accessible toilets for disabled
✈ (ex guide dogs) 🚍 🚬

LONDON W4

Hogarth's House

Hogarth Lane Great West Road W4 2QN
☎ 20 8994 6757 🖷 0845 456 2880

Dir: 50yds W of Hogarth rdbt on Great West Road A4

This early 18th-century house was the country home of artist William Hogarth (1697-1764) during the last 15 years of his life. The house contains displays on the artist's life, and most of his best known engravings, including 'Harlot's Progress', 'Rake's Progress' and 'Marriage á la Mode'. In the gardens you can see Hogarth's famous mulberry tree.

Times: Open Apr-Oct, Tue-Fri 1-5, Sat-Sun 1-6; Nov-Mar, Tue-Fri 1-4, Sat-Sun 1-5. Closed Mon (ex BHs), Jan, Good Fri & 25-26 Dec.
Facilities: 🅿 (25 & 50yds) (spaces marked in Axis Centre car park) ♿ Ground floor, Garden & Grounds accessible toilets for disabled ✈ (ex guide dogs)
🚍 (must pre-book)

LONDON WC1

British Museum

Great Russell Street WC1B 3DG
☎ 20 7323 8000 📄 020 7323 8616
✉ information@thebritishmuseum.ac.uk

Dir: Underground - Russell Sq, Tottenham Court Rd, Holborn

Behind its imposing Neo-Classical façade the British Museum displays the rich and varied treasures which make it one of the great museums of the world. Founded in 1753, displays cover the works of humanity from prehistoric to modern times. The galleries are run by eight departments, including Egyptian, Greek and Roman, Japanese, Prehistory and Europe, Prints and Drawings, and Ethnography. On display are Egyptian mummies, sculptures from the Parthenon, Anglo-Saxon treasure from the Sutton Hoo ship burial and the Vindolanda Tablets from Hadrian's Wall. Regular programme of gallery talks, guided tours and lectures, and special children's trails.

Times: *Open all year, Gallery: Mon-Sat 10-5.30 & Thu-Fri 10-8.30. Great Court: Sun-Wed 9-6, Thu-Sat 9am-11pm. Closed Good Fri, 24-26 Dec & 1 Jan. Facilities: ℗ (5 mins walk) ⬤ ✕ (licenced) ♿ Ground floor only accessible (parking by arrangement) toilets for disabled ✖ (ex guide dogs) ➡ (educational groups must book by phone)

LONDON WC1

Petrie Museum of Egyptian Archaeology

Malet Place Univerity College London WC1E 6BT
☎ 20 7679 2884 📄 020 7679 2886
✉ petrie.museum@ucl.ac.uk

Dir: On 1st floor of the D M S Watson building, in Malet Place, off Torrington Place

One of the largest and most inspiring collections of Egyptian archaeology anywhere in the world. The displays illustrate life in the Nile Valley from prehistory, through the era of the Pharaohs to Roman and Islamic times. Especially noted for its collection of the personal items that illustrate life and death in Ancient Egypt, including the world's earliest surviving dress (c 2800 BC).

Times: *Open all year, Tue-Fri 1-5, Sat 10-1. Closed for 1 wk at Xmas/Etr. Facilities: ℗ (meters) ⬤ ✕ ♿ all parts accessible toilets for disabled ✖ (ex guide dogs) ➡ (max 50 people)

Museums of the Royal College of Surgeons

35-43 Lincoln's Inn Fields WC2A 3PE
☎ 20 7869 6560 ▤ 020 7869 6564
❸ museums@rcseng.ac.uk

Dir: Underground - Holborn

The newly-refurbished Hunterian Museum houses the anatomical and pathological specimens collected by John Hunter FRS (1728-1793), a renowned surgeon and teacher of anatomy. The museum also contains the Science of Surgery Gallery which provides an insight into the development of surgical practice from the 18th century to the present day. The Collection Study Centre holds the museum's reserve collection and provides a dedicated space for learning, exploration and study.

Times: Due to reopen in Feb 2005, Mon-Fri 10-5 **Facilities:** ℗ (15mtrs) (pay & display 8.30-6.30pm) ♿ all parts accessible (prior notice required, external lift) ✖ (ex guide dogs) ➥ (must pre-book)

National Gallery

Trafalgar Square WC2N 5DN
☎ 20 7747 2885 ▤ 020 7747 2423
❸ information@ng-london.org.uk

Dir: Underground - Charing Cross, Leicester Square, Embankment & Piccadilly Circus. Rail: Charing Cross. Located on N side of Trafalgar Sq

All the great periods of Western European painting from 1260-1900 are represented here. The Gallery's particular treasures include Velázquez's 'Toilet of Venus', Leonardo da Vinci's cartoon 'The Virgin and Child with Saints Anne and John the Baptist', Rembrandt's 'Belshazzar's Feast', Van Gogh's 'Sunflowers', and Titian's 'Bacchus and Ariadne'. The British paintings include Gainsborough's 'Mr and Mrs Andrews' and Constable's 'Haywain'.

Times: *Open all year, daily 10-6, (Wed until 9). Special major charging exhibitions open normal gallery times. Closed 24-26 Dec & 1 Jan.
Facilities: ℗ (100yds) ▶ ✖ (licenced) ♿ All parts accessible (wheelchair, induction loop, lift, deaf/blind visitor tours) toilets for disabled ✖ (ex guide & hearing dogs) ➥ (must register on arrival at info desk) ◀

LONDON WC2

National Portrait Gallery

St Martin's Place WC2H 0HE
☎ 20 7306 0055 ▯ 020 7306 0056

Dir: Underground - Charing Cross, Leicester Square. Buses to Trafalgar Square

The National Portrait Gallery is home to the largest collection of portraiture in the world featuring famous British men and woman who have created history from the Middle Ages until the present day. Over 1,000 portraits are on display across three floors form Henry VIII and Florence Nightingale to The Beatles and The Queen. And, if you want to rest those weary feet, visit the fabulous Portrait Restaurant on the top floor with roof-top views across London.

Times: *Open all year, Mon-Wed & Sat-Sun 10-6, Thu-Fri 10-9. Closed Good Fri, 24-26 Dec & 1 Jan. (Gallery closure commences 10mins prior to stated time).
Facilities: Ⓟ (200yds) ● ✗ (licenced) & all parts accessible (stair climber, touch tours, audio guide, large print captions) toilets for disabled ✘ (ex guide dogs) ➡ (10+ must pre-book) ◧

LONDON WC2

Sir John Soane's Museum

13 Lincoln's Inn Fields WC2A 3BP
☎ 20 7405 2107 ▯ 020 7831 3957
✉ jnrock@sloane.org.uk

Dir: Underground - Holborn

Sir John Soane was responsible for some of the most splendid architecture in London, and he built his house in 1812 not only to accommodate his personal household but to display his collections of antiquities, sculpture, paintings, drawings and books. The building was originally three houses, each of them demolished and rebuilt in turn. Amongst his treasures are painting by Hogarth, 'The Rake's Progress' and 'An Election'.

Times: Open all year, Tue-Sat 10-5. Also first Tue of month 6-9pm. (Closed BH). Lecture tour Sat 2.30 (limited no of tickets sold from 2pm)
Facilities: Ⓟ (200yds) (metered parking) & Ground floor only accessible (wheelchair available, phone for details of accessibility) ✘ (ex guide dogs) ➡ (pre-booking essential) ◧

LONDON WC2

Theatre Museum

Russell Street Covent Gardent WC2E 7PR
☎ 20 7943 4700 📄 020 7943 4777
✉ tmenquiries@vam.ac.uk

Dir: Underground - Covent Garden, Leicester Sq

Major developments, events and personalities from the performing arts, including stage models, costumes, prints, drawings, posters, puppets, props and a variety of other theatre memorabilia feature at the Theatre Museum. There are guided tours, demonstrations on the art of stage make-up, and you can dress up in costumes from National Theatre companies. Groups are advised to book in advance. Theatre and walking tours 2pm Saturdays.

Times: *Open all year, Tue-Sun 10-6. Closed 24-26 Dec & 1 Jan.
Facilities: 🅿 (meters, NCP 250yds) ♿ all parts accessible (Braille guides, audio tours) toilets for disabled ✖ (ex guide dogs) 🚌 (parking on embankment) 🚎

BARNET

Museum of Domestic Design & Architecture

Middlesex University Cat Hill EN4 8HT
☎ 20 8411 5244 📄 020 8411 6639
✉ moda@mdx.ac.uk

Dir: From M25, J24 signed A111 Cockfosters to Cat Hill rdbt, straight over onto Chase side. Entrance 1st right opposite Chicken Shed Theatre on Cat Hill Campus

MoDA is a museum of the history of the home. It holds one of the world's most comprehensive collections of decorative design for the period 1870 to 1960, and is a rich source of information on how people decorated and lived in their homes. MoDA has two galleries, a lecture theatre for study days, a seminar room with practical workshops for both adults and children, and a study room which gives visitors access to the collections.

Times: Open Tue-Sat 10-5, Sun 2-5. Closed Mon, Etr, Xmas & New Year.
Facilities: 🅿 ♿ all parts accessible (induction loop fitted in lecture theatre) toilets for disabled ✖ (ex guide dogs) 🚌

BEXLEY

Hall Place

Bourne Road DA5 1PQ
☎ 01322 526574 ▤ 01322 522921

Dir: Near jct of A2 & A233

Hall Place is an attractive Grade I listed mansion of chequered flint and brick, with wonderful gardens. There is topiary in the form of the 'Queen's Beasts'; rose, rock, peat and water gardens; and a herb garden with a fascinating range of plants (labelled in braille) for medicine and cooking. There is also a conservatory, a local studies centre and museum. Please telephone for details of the programme of temporary exhibitions, lectures and concerts in the museum and Great Hall.

Times: Open all year, House: Mon-Sat 10-5, Sun & BHs 11-5 (Apr-Oct); Tue-Sat 10-4.15 (Nov-Mar). Gardens: Mon-Fri 7.30-dusk, Sat & Sun 9-dusk.
Facilities: 🅿 🅿 (100yds) (coaches park in additional parking) 🍽 ✕ (licenced) & all parts accessible toilets for disabled ✖ (ex guide/hearing dogs) ▭

KEW

The National Archives

Ruskin Avenue TW9 4DU
☎ 20 8392 5202 ▤ 020 8487 9202
✉ events@pro.gov.uk

Dir: Underground - Kew Gardens

The National Archives for England, Wales and the United Kingdom houses one of the finest, most complete archives in Europe, comprising the records of the central government and law courts from the Norman Conquest to the present century. It is a mine of information with some fascinating material, including the Domesday Book of 1086, and you can see family documents on microfilm in the Family Record Centre. There are permanent exhibitions in the museum plus a rolling programme of exhibitions. Facilities on site include a restaurant and shop.

Times: *Open Mon, Wed & Fri, 9-4.45; Tue, 10-7; Thu, 9-7. Closed 1st wk in Dec, Sun & public holiday wknds.
Facilities: 🅿 🅿 (100mtrs) 🍽 & All parts accessible (hearing loops & large print text in museum) toilets for disabled ✖ (ex guide dogs) ▭ (advanced booking required)

TWICKENHAM

Orleans House Gallery

Riverside TW1 3DJ
☎ 20 8892 0221 ▤ 020 8744 0501
✉ m.denovellis@richmond.gov.uk

Dir: Richmond road (A305), Orleans Rd is on R just past Orleans Park School

Stroll beside the Thames and through the woodland gardens of Orleans House, where you will find stunning 18th-century interior design and an excellent public art gallery. Visitors of all ages can try out their own artistic talents in pre-booked workshops, and wide-ranging temporary exhibitions are held throughout the year - please telephone for details.

Times: *Open Oct-Mar, Tue-Sat 1-4.30, Sun & BH 2-4.30; Apr-Sep Tue-Sat 1-5.30, Sun & BH 2-5.30.
Facilities: 🅿 🅿 (surrounding areas) (coach space not currently available) ♿ Ground floor, Garden & Grounds accessible (handling objects & large print labels for some exhibitions) toilets for disabled 🐕 (ex guide dogs) ⛲ (booking prefered)

LIVERPOOL

Central Library

William Brown Street L3 8EW
☎ 0151 233 5858 ▤ 0151 233 5824
✉ refham.central.library@liverpool.gov.uk

Dir: Located between museum and art gallery

The Picton, Hornby and Brown buildings, situated in the Victorian grandeur of William Brown Street, house Liverpool's collection of over one million books, forming one of Britain's largest and oldest public libraries. Rarities include 'Birds of America' by Audubon and the original copy of King John's Charter. The Liverpool Record Office is one of the country's largest and most significant County Record offices.

Times: *Open all year, Mon-Thu 9-7.30, Fri 9-5, Sat 10-4 & Sun 12-4. Closed BHs.
Facilities: 🅿 (50 yds) (pay & display parking only) ♿ all parts accessible (lift, text magnification, reading machine) toilets for disabled 🐕 (ex guide dogs) ⛲

LIVERPOOL

Conservation Centre

White Chapel L1 6HZ
☎ 0151 478 4999 ▤ 0151 478 4990

Dir: Follow brown tourist signs to Whitechapel

This award-winning centre, the only one of its kind, gives the public an insight into the world of museum and gallery conservation. It is housed in the former Midland Railway Goods Depot, built in the 1870s, on Queen Square in the heart of the city. Objects of interest on view include a mummified crocodile and a 16th-century copy of the 'Mona Lisa'.

Times: Mon-Sat 10-5, Sun 12-5. Closed 23-26 Dec & 1 Jan.
Facilities: ▣ charged ℙ ➤ ᕦ all parts accessible toilets for disabled ✖ (ex guide dogs) ➡ ➡

LIVERPOOL

HM Customs & Excise National Museum

Merseyside Maritime Museum Albert Dock L3 4AQ
☎ 0151 478 4499 ▤ 0151 478 4590

Dir: Albert Dock - follow brown signs

Enter the exciting world of smuggle busting where everyday items reveal their hidden secrets. Find a fake, rummage for hidden goods and spot a suspect traveller. Look into the illustrious history of HM Customs & Excise, it's the longest battle in history and it's still going on today! Exhibits include the tools of the trade, prints, paintings and photographs, plus some fascinating confiscated goods.

Times: Open daily 10-5.
Closed 23-26 Dec & 1 Jan.
Facilities: ▣ ℙ (100yds) ➤ ✖ (licenced) ᕦ Ground floor only accessible (restricted wheelchair access, no access to basement) toilets for disabled
✖ (ex guide dogs) ➡ (prebooked) ➡

LIVERPOOL

Liverpool Museum

William Brown Street L3 8EN
☎ 0151 478 4393
✉ themuseum@liverpoolmuseums.org.uk

Dir: In city centre next to St George's Hall and Lime St, follow brown signs

One of Britain's most interesting museums, the Liverpool Museum has diverse collections ranging from the Amazonian rain forests to the mysteries of outer space. Special attractions include the award-winning hands-on Natural History Centre and the Planetarium. The museum is undergoing extensive building improvements and refurbishment for its 'Into the Future' project which will lead it to double in size.

Times: Open Mon-Sat 10-5, Sun noon-5. Closed 23-26 Dec & 1 Jan.
Facilities: Ⓟ ☕ ♿ Ground floor only accessible toilets for disabled ✈ (ex guide dogs) 🚌 (book in advance)

LIVERPOOL

Merseyside Maritime Museum

Albert Dock L3 4AQ
☎ 0151 478 4499 🖷 0151 478 4590

Dir: Albert Dock situated near Liverpool's historic waterfront. Entry into dock is from the Strand

Set in the heart of Liverpool's magnificent waterfront, the Merseyside Maritime Museum is located in a former bonded warehouse on Albert Dock. The museum offers a unique insight into the history of the great port of Liverpool, its ships and its people, and the archive has one of the finest collections of merchant shipping records in the UK. There are exhibits on transatlantic slavery, the mass emigration from Liverpool to the New World between 1830 and 1930, and the opulent liners 'Titanic' and 'Lusitania'.

Times: Open daily 10-5. Closed 23-26 Dec & 1 Jan. **Facilities:** Ⓟ ✗ (licenced) ♿ all parts accessible (lifts, wheelchairs, ramps, ex pilot boat & basement) toilets for disabled ✈ (ex guide dogs) 🚌 🚢

LIVERPOOL

Museum of Liverpool Life

Pier Head L3 4AA
☎ 0151 478 4080 🖷 0151 478 4090
✉ liverpoollife@liverpoolmuseums.org.uk

Dir: Follow signs for Albert Dock, museum is on Pier Head side

The Museum of Liverpool Life celebrates the contribution of the people of Liverpool to national life. It recently expanded to include three new galleries: 'City Lives' exploring the richness of Liverpool's cultural diversity, 'The River Room' featuring life around the River Mersey and 'City Soldiers' about the King's Regiment. Other galleries include 'Mersey Culture' from Brookside to the Grand National, 'Making a Living' and 'Demanding a Voice'.

Times: Open daily 10-5. Closed from 2 on 24 Dec and all day 25-26 Dec & 1 Jan)
Facilities: 🅿 charged 🅿 (400yds) ♿ all parts accessible (wheelchairs, audio handsets, subtitles on video terminals) toilets for disabled 🦮 (ex guide/hearing dogs) 🚌 (booked in advance) 🍽

LIVERPOOL

Sudley House

Mossley Hill Road L18 8BX
☎ 0151 724 3245
✉ sudley@liverpoolmuseums.org.uk

Dir: Near Aigburth Station and Mossley Hill Station

Sudley House is the former family home of the Liverpool merchant George Holt in the Liverpool suburb of Mossley Hill. Works on show are drawn mainly from his collection of British paintings including Landseer, Turner, Gainsborough, Reynolds and Romney, as well as major pre-Raphaelite painters. Many of the original Victorian features of the building survive, including tiles, ceramics, stained glass and wallpaper.

Times: Open Mon-Sat 10-5, Sun noon-5. Closed 23-26 Dec & 1 Jan.
Facilities: 🅿 🍽 ♿ Ground floor only accessible 🦮 (ex guide dogs) 🚌

LIVERPOOL

Tate Liverpool

Albert Dock L3 4BB
☎ 0151 702 7400 ▤ 0151 702 7401
✉ liverpoolinfo@tate.org.uk

Dir: Within walking distance of Liverpool Lime Street train station

A converted Victorian warehouse with stunning views across the River Mersey, Tate Liverpool displays the best of the National Collection of 20th-Century Art. A changing programme of exhibitions draws on works from public and private collections across the world.

Times: *Open Tue-Sun, 10-5.30. Closed Mon ex BH Mon, 25-26 Dec, 1 Jan & Good Fri. **Facilities:** P ● & all parts accessible (wheelchairs available, leaflets in Braille, hearing loop) toilets for disabled ▭ ◼

LIVERPOOL

The Walker

William Brown St L3 8EL
☎ 0151 478 4199 ▤ 0151 478 4390

Dir: Follow brown and white signs

For over 120 years, visitors have been surprised, charmed and moved by The Walker's world-famous collection of fine and decorative art, including masterpieces by Rembrandt, Poussin, Rubens and Murillo. The gallery has recently undergone a £4.3 million refurbishment, which has included the development of new temporary exhibition space and a re-hang of the permanent collection. The new galleries promise an exciting and varied programme of must see exhibitions.

Times: Open Mon-Sat 10-5, Sun 12-5. Closed 23-26 Dec & 1 Jan.
Facilities: P charged P (0.25m) ● ✖ & all parts accessible (prior notice appreciated, wheelchair on request) toilets for disabled ✖ (ex guide dogs) ▭

PORT SUNLIGHT

Lady Lever Art Gallery

CH62 5EQ
☎ 0151 478 4136 📄 0151 478 4140
✉ ladyleverartgallery@nmgm.org

Dir: Follow brown heritage signs

Sunlight Soap magnate William Hesketh Lever, the first Lord Leverhulme, founded the Lady Lever Art Gallery in 1922 in memory of his wife. The gallery houses many world famous works of art, including Pre-Raphaelite masterpieces by Millais, Burne-Jones and Rossetti. Dramatic landscapes by the great British painters, Turner and Constable are also displayed alongside portraits by Gainsborough, Romney and Reynolds.

Times: Open all year, Mon-Sat 10-5, Sun 12-5. Closed 23-26 Dec & 1 Jan.
Facilities: 🅿 charged 🅿 (0.25m) 🍴 ♿ all parts accessible (prior notice appreciated, wheelchair on request) toilets for disabled 🐕 (ex guide dogs) 🚗

PRESCOT

Prescot Museum

34 Church Street L34 3LA
☎ 0151 430 7787 📄 0151 430 7219
✉ prescot.museum.dlcs@knowsley.gov.uk

Dir: Situated on corner of High St (A57) & Church St. Follow brown heritage signs

Prescot Museum is located in a handsome Georgian building, formerly a bank. Permanent exhibitions reflect the social, industrial and technological history of the area. Of particular interest is the important collection of watches and clocks, a tribute to the town's horological heritage. It includes a reconstruction of an 18th-century clock maker's home and workshop, and a reconstructed view of a 19th-century watch factory. There is a lively programme of special exhibitions, events and holiday activities. Please contact the museum for details.

Times: *Open all year, Tue-Sat 10-5 (closed 1-2), Sun 2-5. Closed BHs.
Facilities: 🅿 (100 yds) ♿ Ground floor only accessible (ramp to ground floor) 🐕 (ex guide dogs) 🚗

SOUTHPORT

Atkinson Art Gallery

Lord Street PR8 1DH
☎ 01704 533133 ext 2110
🖷 0151 934 2110
✉ atkinson.gallery@leisure.sefton.gov.uk

Dir: Located in centre of Lord St, next to Town Hall

The gallery specialises in 19th and 20th-century oil paintings, watercolours, drawings and prints, as well as 20th-century sculpture. Themed exhibitions of work drawn from the permanent collection are a regular occurrence, along with monthly talks about specific pieces. There is also a programme of temporary exhibitions, so there is always something new to see.

Times: *Open all year, Mon-Wed & Fri 10-5, Thu & Sat 10-1. Closed 25-26 Dec & 1 Jan. **Facilities:** ⓟ (next street) (pay & display) ✕ (licensed) ♿ all parts accessible ✕ (ex guide dogs) 🚌

BACONSTHORPE

Baconsthorpe Castle

NR25 6LN

☎ 1799 322399 **Dir:** 0.75m N of Baconsthorpe off unclass road, 3m E of Holt

The remains of a 15th-century castle, built by Sir John Heydon during the Wars of the Roses. The exact date when the building first begun is not known, since Sir John did not apply for the statutory royal licence necessary to construct a fortified house. In the 1560s Sir John's grandson added the outer gatehouse, which was inhabited until the 1920s when one of the turrets fell down. The remains of red brick and knapped flint are reflected in the lake, which partly embraces the castle as a moat.

Times: *Open all year, any reasonable time. **Facilities:** ⓟ 🚌 ♿

BURGH CASTLE

Burgh Castle

NR31 9PZ

Dir: At far W end of Breydon Water on unclass road, 3m W of Great Yarmouth

Burgh Castle was built in the third century AD by the Romans, as one of a chain of forts along the Saxon Shore - the coast where Saxon invaders landed. Sections of the massive walls still stand: nine feet thick and 14 feet high. On the east wall there are four round towers. The castle is located on Breydon Water, where the Rivers Yare and Waveney meet, and there are some pleasant riverside walks.

Times: *Open any reasonable time.
Facilities: ▭ ✿

CAISTER-ON-SEA

Caister Roman Site

Dir: 3m N of Great Yarmouth

The name Caister has Roman origins, and this was in fact a Roman naval base. The remains include the south gateway, a town wall built of flint with brick courses and part of what may have been a seamen's hostel.

Times: *Open any reasonable time.
Facilities: ▭ ✿

CROMER

Henry Blogg Museum

No 2 Boathouse The Promenade NR27 9HE
☎ 01263 511294 📄 01263 513018
📧 rfmuirhead@csma-netlink.co.uk

Dir: Located at the bottom of East Gangway

A lifeboat has been stationed at Cromer since 1804, and the museum in No 2 boat house at the bottom of The Gangway covers local lifeboat history and the RNLI in general. The main exhibit is the World War II Watson Class lifeboat 'H F Bailey', the boat Henry Blogg coxed. In ten years he helped to save over 500 lives.

Times: *Open Etr-Oct, daily 10-4. Or by appointment with the Curator.
Facilities: 🅿 (pay & display in town) & all parts accessible 🚐 (prior notice preferable)

KING'S LYNN

African Violet Centre

Terrington St Clement PE34 4PL
☎ 01553 828374 📄 01553 828376
📧 info@africanvioletcentre.ltd.uk

Dir: Situated beside A17 5m from Kings Lynn and 3m from A47/A17 jct

A warm and friendly welcome awaits you at the African Violet Centre. As a major plant specialist the centre offers a wide variety of plants for any enthusiast, but is best known for its vast selection and display of African violets. The African Violet Centre is a winner of many Chelsea Gold Medals. Special seasonal events are also a feature.

Times: Open daily Mon-Sat 9-5, Sun 10-5. Closed Xmas & New Year.
Facilities: 🅿 🍽 & all parts accessible (ramps & wide doors) toilets for disabled ✈ (ex guide dogs) 🚐 🍴

N O R F O L K

KING'S LYNN

King's Lynn Arts Centre

27-29 King Street PE30 1HA
☎ 01553 764864 🖷 01553 762141
📧 entertainment_admin@west-norfolk.gov.uk

Dir: Located just off Tuesday Market Place in King Street, next to Globe Hotel

Although it has been used for many purposes, the theatrical associations of this 15th-century guildhall are strongest: Shakespeare himself is said to have performed here. A year round programme of film, performing and visual arts takes place. You can also explore your own artistic potential at one of the courses or workshops run by the centre. Contact the box office for details.

Times: Open Mon-Fri, 10-2. Closed show days, Sun, BHs, Good Fri & 24 Dec-1st Mon in Jan. **Facilities:** Ⓟ (50yds) (pay & display) 🍽 ✕ (licenced) ♿ Ground floor, Garden & Grounds accessible (hearing loop, ramp) ➡ ✹

NORTH CREAKE

Creake Abbey

NR21 9LF

Dir: Off B1355

Originally an almshouse built by the Augustinian order in 1206, it was elevated to an abbey in 1231, though not one of the great wealthy abbeys of the period. It evaded the Dissolution by suffering a different and tragic fate. The church was devastated by a fire, then some 20 years later the order was entirely killed off by the Black Death. The ruins, however, are well worth a visit.

Times: *Open any reasonable time. **Facilities:** ✕ (ex dogs on leads) ➡ ✿

ST OLAVES

St Olave's Priory

Dir: 5.5m SW of Great Yarmouth on A143

These are the remains of an Augustinian priory founded nearly 200 years after the death in 1030 of the patron saint of Norway, after whom it was named. The ruin is located near a bridge on the banks of the River Waveney. The brick-built undercroft can also be visited; the key is available from Priory House.

Times: *Open any reasonable time.
Facilities: 🚌 ♿

THETFORD

Thetford Priory

Dir: On W side of Thetford near station

The Priory of Our Lady of Thetford belonged to the Order of Cluny, and was founded in 1103 by Roger Bigod, an old soldier and friend of William the Conqueror. Little of the original construction remains, but later additions can still be seen, including the gatehouse. The Lady Chapel was added in the 13th century as, according to legend, a vision of the Virgin Mary appeared to local people requesting that this be done.

Times: *Open all year, any reasonable time. Facilities: 🚌 ♿

THETFORD

Thetford Warren Lodge

Dir: 2m W of Thetford, off B1107

These are the remains of a two-storey lodge, built in the early part of the 15th-century of flint with stone dressings. The upper chamber has a fireplace and garderobe. It was built by the Prior of Thetford's for the keeper of the large Westwick rabbit warren, and is set in an attractive wooded area. It can only be viewed from the outside.

Times: *Open any reasonable time. Currently closed for repair, contact regional office on 01233 582700 before visiting.
Facilities: 🚌 🚻

WEETING

Weeting Castle

IP27 0RQ

Dir: 2m N of Brandon off B1106

This ruined 12th-century fortified manor house stands in a rectangular moated enclosure. There are interesting but slight remains of a three-storey cross-wing. The castle was built by Hugh de Plais in 1130, but it was abandoned by the late 14th century.

Times: *Open any reasonable time.
Facilities: 🚌 🚻

KETTERING

Alfred East Gallery

Sheep St NN16 OAN
☎ 01536 534274 📠 01536 534370
✉ museum@kettering.gov.uk

Dir: A43/A6, located in town centre

The art gallery has a permanent exhibition space showing work by Sir Alfred East, Thomas Cooper Gotch and other local artists, as well as selections from the gallery's contemporary collection, including Sir Howard Hodgkin and John Bevan. Two further display spaces are dedicated to monthly changing exhibitions of art, craft and photography, where the pieces are available to purchase.

Times: *Open all year, Mon-Sat 9.30-5 (closed BHs)
Facilities: 🅿 (300yds) ♿ all parts accessible ✘ (ex guide dogs) �

NORTHAMPTON

Northampton Museum & Art Gallery

Guildhall Road NN1 1DP
☎ 01604 838111 📠 01604 838720
✉ museums@northampton.gov.uk

Dir: Situated in town centre, opp Demgate Theatre in Guildhall Rd

Reflecting Northampton's proud standing as Britain's boot and shoe capital, the museum houses a collection of boots and shoes in two new galleries. 'Life and Sole' focuses on the industrial, commercial and health aspects of footwear and includes interactives and an audio-visual display. 'Followers of Fashion' looks at shoe fashion and design. There are galleries and displays with changing programmes, and workshops for children are run during school holidays.

Times: Open all year, Mon-Sat 10-5, Sun 2-5. **Facilities:** 🅿 (200 yds) ♿ all parts accessible (wheelchairs available, large print catalogues) toilets for disabled ✘ (ex guide/assistance dogs) 🚗 (Pre-book) 🚌

NORTHUMBERLAND

CARRAWBROUGH

Temple of Mithras (Hadrian's Wall)

Dir: 3.75m W of Chollerford on B6318

Located south of Hadrian's Wall, designated a World Heritage Site, is this fascinating Mithraic temple, which was uncovered by a farmer in 1949. Its three altars to the god, Mithras, date from the third century AD, and are now in the Museum of Antiquities in Newcastle, but copies have been left on the on site. Mithraism was a cult introduced to the Romans from Persia.

Times: *Open any reasonable time.
Facilities: 🅿 🚻 ♿

MORPETH

Morpeth Chantry Bagpipe Museum

Bridge Street NE61 1PJ
☎ 01670 500717
✉ amoore@castlemorpeth.gov.uk

Dir: Off A1

This unusual museum, housed in the medieval chantry buildings, specialises in the history and development of Northumbrian small pipes and their music. William Alfred Cocks (1892 1971), a clock-maker from Ryton near Newcastle, provided the foundation for the collection. The instruments are set in the context of bagpipes from around the world, from India to Inverness.

Times: Open all year, Mon-Sat, 10-5, open Sun in Aug & Dec. Closed 25-26 Dec, 1 Jan & Etr Mon.
Facilities: 🅿 (100mtrs) ♿ (induction loop, not suitable for wheelchairs) 🚻 ♿

EDWINSTOWE

Sherwood Forest Country Park & Visitor Centre

NG21 9HN
☎ 01623 823202 📄 01623 823202
✉ sherwood.forest@nottscc.gov.uk

Dir: On B6034 N of Edwinstowe between A6075 and A616

At the heart of the Robin Hood legend is Sherwood Forest. Today it offers a country park and visitor centre with 450 acres of ancient oaks and shimmering silver birches. Waymarked pathways are provided to help guide walkers through the forest. A year round programme of events includes the spectacular Robin Hood Festival held annually in late July-early August.

Times: Country Park: open daily dawn to dusk. Visitor Centre: open daily 10-5 (4.30 Nov-Mar)
Facilities: 🅿 charged 🅿 (0.5m) (charges at certain times) ✗ ⅃ all parts accessible (wheelchair loan) toilets for disabled

NEWARK-ON-TRENT

Millgate Museum

48 Millgate NG24 4TS
☎ 01636 655730 📄 01636 655735
✉ museums@nsdc.info

Dir: Easy access from A1 & A46

The Millgate Museum shows some fascinating exhibitions such as recreated streets, shops and houses in period settings. These displays illustrate the working and domestic life of local people from Victorian times to 1950. The mezzanine gallery is used as a temporary exhibition space showcasing the work of local artists, designers and photographers.

Times: *Open all year, Mon-Fri 10-5, Sat & Sun & BH 1-5. (Last admission 4.30).
Facilities: 🅿 (250yds) 🅿 ⅃ Ground floor only accessible toilets for disabled ✈ (ex assistance dogs) 🚃 (pre-book)

NOTTINGHAM

The Lace Centre

Severns Building Castle Road NG1 6AA
☎ 0115 941 3539 📄 0115 941 3539

Dir: Follow signs for Castle, situated opp Robin Hood statue

Exquisite Nottingham lace fills this small 14th-century building to capacity, with panels also hanging from the beamed ceiling. The Lace Centre occupies one of the area's last remaining timber framed houses, close to the castle, in a district known as the Lace Market. The lace is still hand-made today, and there are weekly demonstrations of lace-making on Thursday afternoons from Easter to October.Please telephone for details.

Times: *Open Jan-Mar, daily 10-4; Apr-Nov, 10-5. Every Sun 11-4. Closed Xmas & New Year **Facilities:** 🅿 (100yds) (metered street parking) 🚌 🔺

NOTTINGHAM

The Lace Market Centre

3-5 High Pavement The Lace Market
NG1 1HF
☎ 0115 988 1849 📄 0115 950 5166
✉ info@nottinghamlace.org

Dir: Follow signs for Lace Market. Parking in city centre

'Nottingham Lace and its People' is a free exhibition that includes a photographic story, and hand-made and machine-made lace demonstrations. The Lace Market Trail, which takes about an hour, guides you to all the points of interest around this historical part of the city by means of an audio wand.

Times: *Open Mon-Sat, 10-5: Sun 10.30-4. Closed Xmas.
Facilities: 🅿 (100yds) ♿ Ground floor only accessible (counters at lower level, lift, audio & written tour) ✈ (ex guide dogs) 🚌 (large groups may be split up) 🔺

OLLERTON

Rufford Abbey and Country Park

NG22 9DF
☎ 01623 822944 ▤ 01623 824840
✉ marilyn.louden@nottscc.gov.uk

Dir: 2m S of Ollerton, adjacent to A614

At the heart of the wooded country park stand the remains of a 12th-century Cistercian Abbey, housing an exhibition on the life of a Cistercian Monks at Rufford. Many species of wildlife can be seen on the lake, and there are lovely formal gardens, with sculptures and Britain's first centre for studio ceramics.

Times: Open all year 10.30-5.30 (craft centre closes 4pm Jan & Feb). For further details of opening times telephone establishment.
Facilities: 🅿 charged 🅿(charged for at various times of year) 🍽 ✕ (licenced) ♿ Ground floor, Garden & Grounds accessible (lift to craft centre gallery, free parking,wheelchair loan) toilets for disabled ✖ (ex guide dogs) 🚃 🚃

BANBURY

Banbury Museum

Spiceball Park Road OX16 2PQ
☎ 01295 259855 ▤ 01295 269469
✉ banburymuseum@cherwell-dc.gov.uk

Dir: M40 J11 straight across at first rdbt into Hennef Way, L at next rdbt into Concord Ave, R at next rdbt & L at next rdbt, Castle Quay Shopping Centre & Museum on R

Banbury's stunning new museum is situated in an attractive canal-side location in the centre of town. Exciting modern displays tell of Banbury's origins and historic past. The Civil War, the plush manufacturing industry, the Victorian market town, costume from the 17th century to the present day, Tooley's Boatyard and the Oxford Canal, are just some of the subjects illustrated in this fine development.

Times: *Open all year, Mon-Sat, 10-5, Sun 10.30-4.30.
Facilities: 🅿 (500yds) 🍽 ✕ (licenced) ♿ all parts accessible toilets for disabled ✖ (ex guide dogs) 🚃 (must pre-book) 🚃

DEDDINGTON

Deddington Castle

OX5 4TE

Dir: S of B4031 on E side of Deddington

The large earthworks of the outer and inner baileys of Deddington Castle can still be seen, however, the remains of the 12th-century castle buildings have been excavated - in 1947 and in 1977 - and are not now visible. The grassed-in enclosure provides a pleasant recreational space and is popular with dog walkers.

Times: *Open any reasonable time.
Facilities: ▭ ⚘

MINSTER LOVELL

Minster Lovell Hall & Dovecot

OX8 5RN

Dir: Adjacent to Minster Lovell Church, 3m W of Witney off A40

Home of the ill-fated Lovell family, the ruins of the 15th-century house are steeped in history and legend. The hall is in a lovely setting on the banks of the River Windrush. One of the main features of the estate is the medieval dovecote: stone-built with a conical roof and cupola supported on three wooden pillars.

Times: *Open any reasonable time.
Facilities: ▭ ⚘

NORTH LEIGH

North Leigh Roman Villa

OX8 6QB

Dir: 2m N of North Leigh

These are the remains of a large and well-built Roman villa, located down a track 600 metres from the main road. The villa, which once belonged to a wealthy Roman, is built around a large courtyard, and the most important feature is an almost complete mosaic tile floor, which is intricately patterned in reds and browns and is believed to have been made by workers from Cirencester.

Times: *Open, grounds all year. Viewing window for mosaic tile floor. Pedestrian access only from the main road - 600 yds.
Facilities: 🅿 🚌 🚻

OXFORD

Ashmolean Museum of Art & Archaeology

Beaumont Street OX1 2PH
☎ 01865 278000 📄 01865 278018

Dir: City centre, opposite The Randolph Hotel

The oldest public museum in the country, opened in 1683, the Ashmolean contains Oxford University's priceless collections of art and archaeological artefacts. These are divided into five curatorial areas: Antiquities, the Cast Gallery (casts of sculptures from around the world), Eastern Art, the Heberden Coin Gallery and Western Art. Many important historical art pieces and artefacts are on display, including work from Ancient Greece through to the 20th century.

Times: *Open all year, Tue-Sat 10-5, Sun & BH Mons 2-5. Closed Etr & during St.Giles Fair in early Sep, Xmas & 1 Jan.
Facilities: 🅿 (100-200mtrs) (pay & display) 🅿 ✕ (licenced) ♿ Ground floor only accessible (entry ramp from Beaumont St. Tel. before visit) toilets for disabled 🚌 (big parties split 15 max, booking req) 🍴

OXFORD

Museum of the History of Science

Old Ashmolean Building Broad Street
OX1 3AZ
☎ 01865 277280 ▤ 01865 277288
✉ museum@mhs.ox.ac.uk

Dir: Next to Sheldonian Theatre in city centre, on Bond St

The Museum of the History of Science is located in the first purpose built museum in Britain, the original Ashmolean Museum built in 1683 to accommodate the Ashmolean collection. It is now home to the world's finest collection of early scientific instruments used in astronomy, navigation, surveying, physics and chemistry.

Times: *Open Tue-Sat 12-4, Sun 2-5. Closed Xmas wk.
Facilities: ℙ (300mtrs) (limited street parking, meters) ♿ Ground floor only accessible (lift) toilets for disabled ✱ (ex guide dogs) ▭ (Max 15 people) ◀

OXFORD

Oxford University Museum of Natural History

Parks Road OX1 3PW
☎ 01865 272950 ▤ 01865 272970
✉ info@oum.ox.ac.uk

Dir: Opposite Keble College

Built between 1855 and 1860, this museum of 'the natural sciences' was intended to satisfy a growing interest in biology, botany, archaeology, zoology, entomology and so on. The museum reflects Oxford University's position as a 19th-century centre of learning, with displays of early dinosaur discoveries, Darwinian evolution and Elias Ashmole's collection of preserved animals. Although visitors to the Pitt-Rivers Museum must pass through the University Museum, the two should not be confused.

Times: *Open daily 12-5. Times vary at Xmas & Etr.
Facilities: ℙ (200mtrs) (meter parking) ♿ Ground floor, Garden & Grounds accessible toilets for disabled ▭

OXFORD

Pitt Rivers Museum

South Parks Road OX1 3PP
☎ 01865 270927 📠 01865 270943
📧 prm@prm.ox.ac.uk

Dir: 10 min walk from city centre

The Pitt Rivers Museum is one of the city's most popular attractions, it is part of the University of Oxford and was founded in 1884. The collections held at the museum are internationally acclaimed, and contain many objects from different cultures of the world and from various periods, all grouped by type or purpose. A new research centre for the museum is currently under construction. Special exhibitions and events are regular features.

Times: *Open Mon-Sat 12-4.30 & Sun 2-4.30. Closed Xmas & Etr, open BHs.
Facilities: P (parking for disabled if booked) & Ground floor only accessible (audio guide, wheelchair trail and map to ground floor) toilets for disabled ✈ (ex guide dogs) ⊟

OXFORD

St Edmund Hall

College of Oxford University OX1 4AR
☎ 01865 279000 📠 01865 279090
📧 bursary@seh.ox.ac.uk

Dir: Queen's Lane Oxford at end of High St

This is the only surviving medieval academic hall and has a Norman crypt, 17th-century dining hall, chapel and quadrangle. Other buildings are of the 18th and 20th centuries. It is named after St Edmund of Abingdon, who taught in a house on this site in the 1190s. Within the university it is better known by its nickname 'Teddy Hall'.

Times: *Open all year. Closed 24 Dec-4 Jan, 9-18 Apr & 28-31 Aug.
Facilities: ♥ & Ground floor, Garden & Grounds accessible toilets for disabled ✈ (ex guide dogs) ⊟ (prior notice required)

UFFINGTON

Uffington Castle, White Horse & Dragon Hill

☎ 01793 762209

Dir: S of B4507

The 'castle' is an Iron Age fort on the ancient Ridgeway Path. It covers about eight acres and has only one gateway. On the hillside below the fort is the White Horse, a 375-foot prehistoric figure carved in the chalky hillside and thought to be about 3,000 years old. Dragon Hill is a flat topped mound in the valley below the White Horse and, according to legend, this is where St George slew the dragon.

Times: *Open all year.
Facilities: 🅿 (disabled car park) 🚍 ♿

WOODSTOCK

The Oxfordshire Museum

Fletcher's House OX20 1SN
☎ 01993 811456 📄 01993 813239
✉ oxon.museum@oxfordshire.go.uk

Dir: A44 Evesham-Oxford, follow signs for Blenheim Palace. Museum opposite church

Situated in the heart of the historic town of Woodstock, the award-winning redevelopment of Fletcher's House provides a home for the new county museum. Set in attractive gardens, the new museum celebrates Oxfordshire in all its diversity and features collections of local history, art, archaeology, landscape and wildlife as well as a gallery exploring the country's innovative industries from nuclear power to nanotechnology. Interactive exhibits offer new learning experiences for visitors of all ages. The museum's purpose-built Garden Gallery houses a variety of touring exhibitions of regional and national interest.

Times: Open all year, Tue-Sat 10-5. (Last admission 4.30). Closed Good Fri, 25-26 Dec & 1 Jan. Galleries closed on Mon, but open BH Mons, 2-5. **Facilities:** 🅿 (outside entrance) (free parking) 🍽 ✗ (licenced) ♿ all parts accessible (chair lifts to all galleries) toilets for disabled ✈ (ex guide dogs) 🚍 (pre-booked only)

Oakham Castle

Catmos Street LE15 6HW
☎ 01572 758440 📄 01572 758445
✉ museum@rutland.gov.uk

Dir: Off Market Place

An exceptionally fine Norman great hall of a 12th-century fortified manor house. Earthworks, walls and remains of an earlier motte can be seen along with medieval sculptures and a unique presentation horseshoes forfeited by peers of the realm and royalty to the Lord of the Manor. The castle is licensed for civil marriages. Please enquire for details of the Oakham Festival.

Times: Open all year, Mon-Sat 10.30-5 (closed 1-1.30), Sun 2-4. Closed Good Fri & Xmas.
Facilities: 🅿 (400yds) (disabled parking only by notification) ♿ all parts accessible ✈ (ex guide dogs) 🚌 (pre-booking preferred)

Rutland County Museum

Catmos St LE15 6HW
☎ 01572 758440 📄 01572 758445
✉ museum@rutland.gov.uk

Dir: On A6003, S of town centre

Rutland County Museum displays collections of farming equipment, machinery and wagons, rural tradesmen's tools, domestic artefacts and local archaeology, all housed in a splendid late 18th-century cavalry riding school. The new 'Welcome to Rutland' gallery provides a guide to the history of Rutland and includes a shop and study area.

Times: Open all year, Mon-Sat 10.30-5, Sun 2-4. Closed Good Fri & Xmas.
Facilities: 🅿 (adjacent) (pay & display, free on Sun) ♿ Ground floor only accessible (induction loop in meeting room) toilets for disabled ✈ (ex guide dogs) 🚌 (pre-booking preferred)

RUTLAND

ACTON BURNELL

Acton Burnell Castle

SY5 7PE

Dir: In Acton Burnell on unclass road 8m S of Shrewsbury

What you see today is the warm red sandstone shell of a fortified 13th-century manor house, located near the pretty village of Acton Burnell, by the church. It was built by Robert Burnell, Chancellor of England. King Edward I was a regular visitor and it is believed that he convened the first parliament at which the commons were fully represented here.

Times: *Open at all reasonable times.
Facilities: & all parts accessible 🚍 ✤

BOSCOBEL

Whiteladies Priory

Dir: 1m SW of Boscobel House, off an unclass road between A41 and A5

Only the ruins are left of this Augustinian priory, which dates from 1158 and was destroyed in the Civil War. What you see are parts of the Norman priory church, of simple design but with some lovely carving. After the Battle of Worcester Charles II hid at the priory and in the nearby woods before going on to Boscobel House. The woodland setting is still very attractive.

Times: *Open any reasonable time.
Facilities: 🚍 ✤

COSFORD

The Royal Air Force Museum

TF11 8UP

☎ 01902 376200 📠 01902 376211
📧 cosford@rafmuseum.org

Dir: On A41, 1m S of M54 J3

The Royal Airforce Museum at the Shropshire RAF base has one of the largest aviation collections in the UK. Exhibits include the Victor and Vulcan bombers, the Hastings, York and British Airways airliners, the Belfast freighter and the last airworthy Britannia. The research and development collection includes the notable TSR2, Fairey Delta, Bristol 188 and many more important aircraft.

Times: *Open all year daily, 10-6 (last admission 4). Closed 24-26 Dec & 1 Jan
Facilities: 🅿 ✕ (licenced) ♿ all parts accessible (free loan of 3 manual wheelchairs) toilets for disabled ✖ (ex guide dogs) 🚌 (pre-booked only)

LILLESHALL

Lilleshall Abbey

TF10 9HW

☎ 121 625 6820 **Dir:** Off A518 on unclass road

Lilleshall Abbey was founded shortly before the middle of the 12th century, and its extensive ruins are to be found in the beautiful grounds of Lilleshall Hall. What remains are parts of the church and cloisters, surrounded by ancient yew trees. From the high west front visitors can look down the entire 228-foot length of the abbey church.

Times: *Open any reasonable time.
Facilities: 🚌 ✿

MORETON CORBET

Moreton Corbet Castle

Dir: Off B5063, in Moreton Corbet

The castle was inherited by the Corbets in 1235, and they are thought to have remodelled the great keep, though the castle may already have been over a century old by then. It was remodelled again in the 16th century and then partially demolished to make way for a great Elizabethan mansion House. Although damaged in the civil war, the castle and mansion stand today as one of the most picturesque ruins of the Shropshire Marches.

Times: *Open all reasonable times.
Facilities: 🅿 ♿ all parts accessible 🚍 ▦

OSWESTRY

Old Oswestry Hill Fort

Dir: 1m N of Oswestry, off an unclass road off A483

This impressive Iron Age hill-fort covers an area of 68 acres. It is defended by a series of five ramparts, with an elaborate western entrance and unusual earthwork cisterns. Legend has it that this hill fort was the birth place of Arthur's Queen Guinevere. If you climb to the top you will be rewarded with fabulous views on a clear day.

Times: *Open any reasonable time.
Facilities: 🚍 ▦

AXBRIDGE

King John's Hunting Lodge

The Square BS26 2AP
☎ 1934 732012

Dir: On corner of Axbridge High St, in the Square

Nothing to do with King John or with hunting, this jettied and timber-framed house was built around 1500. It gives a good indication of the wealth of the merchants of that time and is now a museum of local history. On display with the old photographs and paintings are evocative items such as the town stocks and constables' staves.

Times: *Open Apr-Sep, daily 1-4.
Facilities: ♿ Ground floor only accessible 🚌

NUNNEY

Nunney Castle

Dir: 3.5m SW of Frome, off A361

Built in 1373, and supposedly modelled on France's Bastille, this crenellated manor house has one of the deepest moats in England. Following an uneventful few centuries, the castle was wrecked by Parliamentarian forces in the Civil War after a two-day siege. The ruin is located by the medieval parish church in the village of Nunney.

Times: *Open any reasonable time.
Facilities: ♿ Garden & Grounds only accessible 🚌

STOKE SUB HAMDON

Stoke sub Hamdon Priory

North Street TA4 6QP

☎ 1985 843600 **Dir:** Between A303 & A3088

This complex of buildings, used for a time as farm buildings, was originally built in the 14th century to house the priests of the Chantry Chapel of St Nicholas, which has long since been destroyed. The priory's Great Hall is open to visitors.

Times: *Open 27 Mar-Oct, daily 10-6 or dusk if earlier.
Facilities: P (5mtrs) (Braille guides/large print guides) ᾧ

STREET

The Shoe Museum

C & J Clark Ltd High Street BA16 0YA
☎ 01458 842169 ▯ 01458 442226

Dir: M5 J23, A39 to Street, follow signs for Clarks Village

The museum is in the oldest part of the shoe factory set up by Cyrus and James Clark in 1825. Here the company made rugs, mops and chamois leather from sheepskins, before they began producing shoes in 1830. The museum's collections include shoes from Roman times to the present, along with buckles, engravings, fashion plates, machinery, hand tools and advertising material.

Times: Open all year, Mon-Fri 10-4.45, Sat 10-1.30 & 2-5, Sun 11-1.30 & 2-5. Closed 10 days over Xmas.
Facilities: charged P & all parts accessible (access wkdays only) ✈ (ex guide dogs) ⊟

CHEDDLETON

Cheddleton Flint Mill

Beside Caldon Canal Leek Rd ST13 7HL

☎ 1782 502907 **Dir:** 3m S of Leek on A520

Twin water-wheels on the River Churnet drive flint-grinding pans in the two mills. The mill museum shows a collection of machinery used in the preparation of materials for the ceramic industry. This includes a 100 HP Robey horizontal steam engine, a model Newcomen beam engine, an edge-runner mill, and the narrow boat 'Vienna', moored on the Caldon Canal. Display panels explain the processes of winning and treating clays, stone and flint for the pottery industry.

Times: *Open all year, Sat & Sun 2-5, Mon-Fri 10-5 (by arrangement). Phone to check **Facilities:** 🅿 🅿 (in Red Lion pub) (coaches must arrange parking at pub) ♿ Ground floor, Garden & Grounds accessible toilets for disabled ➡ (coaches cannot park on site)

HALFPENNY GREEN

Halfpenny Green Vineyards

DY7 5EP

☎ 01384 221122 📄 01384 221101
✉ enquiries@halfpenny-green-vineyards.co.uk

Dir: 0.5m off B4176 Dudley to Telford road

Using German, French and hybrid varieties that can prosper even in the poorest British summer, this vineyard offers 'The complete English wine experience'. This includes a self-guided vineyard trail as well as guided tours, wine-tasting, a craft centre and a visitor centre. Visitors can purchase wines with personalised labels for special occasions. Coarse fishing is also available.

Times: *Open all year, daily 10.30-5. **Facilities:** 🅿 🍽 ✕ (licenced) ♿ all parts accessible toilets for disabled ✷ (ex guide dogs) ➡ (by appointment) ➡

HIMLEY

Himley Hall & Park

DY3 4DF
☎ 01384 817817 📠 01384 817818
✉ himley.hall@dudley.gov.uk

Dir: Off A449, on B4176

The extensive parkland at Himley Hall offers a range of attractions, including a nine-hole golf course and coarse fishing. A permanent orienteering course is provided with a charge being made for the maps. The hall is open to the public when exhibitions are taking place, and guided tours are available by prior arrangement. Outdoor events and concerts are a feature and the Hall is offered for private hire.

Times: *Open Hall: early Apr-mid Sep, 2-5. Closed Mon ex BH. Park open all year.
Facilities: 🅿 charged <ParkingNearSym>(charge up to £1) 🍵 ♿ Ground floor, Garden & Grounds accessible toilets for disabled ✖ (ex guide dogs & in park) 🚌

STAFFORD

Shire Hall Gallery

Market Square ST16 2LD
☎ 01785 278345 📠 02785 278327
✉ shirehallgallery@staffordshire.gov.uk

Dir: M6 J13, follow signs to Stafford town centre & gallery is signed from there

This fine gallery is housed in the 18th-century Shire Hall; the Grade II listed former Crown Court, and one of Staffordshire's most magnificent buildings. It holds exhibitions of contemporary arts, contains historic courtrooms and a Crafts Council selected craft shop. Also in the building are the town's main library and the Tourist Information Centre.

Times: *Open all year Mon-Sat, 9.30-5. Gallery closes for exhibition changes and at BHs, please call for further details.
Facilities: 🅿 (5 mins walk) ✖ ♿ Ground floor, Garden & Grounds accessible toilets for disabled ✖ (ex guide dogs) 🚌 🛍

STOKE-ON-TRENT

The Potteries Museum & Art Gallery

Bethesda Street Hanley ST1 3DW
☎ 01782 232323 🖷 01782 232500
✉ museums@stoke.gov.uk

Dir: M6 J15/16 take A500 to Stoke-on-Trent. Follow signs for city centre (Hanley), Cultural Quarter & The Potteries Museum

The history of the Potteries under one roof, including a dazzling display of the world's finest collection of Staffordshire ceramics. Other displays introduce natural, local and archaeological history from in and around The Potteries, and a Mark 16 Spitfire commemorating its locally born designer, Reginald Mitchell. The art gallery shows displays of the city's art collection and is a part of the Tate Partnership Scheme.

Times: Open Mar-Oct, Mon-Sat 10-5, Sun 2-5; Nov-Feb, Mon-Sat 10-4, Sun 1-4. Closed 25 Dec-1 Jan.
Facilities: 🅿 charged ℗ (200mtrs) (park & ride 500mtrs away) 💷 ♿ all parts accessible (lift, induction loop, 2 wheelchairs available) toilets for disabled ✖ (ex guide/helping dogs) ⊟ ▣

FLIXTON

Norfolk & Suffolk Aviation Museum

Buckeroo Way The Street NR35 1NZ
☎ 01986 896644 ❸
nsam.flixton@virgin.net

Dir: Off A143, take B1062, 2m W of Bungay

This aviation museum in the Waveney Valley has a collection of over 40 historic aircraft. You can also see a Bloodhound surface-to-air missile, the 446th Bomb Group Museum, RAF Bomber Command Museum, the Royal Observer Corps Museum, RAF Air-Sea Rescue and Coastal Command and a souvenir shop. Among the displays are Decoy Sites and Wartime Deception, Fallen Eagles - Wartime Luftwaffe Crashes - and an ex-Ipswich airport hangar made by Norwich company Boulton and Paul Ltd.

Times: Open Apr-Oct, Sun-Thu 10-5 (last admission 4); Nov-Mar, Tue, Wed & Sun 10-4 (last admission 3). Closed late Dec-early Jan. **Facilities:** 🅿 ℗ (100yds) 💷 ♿ all parts accessible (helper advised, ramps/paths to all buildings) toilets for disabled ✖ (ex guide dogs) ⊟

IPSWICH

Christchurch Mansion

Soane Street IP4 2BE
☎ 01473 253246 & 🖷 01473 210328
✆ mansion@ipswich.gov.uk

Dir: S side of Christchurch Park

The house was built in 1548 on the site of an Augustinian priory. Set in a beautiful park close to the centre of town, it displays period rooms and an art gallery with changing exhibitions. The Suffolk Artists' Gallery has a collection of paintings by Constable and Gainsborough. The large park includes ponds, children's play areas, a bird reserve, arboreta, tennis courts, croquet lawns and a bowling green.

Times: *Open all year, Tue-Sat 10-5 (dusk in winter), Sun 2.30-4.30 (dusk in winter). Closed Good Fri, 24-26 Dec & 1-2 Jan. Open BH Mon.
Facilities: ℗ & Ground floor, Garden & Grounds accessible (tape guide for partially sighted) 🚍

IPSWICH

Ipswich Museum

High St IP1 3QH
☎ 01473 433550 🖷 01473 433558
✆ museum.service@ipswich.gov.uk

Dir: Follow tourist signs to Crown St car park. Museum 3 mins walk from here

The museum has sections on Victorian natural history, Suffolk wildlife (including the Suffolk Biological Records), Suffolk geology, Roman Suffolk, Anglo-Saxon Ipswich and Peoples of the World. There is also one of the best bird collections in the country. Special exhibitions are a regular feature in the museum's galleries and in the adjacent High Street Exhibition Gallery. Children's activities are run in the school holidays and there is an interesting programme of lectures.

Times: *Open all year, Tue-Sat 10-5. Closed Sun, BHs, 24-26 Dec & 1 Jan.
Facilities: ℗ (3 min walk) & Ground floor only accessible (lift) toilets for disabled ✖ (ex guide dogs) 🚍 (telephone in advance)

LEISTON

Leiston Abbey

IP16 4TB
☎ 01728 831354 📄 01728 832500
✉ mo@leistonabbey.fsnet.co.uk

Dir: N of Leiston, off B1069

For hundreds of years this 14th-century abbey, built for the Premonstratensian order of canons, was used as a farm and its church became a barn. A Georgian house, now used as a school for young musicians, was built into its fabric and remains of the choir, the church transepts and parts of the cloisters still stand.

Times: Open any reasonable time.
Facilities: 🅿 🅿 no overnight parking ♿ all parts accessible 🚍

LINDSEY

Lindsey Chapel

Rose Green

Dir: On unclass road 0.5m E of Rose Green

The chapel of St James in this pretty Suffolk village was built mainly in the 13th century, of flint and stone with lancet windows and a thatched roof. It was the chantry to Lindsey Castle, little of which remains beyond the traces of the motte and bailey earthworks. The chapel survived the reformation and was put to use as a barn for 400 years until the owner gave it to the nation in 1930.

Times: *Open all year, daily 10-4.
Facilities: ♿ all parts accessible 🚍 🏢

SUFFOLK

ASH VALE

Army Medical Services Museum

Keogh Barracks GU12 5RQ
☎ 01252 868612 📠 01252 868832
✆ museum@keogh72.freeserve.co.uk

Dir: M3 J4 on A331 to Mytchett then follow tourist signs

The museum, which has recently undergone a major refurbishment, traces the history of Army medicine, nursing, dentistry and veterinary science from 1660 until the present day and the contribution made by the four corps. There is an interactive gallantry display, dioramas, medical equipment and ambulances as well as uniforms and medals.

Times: Open all year, Mon-Fri 10-3.30. Closed Xmas, New Year & BH. Wknds & BH by appointment only.
Facilities: 🅿 🅿 (300yds for coaches) ⅋ all parts accessible (hand rails, wide doors) toilets for disabled ✖ (ex guide dogs) 🚽 (pre-booked only)

GUILDFORD

Guildford House Gallery

155 High Street GU1 3AJ
☎ 01483 444740 📠 01483 444742
✆ guildfordhouse@guildford.gov.uk

Dir: N side of High St, opposite Sainsbury's

An impressive building in its own right, Guildford House dates from 1660 and has been Guildford's art gallery since 1959. A changing selection from the Borough's art collection is on display, including pastel portraits by Guildford-born artist John Russell, topographical paintings and contemporary craftwork, as well as a diverse programme of temporary exhibitions.

Times: Open Tue-Sat 10-4.45. Closed Good Fri & Xmas **Facilities:** 🅿 (100yds) 🍽 ✖ ⅋ Ground floor only accessible ✖ (ex guide dogs) 🚽 🚽

REIGATE

Reigate Priory Museum

Bell Street RH2 7RL

☎ 1737 222550 **Dir:** Next to Bell Street car park

The museum is housed in Reigate Priory, a Grade II listed building, which was originally founded before 1200 and converted into a mansion in Tudor times. Notable features include the magnificent Holbein fireplace, 17th-century oak staircase and murals. The small museum has changing exhibitions on a wide range of subjects, designed to appeal to both adults and children. The collection includes domestic bygones, local history and period costume.

Times: Open Etr-early Dec, Wed & Sat, 2-4.30 in term time.
Facilities: P (50yds) & Ground floor, Garden & Grounds accessible (hands on facilities) ➡ (must pre-book)

BRIGHTON

Booth Museum of Natural History

194 Dyke Road BN1 5AA
☎ 01273 292777 📠 01273 292778
✉ boothmus@pavilion.co.uk

Dir: From A27 Brighton by pass, 1.5m NW of town centre, opp Dyke Rd Park

The museum was built in 1874 to house the bird collection of Edward Thomas Booth (1840-1890). His collection is still on display, but the museum has expanded considerably since Booth's day and now includes thousands of butterfly and insect specimens, geology galleries with fossils, rocks and local dinosaur bones, a magnificent collection of animal skeletons, largely collected by the Brighton solicitor F W Lucas (1842-1932), and an interactive discovery gallery.

Times: Open all year, Mon-Sat (ex Thu) 10-5, Sun 2-5. Closed Good Fri, Xmas & 1 Jan.
Facilities: P (road opposite) (4 hr limit) & all parts accessible ✖ (ex guide dogs) ➡ (booking prefered)

BRIGHTON

Brighton Museum & Art Gallery

Royal Pavilion Gardens BN1 1EE
☎ 01273 290900 🖷 01273 292841

Dir: A23/M23 from London, in city centre near seafront. New entrance in Royal Pavilion Gardens

A £10 million redevelopment has transformed Brighton museum into a state-of-the-art visitor attraction. Dynamic and innovative new galleries, including fashion, 20th-century design and world art, feature exciting interactive displays appealing to all ages. The museum also benefits from a spacious new entrance located in the Royal Pavilion gardens and full disabled access.

Times: *Open all year, Tue 10-7, Wed-Sat 10-5 & Sun 2-5. (Closed Mon ex BHs).
Facilities: P (5 mins walk) (Church St NCP & on street) ● & all parts accessible (lift, tactile exhibits, induction loops, ramps, automatic door) toilets for disabled ✈ (ex guide dogs) ⛟

HASTINGS & ST LEONARDS

Old Town Hall Museum of Local History

Old Town Hall High St TN34 3EW
☎ 01424 781166 🖷 01424 781165
🜨 oldtownmuseum@hastings.gov.uk

Dir: Off A259 coast road into High St in Hastings old town. Signed

Situated in the heart of Hastings Old Town, the Georgian former town hall, built in 1823, provides the setting for this local history museum. It has recently undergone a major refurbishment, with help from the Heritage Lottery Fund, and the smartly presented displays tell the story of Hastings Old Town as a walk back in time, with features including a Cinque Ports ship and interactive exhibits.

Times: Open Apr-Sep, daily 10-5; Oct-Mar, daily 11-4.
Facilities: P (150yds) (parking meters in operation) & all parts accessible (lift, evac chair, low-level displays, audio tour) toilets for disabled ✈ (ex guide dogs) ⛟

BRAMBER

Bramber Castle

BN4 3FB

Dir: On W side of village off A283

Here you can see the remains of a Norman motte and bailey castle built in around 1070 by William De Braose. The gatehouse, still standing almost to its original height, and the walls are still visible. When it was built the coast would have been much further inland, and at high tide the water would have reached the castle walls.

Times: *Open any reasonable time.
Facilities: 🅿 🅿 (limited parking) 🚌 🌠

HIGHDOWN

Highdown Gardens

Highdown Gardens BN12 6PE
☎ 01903 501054 📠 01903 218757
✉ chris.beardsley@worthing.gov.uk

Dir: N off A259 between Worthing & Littlehampton. Access off dual carriageway, when coming from E proceed to rdbt

Set on downland countryside this unique garden overlooks the sea, and has been deemed a National collection due to the unique assortment of rare plants and trees. The garden was the achievement of Sir Frederick and Lady Stern, who worked for fifty years to prove that plants could grow on chalk. Many of the original plants were collected in China and the Himalayas.

Times: Open all year: Apr-Sep, Mon-Fri 10-6. Winter: Oct-Nov & Feb-Mar, Mon-Fri, 10-4.30; Dec-Jan, 10-4.
Facilities: 🅿 🅿 (limited parking for coaches) ♿ All parts accessible toilets for disabled 🐕 (ex guide dogs) 🚌 (by appointment only)

GATESHEAD

The Baltic Centre for Contemporary Art

South Shore Road NE8 3BA
☎ 0191 478 1810 📠 0191 478 1922
✉ info@balticmill.com

Dir: Follow signs for Quayside, Millenium Bridge. 15 mins walk from Gateshead Metro & Newcastle Central Station

Once a 1950s grain warehouse, part of the old Baltic Flour Mills, the Baltic Centre for Contemporary Art is an international centre presenting a dynamic and ambitious programme of complementary exhibitions and events. It comprises five art spaces, cinema, auditorium, library and archive, eating and drinking areas and a shop. Check the website for current events information.

Times: *Please see website for details (www.balticmill.com)
Facilities: 🅿 charged 🅿 🍽 ✗ (licenced) ♿ all parts accessible (wheelchairs/scooters, Braille/large-print guides toilets for disabled 🛇 (ex guide dogs & hearing dogs) 🚌

NEWCASTLE UPON TYNE

Museum of Antiquities

The University NE1 7RU
☎ 0191 222 7849 📠 0191 222 8561
✉ m.o.antiquities@ncl.ac.uk

Dir: Positioned on main campus of Newcastle University between The Haymarket and Queen Victoria Rd

Artefacts from the northeast of England dating from prehistoric times to AD 1600 are on display at Newcastle's Museum of Antiquities, which belongs jointly to the Society of Antiquaries and the University of Newcastle Upon Tyne. The principal museum for Hadrian's Wall, this collection includes models of the wall, life-size Roman soldiers and a recently refurbished reconstruction of the Temple of Mithras.

Times: *Open all year, daily (ex Sun), 10-5. Closed Good Fri, 24-26 Dec & 1 Jan.
Facilities: 🅿 (400yds) ♿ all parts accessible (large print guide) 🛇 (ex guide dogs) 🚌 🚃

SUNDERLAND

Museum & Winter Gardens

Burdon Rd SR1 1PP
☎ 0191 553 2323 📠 0191 553 7828
✉ sunderland.museum@tyne-wear-museums.org.uk

Dir: Situated in Sunderland City Centre

This award-winning attraction re-opened in 2001. The wide-ranging displays, with many hands-on exhibits, cover the archaeology and geology of Sunderland, the coal mines and shipyards of the area and the spectacular glass and pottery made on Wearside. Other galleries show the changes in the lifestyles of Sunderland women over the past century, works by LS Lowry and wildlife from all corners of the globe. The Winter Gardens is a horticultural wonderland where the exotic plants from around the world can be seen growing to their full natural height in a spectacular glass and steel rotunda.

Times: *Open all year, Mon 10-4, Tue-Sat 10-5, Sun 2-5.
Facilities: P (150 yds) ✗ (licenced) & all parts accessible (lifts to all floors, induction loops) toilets for disabled ✗ (ex guide dogs) 🚌 (pre-booking prefered) 🎫

RUGBY

The Webb Ellis Rugby Football Museum

5 Saint Matthew's Street CV21 3BY
☎ 01788 567777 📠 01788 537400
✉ service@webb-ellis.co.uk

Dir: On A428 opposite Rugby School

An intriguing collection of Rugby football memorabilia is housed in the shop in which rugby balls have been made since 1842. Visitors can watch a craftsman at work, hand-stitching the balls. The museum is situated near to Rugby School and its famous playing field, and is named after the pupil who suddenly picked up and ran with the ball during a football match in 1823.

Times: *Open all year, Mon-Sat 9-5. Phone for holiday opening times.
Facilities: P (500yds) & all parts accessible ✗ (ex guide dogs) 🚌 (for comfort, max 30 at one time)

WARWICK

Warwickshire Yeomanry Museum

The Court House Vaults Jury Street CV34 4EW

☎ 01926 492212 📠 01926 494837

Dir: Situated on corner of Jury St & Castle St, 2m E of M40 J15

The vaults of the courthouse display militaria from the county Yeomanry, dating from 1794 to 1945. It includes regimental silver, paintings, uniforms and weapons. A small room in the cellars now houses the HUJ Gun project, a field gun captured by the Yeomanry in 1917.

Times: *Open Good Fri-Sep, Fri-Sun & BHs, 10-1 & 2-4. Other times by prior arrangement.

Facilities: P (300yds) (2hr max in nearby streets) 🚌 (max 15 preferred)

BIRMINGHAM

Aston Hall

Trinity Road Aston B6 6JD

☎ 0121 327 0062 📠 0121 327 7162

✉ bmag-enquiries@birmingham.gov.uk

Dir: M6 J6 follow A38(M) Aston Expressway towards city centre. Leave at Aston Waterlinks and follow brown signs to Aston Hall

Built by Sir Thomas Holte, Aston Hall is a fine Jacobean mansion complete with a panelled Long Gallery, balustraded staircase and magnificent plaster friezes and ceilings. King Charles I spent a night here during the Civil War and the house was damaged by Parliamentarian troops. It was also leased to James Watt Junior, the son of the great industrial pioneer.

Times: *Open Etr-Oct, Tue-Sun 11.30-4. Closed Mon ex BHs.

Facilities: P 🍴 & Garden & Grounds only accessible (ground floor only partially accessible) 🐕 (ex guide dogs) 🚌 (by arrangement)

Birmingham Museum & Art Gallery

Chamberlain Sq B3 3DH
☎ 0121 303 2834 📠 0121 303 1394
✉ bmag-enquiries@birmingham.gov.uk

One of the world's best collections of Pre-Raphaelite paintings can be seen here, including important works by Burne-Jones, a native of Birmingham. Also on display are fine silver, ceramics and glass. The archaeology section has prehistoric Egyptian, Greek and Roman antiquities, and also objects from the Near East, Mexico and Peru.

Times: *Open all year, Mon-Thu & Sat 10-5, Fri 10.30-5 and Sun 12.30-5.
Facilities: P ▶ ✕ (licenced) & all parts accessible (lift) toilets for disabled 🚍 ▄

Museum of the Jewellery Quarter

75-79 Vyse St Hockley B18 6HA
☎ 0121 554 3598 📠 0121 554 9700
✉ bmag-enquiries@birmingham.gov.uk

Dir: Off A41 into Vyse St, museum on L after 1st side street

The museum tells the story of jewellery making in Birmingham from its origins in the Middle Ages right through to the present day. Discover the skill of the jeweller's craft and enjoy a unique tour of an original jewellery factory frozen in time. The Jewellery Quarter is still very much at the forefront of jewellery manufacture in Britain and the museum showcases the work of the city's most exciting new designers.

Times: *Open Etr-Oct, Tue-Sun 11.30-4. (Closed Mon ex BH Mon)
Facilities: P (limited 2hr stay/pay & display) ▶ & all parts accessible (tours for hearing/visually impaired booked in advance) toilets for disabled ✕ (ex guide dogs) 🚍 (prebooked) ▄

BIRMINGHAM

RSPB Sandwell Valley Nature Reserve

20 Tanhouse Avenue Great Barr B43 5AG
☎ 0121 357 7395 📄 0121 358 3013

Dir: Off B4167 Hamstead Rd into Tanhouse Ave

Opened in 1983 on the site of an old colliery, Sandwell Valley is home to hundreds of bird, animal and insect species in five different habitats. Summer is the best time to see the yellow wagtail or reed warblers, while wintertime attracts goosanders, snipe, and redshanks. There are guided walks and bug hunts for the kids in summer, and a shop and visitor centre all year round.

Times: *Open Tue-Fri 9-5, Sat & Sun 10-5 (closes at dusk in winter). Closed Mon, 24 Dec-2 Jan
Facilities: 🅿 🅿 2km ♿ all parts accessible toilets for disabled 🚌

BIRMINGHAM

Sarehole Mill

Cole Bank Road Hall Green B13 0BD
☎ 0121 777 6612 📄 0121 303 2891

Dir: M42 J4. Take A34 towards Birmingham. After 5m turn L on B4146, attraction on L

Birmingham's only working watermill was built in the 1760s. Used for both flour production and metal rolling up to the last century, the mill can still be seen in action during the summer months. The mill was restored with financial backing from J R R Tolkien, who grew up in the area and cites Sarehole as an influence for writing 'The Hobbit' and 'Lord of the Rings'.

Times: *Open Etr-Oct, Tue-Sun 11.30-4. (Closed Mon, ex BH Mon)
Facilities: 🅿 (no coaches) ✈ (ex guide dogs) 🚌 (by arrangement)

BIRMINGHAM

Soho House

Soho Avenue Handsworth B18 5LB
☎ 0121 554 9122 ▤ 0121 554 5929
✉ bmag-enquiries@birmingham.gov.uk

Dir: From city centre follow A41 to Soho Rd, follow brown heritage signs to Soho Ave

Soho House was the elegant home of industrial pioneer Matthew Boulton between 1766 and 1809. Here, he met with some of the most important thinkers and scientists of his day. The house has been carefully restored and contains many of Matthew Boulton's possessions including furniture, clocks, silverware and the original dining table where the Lunar Society met.

Times: *Open Etr-Oct, Tue-Sun 11.30-4. (Closed Mon ex BH Mons)
Facilities: ℗ ➊ ♿ all parts accessible (induction loop) toilets for disabled ✖ (ex guide dogs) ➌ (by arrangement) ◀

COVENTRY

Coventry Transport Museum

Hales Street CV1 1PN
☎ 24 7683 2425 ▤ 024 7683 2465
✉ museum@mbrt.co.uk

Dir: Just off J1, Coventry ring road, Tower St in city centre

Coventry is the traditional home of the motor industry, and the Coventry Transport Museum displays the largest collection of British cars, buses, cycles and motorcycles in the world. Visitors can learn about motoring's early days in 'Landmarques', how royalty travelled, and see Thrust 2 and Thrust SSC, the world land speed record cars.

Times: *Open all year, daily 10-5. Closed 24-26 Dec.
Facilities: ℗ (adjacent) (pay & display) ➊ ♿ all parts accessible (audio tour, tactile floor & models, wheelchairs for hire) toilets for disabled ✖ (ex guide dogs) ➌ (pre-booking preferred) ◀

COVENTRY

Herbert Art Gallery & Museum

Jordan Well CV1 5QP
☎ 24 7683 2381 ▤ 024 7683 2410
✉ artsandheritage@coventry.gov.uk

Dir: In city centre near Cathedral

As Coventry's premier museum hosting a range of exhibitions and events, the Herbert provides a focus for the city's cultural heritage. 'Godiva City' tells Coventry's story over 1,000 years, through interactive exhibits, objects, pictures and words. 'My World' is a fun exhibition for three to five-year-olds. There are also changing displays of art, craft, social and industrial history. The museum is in the midst of a four-year programme of re-development which will bring with it many new facilities.

Times: *Open all year, Mon-Sat 10-5.30, Sun 12-5. Closed 24-26, 31 Dec & 1 Jan
Facilities: ℗ (500yds) ◖ ᖴ all parts accessible (disabled parking, automatic doors, tactile/audio displays) toilets for disabled ✕ (ex guide/assistance dogs) ▱ (pre booking preferred)

COVENTRY

Jaguar Daimler Heritage Centre

Browns Lane Allesley CV5 9DR
☎ 24 7620 3322 ▤ 024 7620 2835
✉ jagtrust@jaguar.com

Dir: On A45, follow signs for Browns Lane Plant

Established in 1983, the Jaguar-Daimler Heritage Trust maintains a unique collection of motor vehicles and artefacts manufactured by Jaguar Cars Ltd, and the many other renowned marques associated with the company. It also maintains a comprehensive archive of photographs and documents related to these great motoring names.

Times: *Open Mon-Thu 9-4, Fri 9-3 & last Sun of month 10-4.
Facilities: ℗ ◖ ᖴ all parts accessible toilets for disabled ✕ (ex guide dogs) ▱

Priory Visitor Centre

Priory Row CV1 5EX
☎ 24 7683 2381 📄 024 7683 2410
✉ artsandheritage@coventry.gov.uk

Dir: In city centre near Cathedral

Earl Leofric and his wife Lady Godiva founded a monastery in Coventry in the 11th century. This priory disappeared somewhere beneath the cathedral that was built on the site, until that in turn was demolished by Henry VIII in the 16th century. Soon after that most of the buildings on the site had been reduced to ground level, leaving modern archaeologists to discover the outlines of history. This visitor centre displays finds from the site as well as telling the story of Coventry's first cathedral.

Times: *Open Mon-Sat 10-5.30, Sun noon-4 Facilities: P (500yds) & Ground floor only accessible toilets for disabled ✖ (ex guide/assistance dogs) ☎

St Mary's Guildhall

Bayley Lane CV1 5QP
☎ 24 7683 2381 📄 024 7683 2410
✉ artsandheritage@coventry.gov.uk

Dir: In city centre near ruined Cathedral

This impressive medieval guildhall has stood in the heart of Coventry for over 650 years, and has played its part in the history of the area. It served as Henry VI's court during the War of the Roses, was a prison to Mary Queen of Scots, and was used as a setting by George Eliot in her novel 'Adam Bede'. The Great Hall contains a Tournai tapestry commissioned for the visit of Henry VII and Queen Elizabeth in 1500.

Times: *Open Etr Sun-Sep, Sun-Thu 10-4 Facilities: P (600yds) & Ground floor, Garden & Grounds accessible ✖ (ex guide/assistance dogs) ☎ (pre-booked)

WEST MIDLANDS

DUDLEY

Museum & Art Gallery

St James's Road DY1 1HU
☎ 01384 815575 ▤ 01384 815576
✉ museum.pls@mbc.dudley.gov.uk

Dir: M5 N J2. Take A4123 signed to Dudley

The museum houses the Brooke Robinson collection of 17th, 18th and 19th century European painting, furniture, ceramics and enamels. A fine geological gallery, 'The Time Trail' has spectacular displays of fossils from the local Wenlock limestone and coal measures. There is also a diverse range of temporary exhibitions. Please telephone for more details.

Times: *Open all year, Mon-Sat 10-4. Closed BHs.
Facilities: ℗ (25mtrs) ⴲ Ground floor only accessible (Braille & large print text. Tactile objects) ✘ (ex guide dogs)
🚌 (pre-booking)

KINGSWINFORD

Broadfield House Glass Museum

Compton Drive DY6 9NS
☎ 01384 812745 ✉
glass.museum@dudley.gov.uk

Dir: Off A491 Stourbridge to Wolverhampton road, just S of Kingswinford Village Centre

This magnificent collection of 19th and 20th-century glass focuses on the cut, etched, engraved and coloured glass made in nearby Stourbridge during the last century. Highlights include cameo glass by Alphonse Lechevrel and George Woodall, and rock crystal engraving by William Fritsche. Also on display are the Michael Parkington collection of 18th, 19th and 20th-century British glass, the Hulbert of Dudley collection, and the Notley/Lerpiniere collection of Carnival Glass.

Times: *Open all year, Tue-Sun & BHs 12-4. Please phone for Xmas/Etr openings
Facilities: ℗ ⴲ Ground floor, Garden & Grounds accessible toilets for disabled ✘ (ex guide dogs) 🚌 🍴

WALSALL

The New Art Gallery Walsall

Gallery Square WS2 8LG
☎ 01922 654400 📠 01922 654401
✉ info@artatwalsall.org.uk

Dir: Signed from all major routes into town centre

This exciting new art gallery has at its core the Garman Ryan Collection, donated to the borough by Lady Kathleen Epstein, and a permanent collection of works acquired by the Walsall Museum and Art Gallery since 1892. Children are very welcome, and an innovative approach is taken in the Children's Discovery Gallery, which offers access to the very best in contemporary art in the only interactive art gallery designed especially for young people. The gallery also has a vibrant programme of temporary exhibitions.

Times: *Open all year Tue-Sat 10-5, Sun noon-5. Closed Mon ex BH Mon.
Facilities: 🅿 🅿 (5 minutes on foot) (on site for disabled) 🍽 ✗ ♿ all parts accessible (lift access to facilities, induction loop, large print) toilets for disabled 🐕 (ex guide dogs) �.

WALSALL

Walsall Leather Museum

Littleton Street West WS2 8EQ
☎ 01922 721153 📠 01922 725827
✉ leathermuseum@walsall.gov.uk

Dir: On Walsall ring-road A4148 on N side of town

An award winning working museum in the saddlery and leathergoods capital of Britain, where you can watch skilled craftsmen and women at work in a restored Victorian leather factory. Displays tell the story of Walsall's leatherworkers past and present. The large shop stocks a range of Walsall made leathergoods, many at bargain prices. The Saddle Room Café serves delicious home-cooked cakes and light lunches. Groups are very welcome and guided tours are available.

Times: *Open all year, Tue-Sat 10-5 (Nov-Mar 4), Sun noon-5 (Nov-Mar 4). Open BH Mon. Closed 24-26 Dec, 1 Jan, Good Fri, Etr Sun & May Day.
Facilities: 🅿 (10mtrs) 🍽 ♿ all parts accessible (staff with sign language skills, tactile activities, parking) toilets for disabled 🐕 (ex guide dogs) 🚌 (max 60 people) 🚌

VENTNOR

Ventnor Botanic Garden

Undercliff Drive PO38 1UL
☎ 01983 855397 🖨 01983 856756
✉ alison.ellsbury@iow.gov.uk

Dir: On A3055 coastal road, 1.5m W of Ventnor

Due to the unique microclimate of the Undercliff, plants that can only survive in a Mediterranean climate thrive on the Isle of Wight. Built on the site of a Victorian hospital for TB sufferers, the garden was founded in 1970 by Sir Harold Hillier, and opened in 1972 by Earl Mountbatten. The garden has plants from Australasia, Africa, America, the Mediterranean, and the Far East, and is a great day out for anyone remotely interested in exotic flora.

Times: Gardens: open all year; Visitor Centre & Green House: Mar-Oct, daily 10-5 & Nov-Feb, wknds only 10-4
Facilities: 🅿 charged 🍽 & All parts accessible (lifts in garden, wheelchairs) toilets for disabled ✈ (ex guide dogs) 🚅 🚅

BRADFORD-ON-AVON

Bradford-on-Avon Tithe Barn

Dir: 0.25m S of town centre, off B3109

This impressive 14th-century tithe barn, over 160 feet long by 30 feet wide, once belonged to Shaftesbury Abbey. It is the biggest and the best of its kind in the country. The roof is of stone slates, supported outside by buttresses and inside by massive beams and a network of rafters. The barn is located in Barton Farm Country Park.

Times: *Open all year, daily 10.30-4. Closed 25 Dec. **Facilities:** 🅿 charged & all parts accessible 🚅 ⌗

LUDGERSHALL

Ludgershall Castle and Cross

SP11 9QR

Dir: 7m NW of Andover on A342

Ruins of an early 12th-century royal hunting palace and medieval cross. The visitor can see large earthworks of the Norman motte-and-bailey castle and the flint walls of the later hunting palace. The stump of a medieval cross stands in the village street.

Times: *Open all reasonable times.
Facilities: 🅿 🅿 (limited parking) ♿ all parts accessible ➡ 🎪

WOODHENGE

Woodhenge

Dir: 1.5m N of Amesbury, off A345 just S of Durrington

A Neolithic ceremonial monument dating from about 2300 BC, consisting of six concentric rings of timber posts, now marked by concrete piles. The long axis of the rings, which are oval, points to the rising sun on Midsummer Day. Woodhenge was discovered by Squadron Leader Insall, an experienced pilot who had been awarded the Victoria Cross during World War I, as he flew above the area in 1925.

Times: *Open all reasonable times.
Facilities: 🅿 ♿ all parts accessible ➡ 🎪

WORCESTER

City Museum & Art Gallery

Foregate St WR1 1DT
☎ 01905 25371 📄 01905 616979
📧 artgalleryandmuseum@cityofworcester.gov.uk

Dir: In city centre, 150m from Foregate St Train Station

The art gallery shows temporary art exhibitions from both local and national sources, while the museum exhibits cover geology, local and natural history. Of particular interest is a complete 19th-century chemist's shop. Also in the building are the Worcestershire Regiment Museum and the Worcestershire Yeomanry Cavalry Museum.

Times: *Open all year, Mon-Fri 9.30-5.30, Sat 9.30-5. Closed Sun, 25-26 Dec, 1 Jan & Good Fri
Facilities: Ⓟ (city centre) 🅿 & all parts accessible (lift, induction loop) toilets for disabled 🚻 (pre-booking advised) 🍴

BURTON AGNES

Burton Agnes Manor House

Dir: In Burton Agnes, 5m SW of Bridlington on A166

This is a rare and well-preserved example of a Norman house. Some interesting Norman architectural features can still be seen, but the building was encased in brick during the 17th and 18th centuries. The house is near Burton Agnes Hall and the gardens are privately owned and not managed by English Heritage.

Times: *Open Apr-Oct, 11-5.
Facilities: ✿

KINGSTON UPON HULL

`Streetlife` - Hull Museum of Transport

High Street HU1 1PS
☎ 01482 613902 📠 01482 613710
✉ museums@hullcc.gov.uk

Dir: A63 from M62, follow signs for Old Town

This purpose built museum uses a 'hands-on' approach to trace 200 years of transport history. With a vehicle collection of national importance, state-of-the-art animatronic displays and authentic scenarios, you can see Hull's Old Town brought vividly to life. The mail coach ride uses the very latest in computer technology to recreate a Victorian journey by four-in-hand.

Times: *Open all year, Mon-Sat 10-5, Sun 1.30-4.30. Closed 24-25 Dec & Good Fri
Facilities: ℗ (500mtrs) ♿ all parts accessible toilets for disabled ✖ (ex guide dogs) 🚌 (pre-booked only)

KINGSTON UPON HULL

Maritime Museum

Queen Victoria Square HU1 3DX
☎ 01482 613902 📠 01482 613710
✉ museums@hullcc.gov.uk

Dir: From M62 follow A63 to town centre, museum is within pedestrian area of town centre

Hull's maritime history is illustrated here, in the former town docks office, with displays on whales and whaling, ships and shipping, and other aspects of this Humber port. There is also a Victorian court room which is used for temporary exhibitions. The restored dock area, with its fine Victorian and Georgian buildings, is well worth exploring too.

Times: *Open all year, Mon-Sat 10-5 & Sun 1.30-4.30. Closed 25 Dec-2 Jan & Good Fri)
Facilities: ℗ (100yds) ♿ all parts accessible ✖ (ex guide dogs) 🚌 (pre-booked only)

KINGSTON UPON HULL

Wilberforce House

23-25 High Street HU1 1NE
☎ 01482 613902 📠 01482 613710
✉ museums@hullcc.gov.uk

Dir: A63 from M62 or A1079 from York, follow signs for Old Town

This early 17th-century merchant's house was the birthplace of William Wilberforce, who became a leading campaigner against slavery. There are Jacobean and Georgian rooms and displays on Wilberforce and the anti-slavery campaign. The house also has secluded gardens, and there is a statue of Wilberforce at the front. Special exhibitions are held throughout the year, and on the nearest weekday to 29 July each year a ceremony is held in the city to commemorate one of its most honoured sons.

Times: *Open all year, Mon-Sat 10-5 & Sun 1.30-4.30. Closed 25-26 Dec, 1 Jan & Good Fri. Facilities: 🅿 (500mtrs) (meters on street) ♿ Ground floor only accessible (large print, video area & audio guides) ✖ (ex guide dogs) 🚍 (prior booking)

THORNTON

Thornton Abbey and Gatehouse

DN39 6TU

Dir: 7m SE of Humber Bridge, on road E of A1077

Thornton Abbey was founded in 1139 for a community of Augustinian cannons, and reconstructed from the 1260s as its prestige and riches grew. The remains of a beautiful octagonal chapter-house are particularly worthy of note. Most impressive is the 14th-century gatehouse, recognised as one of the grandest in England.

Times: *Open Abbey Grounds: Apr-Sep, 10-6. Gatehouse: Apr-Sep, 1st & 3rd Sun of month, 12-6; Oct-Mar, 3rd Sun of month 12-4. Opening times relate to 2004, for further details phone or log onto www.english-heritage.org.uk/visits Facilities: 🅿 ♿ (mostly accessible apart from gatehouse) 🚍 ♿

AYSGARTH

National Park Centre

DL8 3TH
☎ 01969 663424 🖷 01969 663105
✉ aysgarth@ytbtic.co.uk

Dir: Off A684, Leyburn to Hawes road at Falls junct, Palmer Flatt Hotel & continue down hill over river, centre 500yds on L

This is a visitor centre for the Yorkshire Dales National Park, with maps, guides, walks and local information. Interactive displays explain the history and natural history of the area. Plan the day ahead with a light lunch in the coffee shop. Various guided walks set off from here throughout the year.

Times: *Open Apr-Oct, daily 10-5; Winter open Fri-Sun, 10-4.
Facilities: 🅿 charged 🅿 (0.25m) 🍴 & all parts accessible (viewing platform at Falls) toilets for disabled 🐾 (ex guide dogs) 🚻 by previous arrangement 🛍

BEDALE

Bedale Museum

DL8 1AA
☎ 01677 423797 🖷 01677 425393

Dir: On A684, 1.5m W of A1 at Leeming Bar. Opp church, at N end of town

The Bedale is a local history museum situated in a 17th-century building. The central attraction is the Bedale fire engine, which dates back to 1742. The collection also includes documents, toys, craft tools and household utensils, and artefacts associated with agriculture, shoe-making, carpentry and other trades, all of which give a fascinating insight into local life in years past.

Times: *Open Tue & Fri 10-12.30 & 2-4, Wed 2-4, Thu-Sat 10-12
Facilities: 🅿 🅿 (20yds) (2hr disc, long stay 200 yds) & Ground floor, Garden & Grounds accessible 🐾 (ex guide dogs) 🚻 (prior booking preferred)

CLAPHAM

Clapham National Park Centre

LA2 8ED
☎ 015242 51419

Dir: Signed off A65 at Clapham

This visitor centre for the National Park offers a comprehensive information service with displays on the local countryside and limestone scenery. A wide range of maps, guides, information leaflets, gifts and souvenirs are stocked and knowledgeable staff are on duty to answer questions.

Times: *Open Apr-Oct, daily 10-5. Limited opening Nov-Mar.
Facilities: 🅿 charged ঌ Garden & Grounds only accessible (Radar key scheme) toilets for disabled ➡ (Coach parking free) ◀

DANBY

The Moors Centre

Lodge Lane YO21 2NB
☎ 01287 660654 📄 01287 660308
✉ moorscentre@ytbtic.co.uk

Dir: Turn S off A171 signed the Moors Centre Danby. Turn L at cross road in Danby village and follow road for 2m, The Moors Centre is at a bend on the R

The Moors Centre, located in the Esk Valley, is the ideal starting place for exploring the North York Moors National Park. There is an exhibition about the area and a National Park video, as well as a wild flower garden, walks, trails and quizzes. Facilities include a shop, tearooms, wheelchair loan, and an accommodation booking service. Moorsbus Park and Ride operates from this site, please phone for details.

Times: Open all year, Apr-Oct, daily 10-5. Nov, Dec & Mar daily 11-4. Jan & Feb wknds only 11-4.
Facilities: 🅿 charged 🅿£1.50 per day 🍴 ঌ Ground floor only accessible (woodland & garden trails, motorised & manual wheelchairs) toilets for disabled 🐕 (ex guide dogs & in grounds) ➡ (Max 60 people) ◀

EASBY

Easby Abbey

Dir: 1m SE of Richmond off B6271

This Premonstratensian Abbey was founded in 1155 and dedicated to St Agatha. Extensive remains of the monks' domestic buildings can still be seen, attractively set by the River Swale. The Premonstratensians were known as the 'white canons' because of their white habits and, unlike the Cistercians, became involved in the outside community, through preaching and pastoral work.

Times: *Open Apr-Sep, daily, 10-6; Oct, daily, 10-5; Nov-Mar, daily, 10-4. Closed 24-25 Dec.
Facilities: 🅿 🚌 ♿

FAIRBURN

RSPB Nature Reserve

Fairburn Ings The Visitor Centre Newton Lane WF10 2BH
☎ 01977 603796 ✆
chris.drake@rspb.org.uk

Dir: W of A1, N of Ferrybridge. Signed from Allerton Bywater off A656. Signed Fairburn Village off A1

One-third of this 700-acre RSPB Nature Reserve is open water. Over 270 species of birds have been recorded here and it is a great place for seeing wetland birds close up. There are thousands of ducks and geese in winter, and in summer look out for terns, swallows, snipe and lapwings. A visitor centre provides information, and there is an elevated boardwalk, which is suitable for disabled visitors.

Times: *Access to the reserve via car park, open 9-dusk. Centre open 10-5 wknds and 11-4 wkdays. Closed 25-26 Dec.
Facilities: 🅿 ♿ Ground floor, Garden & Grounds accessible (raised boardwalk for wheelchair) toilets for disabled 🐕 (ex guide dogs) 🚌 (booked one month in advance)

GRASSINGTON

National Park Centre

Hebden Road BD23 5LB
☎ 01756 752774 📄 01756 753358
✉ grassington@ytbtic.co.uk

Dir: Situated on B6265 in the main Grassington car park

The centre is a useful introduction to the Yorkshire Dales National Park. It has a video and a display on 'Wharfedale - Gateway to the Park', and maps, guides and local information are available. There is also a 24-hour public access information service through computer screens and a full tourist information service.

Times: *Open Apr-Oct daily, 10-5; Nov-Mar Wed, Fri, & Sat-Sun, 10-4 (also daily in school hols).
Facilities: 🅿 charged & all parts accessible toilets for disabled 🚌 student groups 10 max at once.

MALHAM

Malham National Park Centre

BD23 4DA
☎ 01729 830363 📄 01729 830673
✉ malham@ytbtic.co.uk

Dir: Off A65 at Gargrave opposite petrol station. Malham 7m

The Malham National Park Centre has maps, guides and local information together with displays on the remarkable natural history of the area, the local community and the work of conservation bodies. Audio-visuals are provided for groups and a 24-hour teletext information service is available.

Times: *Open Apr-Oct, daily 10-5. Winter, Fri-Sun, 10-4.
Facilities: 🅿 charged & all parts accessible (Radar key scheme for toilet) toilets for disabled 🚌 🍴

MALTON

Wolds Way Lavender

Deer Farm Park Sandy Lane
Wintringham YO17 8HW
☎ 01944 758641
✉ admin@deerparkfarm.com

Dir: Off A64 between Malton &
Scarborough, follow brown signs

*The medicinal and therapeutic benefits of
lavender are extolled at this 12-acre site
close to the Yorkshire Wolds. Four acres
are currently planted with lavender, and a
recent addition is the wood-burning still for
the extraction of lavender oil. Visitors can
be calmed by the Sensory Areas, enjoy a
cuppa at Lavender Lil's Tearoom, and
purchase all manner of lavender items at
the farm shop.*

Times: Open daily, week before 21 Mar-
Oct, 10-4. Jun-Aug 10-5)
Facilities: 🅿 🍽 ♿ Ground floor, Garden &
Grounds accessible (sensory garden, raised
flower beds) 🐾 (ex guide dogs) 🚌 (please
advise before arrival) ⬛

REDCAR

RNLI Zetland Museum

5 King Street TS10 3AH
☎ 01642 485370

Dir: On corner of King St and
The Promenade

*The museum portrays the lifeboat,
maritime, fishing and local history of the
area, including its main exhibit 'The
Zetland', the oldest lifeboat in the world,
dating from 1802. There is also a replica of
a fisherman's cottage from about 1900 and
almost 2,000 other exhibits. The museum
is housed in an early lifeboat station, now
a listed building.*

Times: *Open May-Sep, Mon-Fri 1-4, Sat &
Sun 12-4. Also Etr. Other times by
appointment.
Facilities: 🅿 (20m) (50p per hour) ♿
Ground floor only accessible (ground floor
accessible only) 🚌

YORK

Guildhall

Coney Street YO1 9QN
☎ 01904 613161 🖷 01904 551052

Dir: 5 mins walk from rail station

The original hall dates from 1446 but in 1942 an air raid virtually destroyed the building. The present guildhall was carefully restored as an exact replica and was re-opened in 1960. There is an interesting arch-braced roof decorated with colourful bosses and supported by 12 solid oak pillars. There are also some beautiful stained-glass windows.

Times: *Open all year, May-Oct, Mon-Fri 9-5, Sat 10-5, Sun 2-5; Nov-Apr, Mon-Fri 9-5.Closed Good Fri, Spring BH, 25-26 Dec & 1 Jan.
Facilities: 🅿 (15-20 mins walk) ♿ all parts accessible (electric chair lift & ramps) toilets for disabled 🐕 (ex guide dogs)

YORK

National Railway Museum

Leeman Road YO26 4XJ
☎ 01904 621261 🖷 01904 611112
✆ nrm@nmsi.ac.uk

Dir: Situated behind railway station. Signed from all major approach roads

York boasts the world's largest railway museum, and families can spend all day exploring the three giant halls that house this impressive collection. Among the exhibits are the huge Chinese Locomotive, built in 1935 and weighing in at 193 tons with tender; the Mallard, which still holds the world speed record for steam traction on rail (126 mph in 1938); the legendary Stephenson's Rocket; and various rail-related items like winding engines, bridges and a horse-drawn ambulance for injured horses.

Times: Open all year, Mon-Sun 10-6. Closed 24-26 Dec.
Facilities: 🅿 charged 🅿 (100 mtrs) (coach parking must be pre-booked) 🍽 ✗ (licenced) ♿ all parts accessible (Please Touch evenings usually in June) toilets for disabled 🐕 (ex guide/hearing dogs) 🚋 (pre-booking desireable) 🚋

BARNSLEY

Monk Bretton Priory

S71 5QD

Dir: 1m E of town centre, off A633

Monk Bretton Priory was an important Cluniac house, founded in 1153. The considerable remains of the gatehouse, church and other buildings can be seen. The priory is in a pleasant open space with views over the wooded valley.

Times: *Open all year, Apr-Sep, daily 10-6; Oct, daily 10-5; Nov-Mar, daily 10-4. Closed 24-26 Dec & 1 Jan.
Facilities: 🅿 🚠 ✿

CUSWORTH

The Museum of South Yorkshire Life Cusworth Hall

Cusworth Lane DN5 7TU
☎ 01302 782342 📠 01302 782342
✉ museum@doncaster.gov.uk

Dir: 3m NW of Doncaster

The Museum of South Yorkshire is located in Cusworth Hall, an 18th-century country house set in a landscaped park. The displays illustrate the way local people lived, worked and entertained themselves over the last 200 years, with a particular focus on the Victorian era. Local industries represented include farming, mining and the railway. Following a grant from the Heritage Lottery Fund, substantial refurbishment of the museum is ongoing.

Times: *Open Mon-Fri 10-5, Sat 11-5 & Sun 1-5. (4 Dec & Jan). Closed Good Fri, Xmas & 1 Jan. Hall & Park undergoing restoration and at times some areas may not be open to the public. Telephone for details.
Facilities: 🅿 ♿(disabled parking only around hall) 🅿 ♿ Ground floor, Garden & Grounds accessible (wheelchair available) toilets for disabled 🐕 (ex guide dogs) 🚠 (prior booking)

DONCASTER

Doncaster Museum & Art Gallery

Chequer Rd DN1 2AE
☎ 01302 734293 📠 01302 735409
✉ museum@doncaster.gov.uk

Dir: Off inner ring road

The wide-ranging collections at the Doncaster Museum & Art Gallery include fine and decorative art and sculpture. There are also ceramics, glass, silver and displays on history, archaeology and natural history. The historical collection of the Kings Own Yorkshire Light Infantry is housed here. Temporary exhibitions are also a feature.

Times: *Open all year, Mon-Sat 10-5, Sun 2-5. Closed Good Fri, 25-26 Dec & 1 Jan.
Facilities: 🅿 🅿 (200yds) (limited periods) ⚓ all parts accessible (lift, hearing loop in lecture room) toilets for disabled ✖ (ex guide dogs) 🚌

SHEFFIELD

Bishops' House

Meersbrook Park Norton Lees Lane S8 9BE
☎ 0114 278 2600
✉ info@sheffieldgalleries.org.uk

Dir: 2m S of Sheffield, on A61 Chesterfield road

This 15th and 16th-century Yeoman's house has been restored and opened as a museum of local and social history. Several rooms have been furnished and there are displays of life in Tudor and Stuart times. Special educational facilities can be arranged for schools and colleges. Please ring for details.

Times: *Open Sat 10-4.30. Sun 11-4.30
Facilities: 🅿 (roadside parking on nearby streets) ⚓ Ground floor, Garden & Grounds accessible ✖ (ex guide dogs) 🚌 (must pre-book)

BRADFORD

Bolling Hall

Bowling Hall Road BD4 7LP
☎ 01274 723057 📄 01274 726220

Dir: 1m from city centre off A650

A classic West Yorkshire manor house, complete with galleried 'housebody' (hall), Bolling Hall dates mainly from the 17th century but has medieval and 18th-century sections. Features to look out for are the panelled rooms, plasterwork in original colours, heraldic glass and a rare Chippendale bed. The house is set in pleasant gardens just a mile from the city centre.

Times: *Open all year, Wed-Fri 11-4, Sat 10-5, Sun 12-5. Closed Mon ex BH, Good Fri, 25-26 Dec.
Facilities: 🅿 🅿 ♿ Ground floor, Garden & Grounds accessible ✘ (ex guide dogs) ▭

BRADFORD

Bradford Industrial Museum and Horses at Work

Moorside Mills Moorside Road
Eccleshill BD2 3HP
☎ 01274 435900 📄 01274 636362

Dir: Off A658

Moorside Mills is an original spinning mill, now part of a museum that brings vividly to life the story of Bradford's woollen industry, with the machinery that once converted raw wool into cloth. The mill yard rings with the sound of iron on stone as shire horses pull trams, haul buses and give rides. There are daily demonstrations and a programme of changing exhibitions.

Times: *Open all year, Tue-Sat 10-5, Sun 12-5. Closed Mon ex BH, Good Fri, 25-26 Dec **Facilities:** 🅿 ♥ (licenced) ♿ All parts accessible (induction loop in lecture theatre, lift) toilets for disabled ✘ (ex guide dogs) ▭

BRADFORD

Cartwright Hall Art Gallery

Lister Park BD9 4NS
☎ 01274 431212 📠 01274 481045
✉ cartwright.hall@bradford.gov.uk

Dir: 1m from city centre on A650

This dramatic Baroque-style art gallery was purpose built in 1904, and is set in its own parkland in the suburbs of Bradford. The Cartwright has permanent collections of 19th and 20th-century British art, contemporary prints, and older works by British and European masters. There is also a notable collection of contemporary South Asian art, Indian silver and Islamic textiles.

Times: *Open all year, Tue-Sat 10-5, Sun 1-5. Closed Mon ex BH, Good Fri, 25-26 Dec.
Facilities: 🅿 🅿 (available for functions & disabled) 🍽 & All parts accessible (wheelchair available, lift) toilets for disabled 🐕 (ex guide dogs) 🚌

BRADFORD

National Museum of Photography, Film & Television

BD1 1NQ
☎ 870 7010200 📠 01274 394540
✉ talk.nmpft@nmsi.ac.uk

Dir: 2m from end of M606, follow signs for city centre

This recently refurbished museum is one of the North of England's most popular attractions. Here you can experience the past, present and future of photography, film and television. Expect amazing interactive displays and a spectacular 3D IMAX cinema. A full programme of events, talks and exhibitions is also offered.

Times: *Open all year, Tue-Sun, BHs & main school hols 10-6. Closed Mon.
Facilities: 🅿 (adjacent) 🍽 ✗ (licenced) & all parts accessible (tailored tours,Braille signs,induction loop,cinema seating) toilets for disabled 🐕 (ex guide dogs) 🚌 🍴

GOMERSAL

Red House

Oxford Road BD19 4JP
☎ 01274 335100 📄 01274 335105

Dir: M62 J26, take A58 towards Leeds then R onto A651 towards Gomersal. Red House is on R hand side

This delightful redbrick house is displayed as the 1830s home of a Yorkshire wool clothier and merchant. The house and family was frequently visited by Charlotte BrontÆ in the 1830s and featured in her novel 'Shirley'. The gardens have been reconstructed in the style of the period and there are exhibitions on the Brontë connection and local history in a restored barn and cartsheds.

Times: *Open all year, Mon-Fri 11-5, Sat-Sun 12-5. Telephone for Xmas opening. Closed Good Fri & 1 Jan.
Facilities: 🅿 🅿 (roadside 100 yds) (difficult between 3-3.30) ﹩ Ground floor, Garden & Grounds accessible (Braille & T-setting hearing aid available) toilets for disabled ✈ (ex guide dogs) ➡ (Booking essential) ➡

HALIFAX

Bankfield Museum

Boothtown Rd Akroyd Park HX3 6HG
☎ 01422 354823 📄 01422 349020
✉ bankfield-museum@calderdale.gov.uk

Dir: On A647 Bradford via Queensbury road, 0.5m from Halifax town centre

Built by Edward Akroyd in the 1860s, this Renaissance-style building is set in parkland on a hill overlooking the town. It has an outstanding collection of costumes and textiles from many periods and parts of the world, including a new gallery featuring East European textiles. There is also a section on toys, and the museum of the Duke of Wellington's Regiment is housed here. Temporary exhibitions are held and there is a lively programme of events, workshops and activities. Please ring for details.

Times: *Open all year, Tue-Sat 10-5, Sun 2-5, BH Mon 10-5. (Extended closing times at Xmas and New Year, phone for details)
Facilities: 🅿 🅿 (50yds) (restricted access for coaches) ﹩ Ground floor, Garden & Grounds accessible (audio guide & tactile objects) toilets for disabled ✈ (ex guide dogs) ➡ ➡

HALIFAX

Piece Hall

HX1 1RE
☎ 01422 358087 📠 01422 349310
✉ karen.belshaw@calderdale.gov.uk

Dir: Follow brown tourist signs, close to railway station

The merchants of Halifax built this elegant and unique hall in 1779, and it has over 300 merchant's rooms around a courtyard, now housing an industrial museum, art galleries and shops selling antiques, books and so on. Open markets are held on Friday and Saturday and a flea market on Thursday. There is a lively programme of exhibitions, workshops, activities and events throughout the year, and a festival in the summer. Please ring for more details.

Times: *Open all year daily. Closed 25-26 Dec. Art Gallery, Tue-Sun & BH Mon 10-5.
Facilities: P (50 yds) ● & all parts accessible (lifts, shopmobility on site & audio guide available) toilets for disabled 🚻 🔊

HUDDERSFIELD

Tolson Memorial Museum

Ravensknowle Park Wakefield Road
HD5 8DJ
☎ 01484 223830 📠 01484 223843

Dir: On A629, 1m from town centre

Displays on the development of the cloth industry and a collection of horse-drawn vehicles are featured at the Tolson Memorial Museum, together with natural history, archaeology, toys and folk exhibits. There is a full programme of events and temporary exhibitions.

Times: *Open all year. Mon-Fri 11-5, Sat & Sun noon-5. Closed Xmas.
Facilities: P & all parts accessible (mini-com, partial stairlift, induction loop, parking) toilets for disabled 🐕 (ex registered guide dogs) 🚻 🔊

ILKLEY

Manor House Gallery & Museum

Castle Yard Church Street LS29 9DT
☎ 01943 600066 🖹 01943 817079

Dir: Behind Ilkley Parish Church, on A65

This Elizabethan manor house, one of Ilkley's few buildings to pre-date the 19th century, was built on the site of a Roman fort. Part of the Roman wall can be seen, together with Roman relics and displays on archaeology. There is a collection of 17th and 18th-century farmhouse parlour and kitchen furniture, and the art gallery exhibits works by contemporary artists and craftsmen.

Times: *Open all year, Tue-Sat 1-5, Sun 1-4. Open BH Mon. Closed Good Fri, 25-28 Dec.
Facilities: ℗ (5mins) ♿ Ground floor only accessible 🐕 (ex guide dogs) 🚌

KEIGHLEY

Cliffe Castle Museum & Gallery

Spring Gardens Lane BD20 6LH
☎ 01535 618231 🖹 01535 610536

Dir: NW of town off A629

French furniture from the Victoria & Albert Museum is displayed at Cliffe Castle, together with collections of local and natural history, ceramics, dolls, geological items and minerals. The grounds of the 19th-century mansion include a play area and an aviary.

Times: *Open all year, Tue-Sat 10-5, Sun 12-5. Open BH Mon. Closed Good Fri & 25-28 Dec.
Facilities: ℗ 🍽 (licenced) ♿ Ground floor only accessible toilets for disabled 🐕 (ex guide dogs) 🚌

LEEDS

City Art Gallery

The Headrow LS1 3AA
☎ 0113 247 8248 ▤ 0113 244 9689

Dir: In city centre, next to town hall and library

The City Art Gallery is home to one of the best collections of 20th-century British art outside London, as well as Victorian and late 19th-century pictures, an outstanding collection of English watercolours, a display of modern sculpture and temporary exhibitions focusing on contemporary work.

Times: *Open all year, Mon-Sat 10-5, Wed until 8, Sun 1-5. Closed BHs.
Facilities: ℙ ❤ ✕ (licenced) ♿ Ground floor only accessible (restricted access to upper floor) toilets for disabled ✱ (ex guide dogs) ➞ (pre-booking advised)

LEEDS

Kirkstall Abbey

Abbey Road Kirkstall LS5 3EH
☎ 0113 230 5492
✉ abbey.house@leeds.gov.uk

Dir: Off A65, W of city centre

Kirkstall is the most complete 12th-century Cistercian Abbey in the country stands on the banks of the River Aire. Many of the original buildings can still be seen, including the cloister, church and refectory. Regular tours take visitors to areas not normally accessible to the public. During the summer the abbey hosts plays, fairs and musical events.

Times: *Open all year. Abbey site open dawn-dusk.
Facilities: ℙ ♿ Ground floor only accessible toilets for disabled ➞ (min 10 people)

LEEDS

Royal Armouries Museum

Armouries Drive LS10 1LT
☎ 0113 220 1999 📠 0113 220 1934
✉ enquiries@armouries.org.uk

Dir: Off A61 close to Leeds centre, follow brown heritage signs

The museum is an impressive contemporary home for the renowned national collection of arms and armour. The collection is divided between five galleries: War, Tournament, Self-Defence, Hunting and Oriental. The Hall of Steel features a 100 foot-high mass of 3,000 pieces of arms and armour. Extensive interactive displays, dramatisations of jousting tournaments, and the chance to see leather workers and armourers at work all make for an exciting day out.

Times: *Open daily, from 10-5.
Closed 24-25 Dec
Facilities: 🅿 charged 🍽 ✗ (licenced) ♿ all parts accessible (induction loops, wheelchairs, signers, low level counter) toilets for disabled ✖ (ex guide & hearing dogs) 🚌 🚃

WAKEFIELD

National Coal Mining Museum For England

Caphouse Colliery New Road WF4 4RH
☎ 01924 848806 📠 01924 844567
✉ info@ncm.org.uk

Dir: On A642 between Wakefield & Huddersfield

A unique opportunity to go 140 metres underground down one of Britain's oldest working mines. Take a step back in time with one of the museum's experienced local miners who will guide parties around the underground workings, where models and machinery depict methods and conditions of mining from the early 1800s to the present day. Other attractions include the pithead baths, Victorian steam winder, nature trail and adventure playground and meet the last ever working pit ponies. You are strongly advised to wear sensible footwear and warm clothing.

Times: Open all year, daily 10-5. Closed 24-26 Dec & 1 Jan.
Facilities: 🅿 🍽 ✗ (licenced) ♿ All parts accessible (nature trail not accessible) toilets for disabled ✖ (ex guide dogs) 🚌 🚃

WAKEFIELD

Wakefield Art Gallery

Wentworth Terrace WF1 3QW
☎ 01924 305796 ▧ 01924 305770
✉ museumsandarts@wakefield.gov.uk

Dir: N of city centre by Wakefield College and Clayton Hospital

Wakefield was home to two of Britain's greatest modern sculptors - Barbara Hepworth and Henry Moore. The Wakefield Art Gallery, which has an important collection of 20th-century paintings and sculptures, has a special room devoted to these two local artists. There are frequent temporary exhibitions of both modern and earlier works.

Times: Open all year, Tue-Sat 10.30-4.30, Sun 2-4.30.
Facilities: Ⓟ (on street) (on street parking restricted to 2hrs) ♿ Ground floor, Garden & Grounds accessible ✻ (ex guide dogs) ▥

CASTLETOWN

Old Grammar School

IM9 1LE
☎ 01624 648000 ▧ 01624 648001
✉ enquiries@mnh.gov.im

Dir: Centre of Castletown, opposite the castle

This small whitewashed building, built around AD 1200, was originally the church in the former capital, Castletown. Its main wing is the oldest roofed building on the island. St Mary's has played a significant role in Manx education. It was used as a school from at least 1570, and exclusively so from 1702 until 1930, and these days recalls the experience of Victorian school life.

Times: *Open daily 10-5, Apr-late Oct.
Facilities: Ⓟ Ⓟ 30 yards Disc Zone Parking ✻ (ex guide dogs) ▥ (pre-booking advised)

DOUGLAS

Manx Museum

IM1 3LY
☎ 01624 648000 📠 01624 648001
✉ enquiries@mnh.gov.im

Dir: Signed in Douglas

The island's treasure house provides an exciting introduction to the 'Story of Mann' where a specially produced film portrayal of Manx history complements the award winning displays. Galleries depict natural history, archaeology and the social development of the Island. There are also examples of famous Manx artists in the National Art Gallery together with the island's national archive and reference library.

Times: *Open daily all year, Mon-Sat 10-5. Closed 25-26 Dec & 1 Jan.
Facilities: 🅿 🅿 (30 yds) (2 hourly barge parking) ✗ (licenced) ♿ Ground floor, Garden & Grounds accessible (lift) toilets for disabled ✖ (ex guide dogs) 🚌 (pre-booking advised) 🍴

VALE

Rousse Tower

Rousse Tower Headland
☎ 01481 726518 📠 01481 715177
✉ peter@museum.guernsey.net

Dir: On Island's W coast, signed

The Rousse Tower is one of the original 15 towers built in 1778 and 1779 in prime defensive positions around the coast of Guernsey. The towers were designed primarily to prevent the landing of troops on nearby beaches. Musket fire could be directed on invading forces through the loopholes. An interpretation centre displays replica guns.

Times: *Open Apr-Oct 9-dusk, Nov-Mar Wed, Sat & Sun 9-4.
Facilities: 🅿 🅿 (50mtrs) ✖ (ex guide dogs) 🚌

LA GREVE DE LECQ

Greve de Lecq Barracks

JE3 3EN
☎ 01534 483193 🖨 01534 485873
✉ enquiries@nationaltrustjersey.org.je

Dir: On R hand side of valley, overlooking beach

Originally serving as an outpost of the British Empire, these barracks, built in 1810, were used for civilian housing from the end of World War I to 1972, when they were bought by the National Trust and made into a museum that depicts the life of soldiers who were stationed here in the 19th century. Also on site is a collection of old horse-drawn carriages.

Times: *Open 4 May-26 Sep, Tue-Sat 11-5 & Sun 2-5. (Closed Mon).
Facilities: 🅿 🅿 (100mtrs) & Ground floor, Garden & Grounds accessible (wheelchair ramps) toilets for disabled 🦮 (ex guide dogs)

ST OUEN

Kempt Tower Visitor Centre

Five Mile Road
☎ 01534 483651 🖨 01534 485289
✉ marketing@jerseyheritagetrust.org

The visitor centre has displays on the history and wildlife of St Ouen's Bay, including Les Mielles, which is Jersey's miniature national park. Facilities include a shop and picnic areas, and education packs are available. Nature walks are held every Thursday (May to September). Check local press for details.

Times: *Open BHs, Apr & Oct, Thu & Sun only 2-5; May-Sep, daily (ex Mon) 2-5.
Facilities: 🅿 🅿 🚻

ABERDEEN

Aberdeen Art Gallery

Schoolhill AB10 1FQ
☎ 01224 523700 📠 01224 632133
✉ info@aagm.co.uk

Dir: Located in city centre

One of the city's most popular tourist attractions, Aberdeen's splendid art gallery houses an important fine art collection with many 19th and 20th century works by the likes of Stanley Spencer, Paul Nash and Christopher Wood. There are also some French Impressionist paintings, plus a programme of special exhibitions and events.

Times: *Open all year Mon-Sat 10-5, Sun 2-5. Closed Xmas & New Year
Facilities: ℗ (500yds) 🍽 ♿ all parts accessible (ramp, lift) toilets for disabled ✈ (ex guide dogs) 🚐

ABERDEEN

Aberdeen Maritime Museum

Shiprow AB11 5BY
☎ 01224 337700 📠 01224 213066
✉ info@aagm.co.uk

Dir: Located in city centre

The museum is located in Provost Ross's House, Aberdeen's oldest building dating from 1593, which has fabulous views over the harbour. It highlights the city's maritime history, oil industry, and shipbuilding, so you can find out about life on a North Sea oil platform and see some beautifully made ship models and displays on fishing. Marine art is also featured.

Times: *Open all year Mon-Sat 10-5, Sun 12-3. Closed Xmas & New Year.
Facilities: ℗ (250yds) 🍽 ✗ (licenced) ♿ all parts accessible (ramps, lifts) toilets for disabled 🚐 🚃

ABERDEEN

Cruickshank Botanic Garden

University of Aberdeen
St Machar Drive AB24 3UU
☎ 01224 272704 📠 01224 272703
✉ pss@abdn.ac.uk

Dir: Enter by gate in Chanonry, in Old Aberdeen

Developed at the end of the 19th century, the 11 acres include rock and water gardens, a rose garden, a fine herbaceous border, an arboretum and a patio garden. There are collections of spring bulbs, gentians and alpine plants, and a fine array of trees and shrubs. The garden is part of the University of Aberdeen and is used for teaching and research purposes.

Times: *Open all year, Mon-Fri 9-4.30; also Sat & Sun, May-Sep 2-5.
Facilities: P (200mtrs) & All parts accessible 🚌 (by appointment)

ABERDEEN

Provost Skene's House

Guestrow off Broad St AB10 1AS
☎ 01224 641086
✉ info@aagm.co.uk

Experience the epitome of style and elegance in this 16th-century townhouse, which has been furnished and decorated in a series of period styles. These include the 17th-century great hall, parlour and bedroom; 18th-century dining room and bedroom, and a 19th-century nursery. You can see changing fashions in the Costume Gallery and view an important cycle of religious paintings in the gallery.

Times: *Open all year Mon-Sat 10-5, Sun 1-4. Closed Xmas & New Year.
Telephone for details.
Facilities: P (200yds) ☕ 🐕 (ex guide dogs) 🚌

BANCHORY

Banchory Museum

Bridge Street AB31 5SX
☎ 01771 622906 🖷 01771 622884
✉ heritage@aberdeenshire.gov.uk

Dir: In Bridge St beside tourist
information centre

*The museum has displays on Scott Skinner,
the Banchory born musician and composer,
known locally as the 'Strathspey King'.
Other features are 19th-century tartans,
royal commemorative china and local silver
artefacts, alongside a variety of natural
history and local history displays.*

Times: *Open May, Jun & Sep, Mon-Sat
11-1 & 2-4.30; Jul-Aug, Mon-Sat 11-1, 2-
4.30 & Sun 2-4.30. Telephone for Apr & Oct
opening times.
Facilities: ℗ (100yds) (limited) & all parts
accessible toilets for disabled ✖ (ex guide
dogs) 🚌 (pre-booking preferred)

BANFF

Banff Museum

High Street AB45 1AE
☎ 01771 622906 🖷 01771 622884
✉ heritage@aberdeenshire.gov.uk

*This is one of Scotland's oldest museums,
founded in 1828. There are displays
relating to two celebrated sons of
Banffshire, James Ferguson, the 18th-
century astronomer, and Thomas Edward,
the 19th-century naturalist. Other exhibits
include geology, natural history, local
history, Banff silver, arms and armour.*

Times: *Open Jun-Sep, Mon-Sat 2-4.30.
Facilities: ℗ (200yds) & Ground floor only
accessible ✖ (ex guide dogs)
🚌 (pre-booking preferred)

HUNTLY

Brander Museum

The Square AB54 8AE
☎ 01771 622906 📠 01771 622884
✉ heritage@aberdeenshire.gov.uk

Dir: In centre of Huntly, sharing building with library, museum on ground floor

This recently refurbished museum has displays of local and church history, archaeological finds from Huntly Castle, plus 19th-century arms and armour from the Anderson Bey and the Sudanese campaigns. Exhibits connected with Huntly-born George MacDonald, author and playwright, can also be seen.

Times: *Open all year, Tue-Sat 2-4.30. **Facilities:** 🅿 (25yds) ♿ all parts accessible (access difficult due to 3 large steps at entrance) 🚫 (ex guide dogs) 🚌 (pre-booking necessary)

INVERURIE

Carnegie Museum

Town House The Square AB51 3SN
☎ 01771 622906 📠 01771 622884
✉ heritage@aberdeenshire.gov.uk

Dir: In centre of Inverurie, on L side of townhouse building, above library

This fine museum contains displays on local history and archaeology, including Pictish stones, Bronze Age material and Great North of Scotland Railway memorabilia. A particularly interesting aspect of the museum is the collection of internationally important Inuit carvings.

Times: *Open all year, Mon & Wed-Fri 2-4.30, Sat 10-1 & 2-4. Closed Tue & public hols. **Facilities:** 🅿 (50yds) 🚫 (ex guide dogs) 🚌 (pre-booking preferred)

MINTLAW

Aberdeenshire Farming Museum

Aden Country Park AB42 5FQ
☎ 01771 622906 📠 01771 622884
✉ heritage@aberdeenshire.gov.uk

Dir: 1m W of Mintlaw on A950

The farm museum is housed in 19th-century farm buildings, once part of the estate which now makes up the Aden Country Park. Two centuries of farming history and innovation are illustrated, and the story of the estate is also told. The reconstructed farm of Hareshowe shows how a family in the northeast farmed during the 1950s. Access is by guided tour only.

Times: Open May-Sep, daily 11-4.30; Apr & Oct, wknds only noon-4.30. (Last admission 30 mins before closing). Park open all year, Apr-Sep 7-10, winter 7-7.
Facilities: 🅿 charged 🅿 (200yds) 🍽 & Ground floor, Garden & Grounds accessible (sensory garden) toilets for disabled 🐕 (ex guide dogs) 🚌 (pre-booking essential)

OLD DEER

Deer Abbey

☎ 01466 793191

Dir: 2m W of Mintlaw on A950

Deer was a Cistercian abbey, founded in 1218 by William Comyn, Earl of Buchan. The remains include the infirmary, Abbot's House and the southern claustral range. The University Library at Cambridge now houses the famous Book of Deer, an 84-page illuminated manuscript written in Latin and an early form of Scottish Gaelic.

Times: *Open at all reasonable times.
Facilities: 🅿 ♨

PETERHEAD

Arbuthnot Museum

St Peter Street AB42 1QD
☎ 01771 622906 📄 01771 622884
✉ heritage@aberdeenshire.gov.uk

Dir: At St Peter St & Queen St x-roads, above library

Specialising in local exhibits, particularly those relating to the fishing industry, the Arbuthnot Museum also displays Arctic and whaling specimens, an important collection of Inuit artefacts, and a British coin collection. The exhibitions gallery offers a regular programme of temporary exhibitions.

Times: *Open all year, Mon, Tue & Thu-Sat 11-1 & 2-4.30, Wed 11-1. Closed Sun and BHs. **Facilities:** P (150 yds) ✕ (ex guide dogs) 🚌 (pre-booking prefered)

STONEHAVEN

Tolbooth Museum

Old Pier AB39 2JU
☎ 01771 622906 📄 01771 622884
✉ heritage@aberdeenshire.gov.uk

Dir: On harbour front

Stonehaven's oldest building, located right on the harbourside, was built in the late 16th century as a storehouse for the Earls Marischal at Dunnottar Castle. The building was also the Kincardineshire County Tollbooth from 1600-1767. Now the town's museum it shows displays on local history and fishing.

Times: *Open May-Oct, Wed-Mon, 1.30-4.30. Closed Tue.
Facilities: P (20yds) ♿ Ground floor only accessible ✕ (ex guide dogs) 🚌 (pre-booking preferred)

ARBROATH

Arbroath Museum

Signal Tower Ladyloan DD11 1PU
☎ 01241 875598 📄 01241 439263
✉ signal.tower@angus.gov.uk

Dir: On A92 adjacent to harbour. 16m NE of Dundee

Fish and Arbroath Smokies, textiles and engineering feature at this local history museum housed in the 1813 shore station of Stevenson's Bell Rock lighthouse. There are also exhibits of fine and decorative art, Arbroath silver and natural sciences.

Times: Open all year, Mon-Sat 10-5; Jul-Aug, Sun 2-5. Closed 25-26 Dec & 1-2 Jan.
Facilities: 🅿 🅿 (100yds) ♿ Ground floor only accessible (induction loop) 🐕 (ex guide dogs) 🚌 (pre-booking required)

FORFAR

The Meffan Art Gallery & Museum

20 West High Street DD8 1BB
☎ 01307 464123 📄 01307 468451
✉ the.meffan@angus.gov.uk

Dir: Off A90, 13m N of Dundee. Attraction in town centre

This lively, ever-changing contemporary art gallery and museum is full of surprises. Walk down a cobbled street full of shops and end up at a witch-burning scene! Carved Pictish stones and a diorama of an archaeological dig complete the vibrant displays. There is also a programme of temporary exhibitions.

Times: Open all year. Closed 25-26 Dec & 1-2 Jan.
Facilities: 🅿 (150yds) (30 mins limit on street) ♿ Ground floor only accessible (handrails, wide door, portable ramp) toilets for disabled 🐕 (ex guide dogs) 🚌 (pre-booking required) 🍴

ANGUS

MONTROSE

Montrose Museum & Art Gallery

Panmure Place DD10 8HE
☎ 01674 673232
✉ montrose.museum@angus.gov.uk

Dir: Opp Montrose Academy in town centre, approach via A92 from Aberdeen or Dundee

This is one of Scotland's oldest town museums in its original 1842 building. Its extensive local collections cover the history of Montrose from prehistoric times, the maritime history of the port, the natural history of Angus, and local art. Items of particular fascination are the Inchbrayock Pictish stones and the witch's branks - metal face masks.

Times: Open all year, Mon-Sat 10-5. Closed 25-26 Dec & 1-2 Jan.
Facilities: P & Ground floor only accessible ✘ (ex guide dogs) ⊟ (pre-booking required)

ARROCHAR

Argyll Forest Park

Forest Enterprise Ardgartan Visitor Centre G83 7AR
☎ 01301 702597 📄 01301 702597
✉ robin.kennedy@forestry.gsl.gov.uk

Dir: On A83 at foot of The Rest and Be Thankful

The Argyll Forest Park extends over a large area of mountains, glens, lochs and forest, and is noted for its rugged beauty. It was the first Forest Park to be established for public enjoyment, as far back as 1935. Numerous forest walks and picnic sites allow for plenty of exploration; the arboretum walks and the route between the Younger Botanic Gardens and Puck's Glen are particularly lovely.

Times: *Open all year.
Facilities: P (no overnight parking) ⊟

CARNASSERIE CASTLE

Carnasserie Castle

PA31 8RQ

Dir: 2m N of Kilmartin off A816

Carnasserie Castle is a handsome combined tower house and hall, built in 1565 by John Carswell, first Protestant Bishop of the Isles and translator of the first book printed in Gaelic. The castle was captured and demolished by MacLaine of Torloisk in 1685 because its owner, a Campbell, was part of the Monmouth Rising. Fine architectural details from the late 16th century can still be seen in the ruins.

Times: *Open at all reasonable times.
Facilities: ☻

KILMARTIN

Dunadd Fort

Dir: 2m S of Kilmartin on A816

Dunadd was one of the ancient capitals of Dalriada from which the Celtic kingdom of Scotland was formed. Near to this prehistoric hill fort (now little more than an isolated hillock) are carvings of a boar and a footprint; these probably marked the spot where early kings were invested with their royal power.

Times: *Open at all reasonable times.
Facilities: ☻

EDINBURGH

City Art Centre

2 Market Street EH1 1DE
☎ 0131 529 3993 📠 0131 529 3986
✉ enquiries@city-art-centre.demon.uk

Dir: Opposite rear of Waverley Stn

The City Art Centre houses Edinburgh's permanent fine art collection and stages a constantly changing programme of temporary exhibitions from all parts of the world. It has six floors of display galleries linked by an escalator and around 3,500 pieces of work by Scottish artists. Exhibitions drawn from the collection are also a regular feature. Bequests and funding from the Scottish Arts Council have enabled the centre to keep up to date with the acquisition of work by contemporary Scottish artists.

Times: *Open Mon-Sat 10-5 & Sun 12-5 Jul-Aug
Facilities: 🅿 (500yds) (single yellow lines) 🍽 & all parts accessible (induction loop, lifts, Braille signage, escalator) toilets for disabled ✈ (ex guide dogs) 🚌 (pre-booking preferred) 🛥

EDINBURGH

Dean Gallery

73 Belford Rd EH4 3DS
☎ 0131 624 6200 📠 0131 343 3250
✉ enquiries@nationalgalleries.org

Dir: 20 min walk from Edinburgh Haymarket stn & Princes St

Opened in March 1999, the Dean Gallery provides a home for the Eduardo Paolozzi gift of sculpture and graphic art, the Gallery of Modern Art's renowned Dada and Surrealist collections, and a major library and archive centre. There is also a temporary exhibition space for modern and contemporary art.

Times: *Open all year, Mon-Sat 10-5, Sun 12-5. Extended opening during Edinburgh Festival. Closed 25-26 Dec.
Facilities: 🅿 🅿 🍽 (licenced) & all parts accessible (ramps & lift) toilets for disabled ✈ (ex guide dogs) 🚌 🛥

EDINBURGH

Museum of Childhood

42 High Street, Royal Mile, EH1 1TG
☎ 0131 529 4142 📠 0131 558 3103

Dir: On the Royal Mile

The Museum of Childhood was one of the first museums of its kind, and was massively expanded in the mid 1980s. Children and adults alike will be delighted by this wonderful collection of toys, games and other belongings of children through the ages. A programme of temporary exhibitions and special events means that there is always something new to enjoy. Please ring for details.

Times: *Open all year, Mon-Sat, Jun-Sep 10-6; Oct-May 10-5; (also Sun 12-5 in Jul-Aug).

Facilities: Ⓟ ♿ (3 floors only) toilets for disabled ✖ (ex guide dogs) 🚌 (advance notice preferred)

EDINBURGH

Museum of Edinburgh

142 Canongate Royal Mile EH8 8DD
☎ 0131 529 4143 📠 0131 557 3346

Dir: On the Royal Mile

The Museum of Edinburgh is housed in one of the best-preserved 16th-century buildings in the Old Town. It was built in 1570 and later became the headquarters of the Incorporation of Hammermen. Now a museum of local history, it has collections of silver, glassware, pottery, and other items such as street signs.

Times: *Open all year, Mon-Sat 10-5. During Festival period only, Sun 2-5.

Facilities: Ⓟ (200yds) (parking meters, limited spaces) ♿ Ground floor only accessible ✖ (ex guide dogs) 🚌 (pre-booking required)

EDINBURGH

Museum of Scotland

Chambers Street EH1 1JF
☎ 0131 247 4219 🖷 0131 220 4819
✉ info@nms.ac.uk

The museum is a striking new landmark in Edinburgh's historic Old Town. It houses more than 10,000 of the nation's most precious artefacts, as well as everyday objects that throw light on life in Scotland through the ages. Admission to the Royal Museum, which is adjacent to the Museum of Scotland, is also free. Please telephone for details of special events.

Times: *Open all year, Mon, Wed-Sat 10-5, Tue 10-8 & Sun 12-5.
Facilities: ℗ ♥ ✗ (licenced) ♿ all parts accessible toilets for disabled ✕ (ex assist dogs) ▭ ◀

EDINBURGH

National Gallery of Scotland

The Mound EH2 2EL
☎ 0131 624 6200 🖷 0131 343 3250
✉ enquiries@nationalgalleries.org

Dir: Off Princes St

Occupying a handsome neo-classical building designed by William Playfair, the gallery is home to Scotland's greatest collection of European paintings and sculpture from the Renaissance to Post-Impressionism. It contains notable collections of works by Old Masters, Impressionists and Scottish artists. Special exhibitions at the National Gallery of Scotland focus on European and British art from the 14th to the 19th century.

Times: *Open all year, Mon-Sat 10-5, Sun 12-5. Extended opening hours during the Edinburgh Festival period.
Closed 25-26 Dec.
Facilities: ℗ (150yds) ♿ all parts accessible (ramps & lift, room A1 not accessible) toilets for disabled ✕ (ex guide dogs) ▭ (prior booking prefered) ◀

EDINBURGH

Parliament House

Supreme Courts 2-11 Parliament Square
EH1 1RQ
☎ 0131 225 2595 ▯ 0131 240 6755

Dir: Behind St Giles Cathedral

Scotland's independent parliament last sat in 1707, in this 17th-century building hidden behind an 1829 façade, now the seat of the Supreme Law Courts of Scotland. A large stained glass window depicts the inauguration of the Court of Session in 1540.

Times: *Open all year, Mon-Fri 10-4.
Facilities: ℙ (400mtrs) (metered parking in high street) ▯ ✕ & Ground floor only accessible toilets for disabled
✕ (ex guide dogs) ▭

EDINBURGH

Royal Botanic Garden Edinburgh

20A Inverleith Row EH3 5LR
☎ 0131 552 7171 ▯ 0131 248 2901
✉ info@rbge.org.uk

Dir: 1m N of city centre, off A902

Established in 1670, on an area the size of a tennis court, the Royal Botanic Garden in Edinburgh now extends over 70 acres of beautifully landscaped grounds. Spectacular features include the Rock Garden and the Chinese Hillside. The amazing glasshouses feature Britain's tallest palm house and there are magnificent woodland gardens and an arboretum.

Times: *Open all year, daily; Apr-Sep, 10-7; Mar & Oct, 10-6; Nov-Feb, 10-4. Closed 25 Dec & 1 Jan. (Facilities close 30 mins before Garden)
Facilities: ℙ (restricted at certain times) ▯ ✕ (licenced) & All parts accessible (wheelchairs available at east/west gates) toilets for disabled
✕ (ex guide dogs) ▭ ▭

EDINBURGH

Royal Museum

Chambers St EH1 1JF
☎ 0131 247 4219 (info)
🖷 0131 220 4819
✉ info@nms.ac.uk

Dir: 5 min from Edinburgh Castle and Royal Mile

This magnificent museum houses 36 galleries, containing extensive international collections covering the Decorative Arts, Natural History, Science, Technology and Working LIfe, and Geology. Look out for the Bersudsky's Millennium Clock which dominates the main hall. The clock was started on January 1st, 2000, and gives a five-minute mechanical performance every day at 11am (except Sunday), 12 noon, 2pm and 4pm. Temporary exhibitions, films, lectures and concerts take place throughout the year.

Times: *Open all year, Mon-Sat 10-5, Sun 12-5 (Tue late opening till 8). Closed 25 Dec. Phone for times on 26 Dec/1 Jan.
Facilities: 🅿 🍽 ✗ (licenced) ⅗ all parts accessible (induction loops) toilets for disabled ✘ (ex assist dogs) 🚐 🚋

EDINBURGH

Scottish National Gallery of Modern Art

Belford Rd EH4 3DR
☎ 0131 624 6200 🖷 0131 343 3250
✉ enquiries@nationalgalleries.org

Dir: In West End, 20 min walk from Haymarket station

An outstanding collection of 20th-century painting, sculpture and graphic art is shown at the Scottish National Gallery of Modern Art. It includes major works by Matisse, Picasso, Bacon, Moore and Lichtenstein and an exceptional group of Scottish paintings. The gallery is set in leafy grounds with a sculpture garden. Facilities include a good bookshop and café.

Times: *Open all year, Mon-Sat 10-5 & Sun 12-5. Extended opening hours during the Edinburgh Festival. Closed 25-26 Dec.
Facilities: 🅿 🍽 (licenced) ⅗ all parts accessible (ramps & lift) toilets for disabled ✘ (ex guide dogs) 🚐 🚋

Scottish National Portrait Gallery

1 Queen Street EH2 1JD
☎ 0131 624 6200 🖷 0131 558 3691
✉ enquiries@nationalgalleries.org

Dir: Parallel to Princes St, just behind St Andrew Square

The collection at the Scottish National Portrait Gallery provides a visual history of Scotland from the 16th century to the present day, told through the portraits of the people who shaped it. Among the most famous are Mary, Queen of Scots, Ramsay's portrait of David Hume and Raeburn's Sir Walter Scott. The building also houses the National Collection of Photography.

Times: *Open all year, daily, Mon-Sat 10-5, Sun 12-5. Extended opening hours during Edinburgh Festival. Closed 25-26 Dec.
Facilities: ℗ (200yds) ⬤ ♿ all parts accessible (ramps & lift) toilets for disabled ✻ (ex guide dogs) 🚍 (prior booking prefered) ▣

The People's Story

Canongate Tolbooth 163 Canongate Royal Mile EH8 8BN
☎ 0131 529 4057 🖷 0131 556 3439

Dir: On the Royal Mile

The museum, housed in the 16th-century Canongate Tolbooth, tells the story of the ordinary people of Edinburgh from the late 18th century to the present day, their home life, working life and leisure time. Reconstructions include a prison cell, a 1930s pub, a 1940s kitchen and a wash house, supported by photographs, displays, sounds and smells.

Times: *Open, Mon-Sat 10-5. Also open Sun during Edinburgh Festival 2-5.
Facilities: ℗ (100yds) (parking meters) ♿ Ground floor only accessible (lift, induction loop in video room, touch facilities) toilets for disabled ✻ (ex guide dogs) 🚍

EDINBURGH

The Writer's Museum

Lady Stair's House, Lady Stair's Close
Lawnmarket EH1 2PA
☎ 0131 529 4901 📠 0131 220 5057
✉ enquiries@writersmuseum.demon.co.uk

Dir: Off the Royal Mile

Situated in the historic Lady Stair's House which dates from 1622, the museum houses various objects associated with Robert Burns, Sir Walter Scott and Robert Louis Stevenson. Temporary exhibitions are planned throughout the year featuring Scottish writers including contemporary names. The courtyard outside the museum, called Makers Court, is inscribed to commemorate writers from the 14th century to the present day.

Times: *Open all year, Mon-Sat 10-5. (During Festival period only, Sun 2-5).
Facilities: ℗ (500mtrs) (parking meters) ✈ (ex guide dogs) 🚌 (pre-booking required)

SOUTH QUEENSFERRY

Queensferry Museum

53 High Street EH30 9HP
☎ 0131 331 5545 📠 0131 557 3346

Dir: A90 from Edinburgh

The museum commands magnificent views of the two great bridges spanning the Forth and traces the history of the people of Queensferry and Dalmeny, the historic passage to Fife, the construction of the rail and road bridges and the wildlife of the Forth estuary. An ancient annual custom, in August, is Burry Man, who is clad from head to toe in burrs, and parades through the town. See the full size model of the Burry Man in the museum.

Times: *Open all year, Mon & Thu-Sat 10-1, 2.15-5, Sun noon-5. (Last admission ½ hour before closing).
Closed 25-26 Dec & 1-2 Jan
Facilities: ℗ (0.25m) (induction loop at reception) ✈ (ex guide dogs) 🚌 (up to 40 people)

GLASGOW

Burrell Collection

2060 Pollokshaws Rd G43 1AT
☎ 0141 287 2550 📠 0141 287 2597
📧 museums@cls.glasgow.gov.uk

Dir: 3.5m S of city centre

Set in Pollok Country Park, this award-winning building makes the priceless works of art on display seem almost part of the woodland setting. Shipping magnate Sir William Burrell's main interests were medieval Europe, Oriental art and European paintings. Colourful pictures and stained glass depict details of medieval life; rugs, ceramics and metalwork represent the art of Islam, and there is an impressive collection of Chinese and other Oriental ceramics. Furniture, sculpture, armour and weapons complete the picture. Notable paintings on display include works by Bellini, Rembrandt and the French Impressionists.

Times: Open all year, Mon-Thu & Sat 10-5,
Fri & Sun 11-5.
Closed 24-25 & 31 pm Dec & 1-2 Jan
Facilities: 🅿 charged 🍽 ✕ (licenced) ♿ all
parts accessible (wheelchairs available,
tape guides, lifts) toilets for disabled 🚌

GLASGOW

Gallery of Modern Art

Royal Exchange Square G1 3AH
☎ 0141 229 1996 📠 0141 204 5316
📧 museums@cls.glasgow.gov.uk

Dir: Just off Buchanan St & close to
Central Station & Queen St Stn

Glasgow's Gallery of Modern Art is located in the heart of the city in the historic Royal Exchange building. It shows work by local and international artists, as well as addressing contemporary social issues through its major biannual projects. A thought-provoking programme of temporary exhibitions and workshops helps to maintain the vitality of this impressive post-war collection.

Times: Open all year, Mon-Tue & Sat 10-5,
Thu 10-8, Fri & Sun 11-5.
Facilities: 🅿 (200yds) 🍽 ♿ all parts
accessible toilets for disabled ✖ (ex guide
dogs) 🚌

GLASGOW

Glasgow Botanic Gardens

730 Great Western Road G12 0UE
☎ 0141 334 2422 ▤ 0141 339 6964
✆ gbg@land.glasgow.gov.uk

Dir: From M8 J17 onto A82 Dumbarton. Approx 2-3m the Botanic Gardens are on the R

The Botanic Gardens occupy 2,137 square miles of parkland in the West End of the city, and are renowned for their huge glasshouses, including the Kibble Palace built in 1873, which is among the biggest in Britain. The gardens are home to the national collections of dendrobium orchids, begonias and tree ferns, and also include an arboretum, herbaceous borders, a herb garden and unusual vegetables.

Times: Open all year. Gardens open daily 7-dusk, Glasshouses 10-4.45 (4.15 in winter). The Kibble Palace is closed for restoration until 2006, this includes the Coffee shop & picnic area.
Facilities: Ⓟ street parking & all parts accessible toilets for disabled ✖ (ex in grounds) ▭

GLASGOW

Glasgow Cathedral

Castle St G4 0QZ
☎ 0141 552 6891

Dir: M8 J15, in centre of Glasgow

Glasgow is the only Scottish mainland medieval cathedral to have survived the Reformation complete (apart from its western towers). It was built during the 13th to 15th centuries over the supposed site of the tomb of St Kentigern. Notable features of the splendid building are the elaborately vaulted crypt, which includes an introductory display and collection of carved stones, the stone screen of the early 15th century and the unfinished Blackadder Aisle.

Times: *Open all year, Apr-Sep daily 9.30-6.30; Oct-Mar daily 9.30-4.30. Closed 25-26 Dec & 1-2 Jan.
Facilities: & (telephone for disabled access details) ♨

GLASGOW

Glasgow Museums Resource Centre

200 Woodhead Road South Nitshill Ind Estate G53 7NN
☎ 0141 276 9300 ▧ 0141 276 9305

Dir: On S side, close to Rail Stn

Glasgow Museums Resource Centre is the first publicly accessible store for the city's museum service, offering a behind-the-scenes look at 200,000 treasures held in storage. Please note that access to the stores is by guided tour only. Viewings of a specific object can be arranged with two weeks prior notice. Activities, tours and talks are held throughout the year - please see the website or phone for details.

Times: *Open all year Mon-Thu & Sat 10-5, Fri-Sun 11-5.
Guided tours for public at 2.30
Facilities: ▣ & All parts accessible toilets for disabled ✖ (ex guide dogs)
🚍 please pre-book

GLASGOW

Hunterian Art Gallery

82 Hillhead Street The University of Glasgow G12 8QQ
☎ 0141 330 5431 ▧ 0141 330 3618
✉ hunter@museum.gla.ac.uk

Dir: On University of Glasgow Campus in Hillhead District, 2m W of city centre

The founding collection is made up of paintings bequeathed in the 18th century by Dr William Hunter, including works by Rembrandt and Stubbs. The gallery now has works by James McNeill Whistler, major displays of paintings by the Scottish Colourists, and a graphics collection holding some 300,000 prints. A popular feature of the Charles Rennie Mackintosh collection is the re-construction of the interiors of The Mackintosh House.

Times: Open Mon-Sat 9.30-5. Telephone for BH closures.
Facilities: ▣ (500 yds) (pay & display) 🍽
& Ground floor only accessible (lift, wheelchair available) toilets for disabled ✖ (ex guide dogs)
🚍 (advance booking essential) 🚍

GLASGOW

Hunterian Museum

Gilbert Scott Building The University of Glasgow G12 8QQ
☎ 0141 330 4221 ▤ 0141 330 3617
✉ hunter@museum.gla.ac.uk

Dir: On University of Glasgow campus in Hillhead District, 2m W of city centre

The museum is named after the 18th-century physician, Dr William Hunter, who bequeathed his large and important collections of coins, medals, fossils, geological specimens and archaeological and ethnographic items to the university. The exhibits are shown in the main building of the university, and temporary exhibitions are also held.

Times: Open all year, Mon-Sat 9.30-5. Closed certain BHs phone for details.
Facilities: ℙ (100yds) (pay & display) & Ground floor only accessible (lift) toilets for disabled ✖ (ex guide dogs) ▭ ◼

GLASGOW

McLellan Galleries

270 Sauchiehall Street G2 3EH
☎ 0141 565 4137 ▤ 0141 565 4111
✉ museums@cls.glasgow.gov.uk

Dir: N side of Sauchiehall St, close to Glasgow School of Art

The McLellan Galleries first opened in 1854 and featured the personal collection of Glasgow industrialist and coachbuilder Archibald McLellan. With over 1,200 square metres of top gallery space, the McLellan Galleries provide Glasgow Museums with the opportunity to bring to Glasgow major exhibitions and establish Glasgow as Britain's second art city. With Kelvingrove Art Gallery closed for refurbishment until Spring 2006, the McLellan Galleries are showing 200 of Kelvingrove's famous paintings and objects in the exhibition 'Art Treasures of Kelvingrove' (closes Nov 2005).

Times: Open all year, Mon-Thu & Sat 10-5, Fri & Sun 11-5. Closed 24-25 & 31 Dec pm & 1-2 Jan
Facilities: ℙ (500mtrs) ☕ & all parts accessible (assistance available, lift) toilets for disabled ▭

Museum of Transport

1 Bunhouse Road G3 8DP
☎ 0141 287 2720 📠 0141 287 2692
✉ museums@cls.glasgow.gov.uk

Dir: 1.5m W of city centre

Visit the Museum of Transport and the first impression is of gleaming metalwork and bright paint. All around you there are cars, caravans, carriages and carts, fire engines, buses, steam locomotives, prams and trams. The museum uses its collections of vehicles and models to tell the story of transport by land and sea, with a unique Glasgow flavour. Visitors can even go window shopping along the recreated Kelvin Street of 1938. Upstairs, 250 ship models tell the story of the great days of Clyde shipbuilding.

Times: Open all year, Mon-Thu & Sat 10-5, Fri & Sun 11-5.
Facilities: 🅿 charged 🅿 (100yds) 🍽 & all parts accessible (assistance available) toilets for disabled 🐕 (ex guide dogs) 🚐

People's Palace & Winter Gardens

Glasgow Green G40 1AT
☎ 0141 271 2951 📠 0141 271 2960
✉ museums@cls.glasgow.gov.uk

Dir: 1m SE of city centre

Glasgow grew from a medieval town by the cathedral to the second city of the British Empire.Trade with the Americas, and later industry, made the city rich. But not everyone shared in Glasgow's wealth. The People's Palace on historic Glasgow Green shows how ordinary Glaswegians worked, lived and played. Visitors can discover how a family lived in a typical one-room Glasgow 'single end' tenement flat, see Billy Connolly's amazing banana boots, learn to speak Glesga, take a trip 'doon the watter' and visit the Winter Gardens.

Times: Open all year, Mon-Thu & Sat 10-5, Fri & Sun 11-5. Closed 24-25 & 31 Dec pm & 1-2 Jan **Facilities:** 🅿 (50yds) 🍽 & all parts accessible (lifts) toilets for disabled 🚐

GLASGOW

Provand's Lordship

3 Castle Street G4 0RB
☎ 0141 552 8819 📄 0141 552 4744
✉ museums@cls.glasgow.gov.uk

Dir: 1m E of city centre

Provand's Lordship is the only house to survive from medieval Glasgow. For over five hundred years it has watched the changing fortunes of the city and the nearby cathedral. Bishop Andrew Muirhead built the house as part of St Nicholas' Hospital in 1471. The prebendary of Barlanark later bought it for use as a manse. Inside, the displays recreate home life in the middle ages. Behind the house is the St Nicholas Garden, built in 1997. It is a medical herb garden, in keeping with the original purpose of the house.

Times: Open all year, Mon-Thu & Sat 10-5, Fri & Sun 11-5.
Facilities: 🅿 (50 yds) 🍽 & Ground floor, Garden & Grounds accessible (please contact for details) ✖ (ex guide dogs) 🚍

GLASGOW

St Mungo Museum of Religious Life & Art

2 Castle Street G4 0RH
☎ 0141 553 2557 📄 0141 552 4744
✉ museums@cls.glasgow.gov.uk

Dir: 1m NE of city centre

The award-winning St Mungo Museum explores the importance of religion in people's everyday lives and art. It aims to promote understanding and respect between people of different faiths and of none. Highlights of the collection include the Salvador Dali painting 'Christ of St John of the Cross'. The museum also features stained glass, objects, statues and video footage. Within the grounds is Britain's first Japanese zen garden.

Times: Open all year, Mon-Thu & Sat 10-5, Fri & Sun 11-5.
Facilities: 🅿 (50yds) 🍽 (licenced) & all parts accessible (taped information & lift) toilets for disabled ✖ (ex guide dogs) 🚍

GLASGOW

University of Glasgow Visitor Centre

University Avenue G12 8QQ
☎ 0141 330 5511 🖷 0141 330 5225
✉ visitorcentre@gla.ac.uk

Dir: M8 J19 E or J18 W

The visitor centre is spacious and pleasant, with leaflets, publications and video displays explaining how the university works and its history, plus what courses are available and which university events are open to the public. It forms the starting point for guided tours of the university's historic attractions, including the Memorial Chapel, Bute and Randolph Halls, Professors' Square and Lion and Unicorn Staircase. The Hunterian Museum is not part of the tour but visitors are welcome to view the museum on their own.

Times: *Open all year, Mon-Sat 9.30-5. Also May-Sep, Sun 2-5.
Facilities: P (880yds) (few spaces available) 🍴 ᕫ All parts accessible (designated seating) toilets for disabled 🐾 (ex guide dogs) 🚍 🚢

ALVA

Mill Trail Visitor Centre

Glentana Mill West Stirling St FK12 5EN
☎ 01259 769696 🖷 01259 763100

Dir: On A91 approx 8m E of Stirling

In the heart of Scotland's woollen mill country, the centre recounts the history of Scotland's woollen and tweed traditions, and features machines ranging from spinning wheels to large motorised looms of the type in use today. Hear 12-year-old Mary describe her working day as a mill girl 150 years ago, and then contrast her story with our modern working woollen mill. Factory bargains and local crafts are for sale and there is a tourist information centre and café.

Times: *Open all year, Jan-Jun 10-5; Jul-Aug 9-5; Sep-Dec 10-5.
Facilities: P 🍴 ᕫ all parts accessible toilets for disabled 🐾 (ex guide dogs) 🚍 (prebooked) 🚢

DRUMCOLTRAN TOWER

Drumcoltran Tower

Dir: 7m NE of Dalbeattie, in farm buildings off A711

Drumcoltran is a well-preserved tower of mid 16th-century date, simply planned and built, which these days sits amid a busy modern farmyard. A sign-posted pathway leads you round the side of the tower to its main entrance. If you climb to the top you can enjoy the parapet walk round three sides of the tower, some 40 feet up.

Times: *Open at any reasonable time.
Facilities: ◨ ☒

DUMFRIES

Burns Mausoleum

St Michael's Churchyard
☎ 01387 255297 ▤ 01387 265081
✉ dumfriesmuseum@dumgal.gov.uk

Dir: At jct of Brooms Rd ATS and St Michael's St B725

The mausoleum is in the form of a Greek temple, and contains the tombs of Robert Burns, his wife Jean Armour, and their five sons. A sculptured group shows the Muse of Poetry flinging her cloak over Burns at the plough, a fitting tribute to Scotland's favourite poet. Burns was originally buried in a more modest grave in this graveyard, but was moved to the mausoleum 20 years after his death.

Times: Unrestricted access.
Facilities: ℗ (50yds) ⟐ all parts accessible (visitors with mobility difficulties tel 01387 255297) ⊟

DUMFRIES

Dumfries Museum & Camera Obscura

The Observatory Rotchell Rd DG2 7SW
☎ 01387 253374 📠 01387 265081
✉ dumfriesmuseum@dumgal.gov.uk

Dir: A75 from S Carlisle or SW from Castle Douglas, museum in Maxwellton area of Dumfries

Situated in and around an interesting 18th century windmill tower, the museum's collections were started over 150 years ago and exhibitions trace the history of the people and landscape of Dumfries & Galloway. Visitors will find prehistoric footprint fossils, Solway wildlife, tools and wepons of the earliest local people, stone carvings by early Christians, and a collection of everyday items from Victorian farmlife. The Camera Obscura was installed in 1836 and offers incredible views of Dumfries and surrounding countryside. Although the museum is free, there is a small fee for the Camera Obscura.

Times: Open all year, Apr-Sept Mon-Sat 10-5, Sun 2-5; Oct-Mar Tue-Sat 10-1 & 2-5.
Facilities: 🅿 ♿ (camera obscura, parking available) toilets for disabled shop

DUMFRIES

Old Bridge House Museum

Mill Road DG2 7BE
☎ 01387 256904 📠 01387 265081
✉ dumfriesmuseum@dumgal.gov.uk

Dir: At W end of Devorgilla's Bridge

The Old Bridge House was built in 1660, and is the oldest house in Dumfries. It is a museum of everyday life in the town and includes among it exhibits an early 20th-century dentist's surgery, a Victorian nursery and kitchens of the 1850s and 1900s.

Times: Open Apr-Sep, Mon-Sat 10-5 & Sun 2-5.
Facilities: 🅿 🅿 (50yds) (discs needed to park-ask at museum) ♿ Ground floor only accessible 🚗

DUMFRIES

Robert Burns Centre

Mill Road DG2 7BE
☎ 01387 264808 📄 01387 265081
✉ dumfriesmuseum@dumgal.gov.uk

Dir: On Westbank of River Nith

This award-winning centre explores the connections between the poet Robert Burns and the town of Dumfries. Situated in the town's 18th-century watermill, the centre tells the story of Burns' last years spent in the busy streets and lively atmosphere of Dumfries in the 1790s. In the evening the centre shows feature films in the Film Theatre.

Times: Open all year, Apr-Sep, daily 10-8 (Sun 2-5); Oct-Mar, Tue-Sat 10-1 & 2-5.
Facilities: 🅿 🅟 (50yds) (parking disc required-ask at museum) 🍽 ✕ ♿ all parts accessible (induction loop hearing system in auditorium, chairlift) toilets for disabled 🚍 ◄

DUMFRIES

Robert Burns House

Burns St DG1 2PS
☎ 01387 255297 📄 01387 265081
✉ dumfriesmuseum@dumgal.gov.uk

Dir: Signed from Brooms Rd ATS car park

It was here that Robert Burns spent the last three years of his short life; he died here in 1796. The house retains much of its 18th-century character and contains many fascinating items connected with the poet. There is the chair in which he wrote his last poems, many original letters and manuscripts, and the famous Kilmarnock and Edinburgh editions of his work.

Times: Open all year, Apr-Sep, Mon-Sat 10-5, Sun 2-5; Oct-Mar Tue-Sat 10-1 & 2-5.
Facilities: 🅿 (opposite) 🚍

KIRKCUDBRIGHT

Stewartry Museum

St Mary Street DG6 4AQ
☎ 01557 331643 📠 01557 331643
✉ davidd@dumgal.gov.uk

Dir: From A711 through town, pass
parish church, museum approx 200mtrs
on R

*A large and varied collection of
archaeological, social history and natural
history exhibits relating to the Stewartry
district - the eastern half of Galloway - is
shown in the Stewartry Museum, which
dates from 1893. Local and family history
services are provided.*

Times: *Open May, Jun & Sep, Mon-Sat
11-5 Sun 2-5; Jul-Aug, Mon-Sat 10-5 Sun
2-5; Oct Mon-Sat 11-4 Sun 2-5; Nov-Apr
Mon-Sat 11-4
Facilities: 🅿 (outside) ঌ Ground floor only
accessible ✖ (ex guide dogs) ▄

KIRKCUDBRIGHT

Tolbooth Art Centre

High Street DG6 4JL
☎ 01557 331556 📠 01557 331643
✉ davidd@dumgal.gov.uk

Dir: From A711, through town pass
parish church & Stewartry Museum, 1st R
into High St

*The Tolbooth, dating from 1629, provides
interesting accommodation for this
engaging arts centre. It offers an
interpretive introduction to the
Kirkcudbright artists's colony, which
flourished in the town from the 1880s. It
also provides studio and exhibition space
for contemporary local and visiting artists.
There is a programme of exhibitions from
March to October.*

Times: *Open May, Jun & Sep, Mon-Sat
11-5 Sun 2-5; Jul & Aug, Mon-Sat 10-6 Sun
2-5; Oct, Mon-Sat 11-4 Sun 2-5; Nov-Apr,
Mon-Sat 11-4
Facilities: 🅿 (on street parking) 🍽 ঌ all
parts accessible (lift for access to upper
floors) toilets for disabled
✖ (ex guide dogs) ▄ 30 max

DUMFRIES & GALLOWAY

PALNACKIE

Orchardton Tower

Dir: 6m SE of Castle Douglas on A711

Of all the thousands of tower houses scattered about Scotland, this one has a unique feature - it is round. It is a charming structure dating from the mid 15th century, built by John Cairns. The tower, which stands at 33 feet, tapers as it rises from a base diameter of 29 feet to a top diameter of 27 feet 6 inches, with a very tight spiral staircase within. A wall walk can also be accessed.

Times: *Open all reasonable times. Closed 25-26 Dec.
Facilities: 🅿 ♨

RUTHWELL

Ruthwell Cross

Dir: Sited within the parish church on B724

Now in a specially built apse in the parish church, the carved cross dates from the 7th or 8th centuries. Two faces show scenes from the Life of Christ; the others show scroll work, and parts of an ancient poem in Runic characters. It was broken up in the 18th century, but pieced together by a 19th-century minister.

Times: *Open all reasonable times. Contact Key Keeper for access on 01387 870249.
Facilities: 🅿 ♨

RUTHWELL

Savings Banks Museum

DG1 4NN
☎ 01387 870640
✆ tsbmuseum@btinternet.com

Dir: Off B724, 10m E of Dumfries & 6m W of Annan

Housed in the building where savings banks first began, the museum traces their growth and development from 1810 up to the present day. The museum also has an exhibit on the life of Dr Henry Duncan, the father of savings banks, and restorer of the Ruthwell Cross. Multi-lingual leaflets are available.

Times: *Open all year, daily (ex Sun & Mon Oct-Etr), 10-1 & 2-5.
Facilities: 🅿 🅿 (adjacent) ♿ all parts accessible (touch facilities for blind, guide available) ✖ (ex guide dogs) 🚌 (advanced notification required)

SANQUHAR

Sanquhar Tolbooth Museum

High Street DG4 6BN
☎ 01659 250186 📠 01387 265081
✆ dumfriesmuseum@dumgal.gov.uk

Dir: On A76 Dumfries-Kilmarnock road

Housed in the town's fine 18th-century Tolbooth, the museum tells the story of the mines and miners of the area, its earliest inhabitants, native and Roman, the history and customs of the Royal Burgh of Sanquhar and local traditions. A particularly interesting feature is an exhibit on Sanquhar knitting, which is known throughout the world.

Times: Open Apr-Sep, Tue-Sat 10-1 & 2-5, Sun 2-5.
Facilities: 🅿 🅿 (50yds) (museum up steps, phone for info) 🚌

DUNDEE

Broughty Castle Museum

Broughty Ferry DD5 2TF
☎ 01382 436916 📠 01382 436951
✉ broughty@dundeecity.gov.uk

Dir: Turn S off A930 at traffic lights by Eastern Primary School in Broughty Ferry

The 15th-century castle was rebuilt to defend the Tay estuary in the 19th century. It now houses fascinating displays on Dundee's whaling history, arms and armour, local history and seashore life. There are superb views across the Tay estuary from the observation room.

Times: *Open all year Apr-Sep, Mon-Sat 10-4, Sun 12.30-4; Oct-Mar, Tue-Sat 10-4, Sun 12.30-4. Closed Mons, 25-26 Dec & 1-3 Jan.
Facilities: 🅿 🅿 (50yds) 🍽 (unsuitable for wheelchairs) ✈ (ex guide dogs) 🚌 (pre-booking preferred)

DUNDEE

McManus Galleries

Albert Square DD1 1DA
☎ 01382 432350 📠 01382 432369
✉ mcmanus.galleries@dundeecity.gov.uk

Dir: Off A90, attraction in city centre

A remarkable Gothic building housing one of Scotland's most impressive collections of fine and decorative art. There are also displays on local archaeology, civic and social history, trades and industries and wildlife and the environment. Touring exhibitions are a regular feature.

Times: Open all year. Mon-Sat 10.30-5, Thu 10.30-7, Sun 12.30-4. Closed 25-26 Dec & 1-3 Jan. Closed for refurbishment in Sept 2005, please check for details.
Facilities: 🅿 (100 yds) 🍽 ♿ all parts accessible (wheelchair available, lift, high arm chairs & audio loop) toilets for disabled ✈ (ex guide dogs) 🚌 (drop off/pick up on N-side of building) 🍴

KILMARNOCK

Dick Institute Museum & Art Galleries

Elmbank Ave KA1 3BU
☎ 01563 554343 📠 01563 554344

Dir: Follow brown tourist signs from A77 S of Glasgow, into town centre

Temporary and permanent exhibitions are spread over the two floors of this grand Victorian building. Fine art, social and natural history are shown upstairs, while the downstairs galleries house temporary exhibitions of art and craft. Exhibits of beautiful Ayrshire embroidery are a particular feature.

Times: *Open all year, Gallery & Museum: Mon-Tue, Thu-Fri 10-8, Wed & Sat 10-5. Closed Sun & PHs.
Facilities: 🅿 🅿 (300yds) (limited disabled parking) ♿ all parts accessible (wheelchair available) toilets for disabled ✖ (ex guide dogs) 🚌

BEARSDEN

Antonine Wall: Bearsden Bath-house

Roman Road G61 2SG

Dir: Signed from Bearsden Cross on A810

Considered to be the best surviving visible Roman building in Scotland, the bath-house was discovered in 1973 during excavations for a construction site. It was originally built for use by the Roman garrison at Bearsden Fort, which is part of the Antonine Wall defences. This building dates from the second century AD. Visitors should wear sensible footwear.

Times: *Open all reasonable times.
Facilities: ♿ all parts accessible 🏆

MILNGAVIE

Mugdock Country Park

Craigallian Rd G62 8EL
☎ 0141 956 6100 ▤ 0141 956 5624
✉ lain@mcp.ndo.co.uk

Dir: N of Glasgow on A81, signed

This country park incorporates the remains of Mugdock and Craigend castles, and is set in beautiful landscapes. Facilities at the park include an exhibition centre and craft shops, an orienteering course and many walks. There are over 30 organised activities throughout the year, plus barbecue site hire, pond dipping and mini beast studies.

Times: Open all year, daily.
Facilities: ▣ ▣ ▶ & Ground floor, Garden & Grounds accessible toilets for disabled ▭ (pre-booking preferred) ▭

EAST LINTON

Hailes Castle

Dir: 1.5m SW of East Linton on A1

Hailes Castle is an impressive ruin incorporating a fortified manor of 13th-century date, extended in the 14th and 15th centuries. It is beautifully situated by the River Tyne, to its north, while to the south the ground rises up toward the ancient hill fort on the top of Traprain Law. The remains of the castle include two vaulted pit prisons.

Times: *Open at all reasonable times.
Facilities: ▣ ▮

PRESTONPANS

Prestongrange Museum

Prestongrange
☎ 0131 653 2904 📠 01620 828201
✉ elms@eastlothian.gov.uk

Dir: On B1348

The oldest documented coal mining site in Scotland is at Prestongrange, with 800 years of history, and this museum shows a Cornish Beam Engine and on-site evidence of associated industries such as brick-making and pottery. It is located next to a 16th-century customs port. Special events for all the family are held at weekends during July and August.

Times: *Open end Mar-mid Oct, daily 11-4. Last tour 3pm.
Facilities: 🅿 🍽 ♿ Ground floor only accessible (grounds partly accessible) toilets for disabled
🐕 (ex guide dogs or outside) 🚐

BO'NESS

Kinneil Museum & Roman Fortlet

Duchess Anne Cottages Kinniel Estate
EH51 0PR
☎ 01506 778530

Dir: Follow tourist signs from Heritage Railway, off M9. Establishment at E end of town accessed via Dean Rd

The museum is located in a converted stable block of Kinneil House. The ground floor has displays on the industrial history of Bo'ness, while the upper floor looks at the history and environment of the Kinneil estate. An audio visual presentation shows 2,000 years of history. The remains of the Roman fortlet can be seen nearby.

Times: *Open all year, Mon-Sat 12.30-4.
Facilities: 🅿 ♿ Ground floor only accessible 🐕 (ex guide dogs) 🚐

FALKIRK

Rough Castle

Dir: 1m E of Bonnybridge, signed from B816

The impressive earthworks of a large Roman fort on the Antonine Wall can be seen here. The buildings have disappeared, but the mounds and terraces are the sites of barracks, and granary and bath buildings. Running between them is the military road, which once linked all the forts on the wall and is still well defined.

Times: *Open any reasonable time.
Facilities: 🅿 ⛲

BURNTISLAND

Burntisland Edwardian Fair Museum

102 High Street KY3 9AS
☎ 01592 412860 📠 01592 412870

Dir: In the centre of Burntisland

Burntisland Museum, located within the public library, has recreated a walk through the sights and sounds of the town's fair in 1910, based on a painting of the scene by local artist Andrew Young. You can see reconstructed rides, stalls and side shows of the time. There is also a local history gallery.

Times: *Open all year, Mon, Wed, Fri & Sat 10-1 & 2-5; Tue & Thu 10-1 & 2-7. Closed PHs)
Facilities: 🅿 (20m) (on street parking) ✈ (except guide dogs) 🚌 (phone in advance)

DUNFERMLINE

Pittencrieff House Museum

Pittencrieff Park KY12 8QH
☎ 01383 722935 ▤ 01383 313837

Dir: Off A994 on to Coal Rd, L into Pittencrieff Park Car Park. Museum on W edge of town

Pittencrieff is a fine 17th-century house standing in a beautiful park, given to the town by Andrew Carnegie, the Victorian philanthropist who made his fortune through his steel company in the USA, but was born in Dunfermline. Accessible displays tell the story of the park's animals and plants, with plenty of photographs of people enjoying the park over the last 100 years.

Times: *Open daily Apr-Sep, 11-5
Facilities: 🅿 (800yds) ♿ All parts accessible (ramp) toilets for disabled ✲ (ex guide dogs) 🚍

KIRKCALDY

Kirkcaldy Museum & Art Gallery

War Memorial Gardens KY1 1YG
☎ 01592 412860 ▤ 01592 412870
✉ kirkcaldy.museum@fife.gov.uk

Dir: Next to train station

Set in the town's lovely memorial gardens, the museum houses a collection of fine and decorative art, including 18th to 21st-century Scottish paintings; among them the works of William McTaggart and S J Peploe. An award-winning display, 'Changing Places', tells the story of the social, industrial and natural heritage of the area.

Times: *Open all year, Mon-Sat 10.30-5, Sun 2-5. Closed local hols
Facilities: 🅿 🅿 (station car park) 🍽 ♿ all parts accessible (ramp to main entrance & lift to 1st floor galleries) toilets for disabled ✲ (ex guide dogs)
🚍 (contact museum in advance)

HIGHLAND

CLAVA CAIRNS

Clava Cairns

☎ 01667 460232

Dir: 6m E of Inverness, signed from B9091

The Clava Cairns, otherwise known as the Balnuaran Cairns, are the remains of one of Scotland's best preserved Bronze Age burial sites, with a complex of passage graves, ring cairns, a kerb cairn and standing stones in a beautiful setting by the River Nairn. In addition, the remains of a chapel of unknown date can be seen at this site.

Times: *Open at all reasonable times.
Facilities: ▣ ➡ ☙

FORT WILLIAM

Inverlochy Castle

PH33 6SN

Dir: 2m NE of Fort William, off A82

A fine well-preserved 13th-century castle of the Comyn family; in the form of a square, with round towers at the corners. The largest tower was the donjon or keep. This is one of Scotland's earliest castles, now fairly ruined, with a more modern castle of the same name nearby, which is now a hotel.

Times: *Open at all reasonable times.
Facilities: ▣ ☙

KINGUSSIE

Ruthven Barracks

☎ 01667 460232

Dir: 1m SE from Kingussie, signed from A9 and A86

These are the remains of infantry barracks erected in 1719 by General Wade following the Jacobite rising of 1715, with the aim of keeping the Scots under control. The buildings comprise two ranges of quarters and a stable block. The barracks were captured and burnt by Prince Charles Edward Stuart's army in 1746, on their retreat to Culloden.

Times: *Open at any reasonable time.
Facilities: 🅿 ☼

NEWTONMORE

Clan Macpherson House & Museum

Main Street PH20 1DE
☎ 01540 673332 🗒 01540 673332

Dir: Off A9 at jct of Newtonmore and Kingussie, museum on L after entering village

This museum contains the relics and memorials of the clan chiefs and other Macpherson families, as well as those of Prince Charles Edward Stuart. On display are the Prince's letters to the Clan Chief of 1745, and one to the Prince from his father the Old Pretender, along with royal warrants and the green banner of the clan. Other interesting historic exhibits include James Macpherson's fiddle, swords, pictures, decorations and medals.

Times: Open Apr-Oct, Mon-Sat 10-5, Sun 2-5. Other times by appointment.
Facilities: 🅿 🅿 (short distance) ♿ all parts accessible (ramp entrance from car park) toilets for disabled 🐕 (ex guide dogs) 🚌 (donation requested) ◀

ROSEMARKIE

Groam House Museum

High Street IV10 8UF
☎ 01381 620961 & 🖷 01381 621730
🖲 groamhouse@ecosse.net

Dir: Off A9 at Tore onto A832

Opened in 1980, this community-based museum explores the history, culture and crafts of the mysterious Picts, who faded from history over a thousand years ago. Visitors can see the Rosemarkie Stones, large slabs that show Pictish carvings; paintings, a replica Pictish harp, and a collection of photographs of Pictish stones all over the country and interactive computer programmes. Temporary exhibitions take place, often with loans from other major museums.

Times: Open Etr week, daily 2-4.30; May-Sep, Mon-Sat, 10-5, Sun 2-4.30; Oct-Apr, Sat-Sun 2-4.30. Other times by appointment. Closed 13 Dec-5 Mar.
Facilities: 🅿 🅟 (50mtrs) ♿ Ground floor only accessible 🐕 (ex guide dogs) 🚍 40 people max 🍽

WICK

Castle of Old Wick

☎ 01667 460232

Dir: 1m S on Shore Rd

These are the ruins of the best-preserved Norse castle in Scotland, dating from the 12th-century. The location is spectacular, on a spine of rock protecting the sea between two deep, narrow gullies. Visitors exploring the castle must take great care and wear sensible shoes.

Times: *Open at all reasonable times.
Facilities: 🍽

GREENOCK

McLean Museum & Art Gallery

15 Kelly Street PA16 8JX
☎ 01475 715624 ▤ 01475 715626
✉ museum@inverclyde.gov.uk

Dir: Close to Greenock West Railway Station and Greenock Bus Station

James Watt, the engineer who developed the steam engine, was born in Greenock, and various exhibits connected with him are shown. The museum also has displays on shipping, local and natural history, Egyptology and ethnography. The art galleries show both the permanent collection of fine art and temporary exhibitions.

Times: Open all year, Mon-Sat 10-5. Closed local & national PHs.
Facilities: ℙ (200mtrs) ♿ Ground floor, Garden & Grounds accessible (induction loop) toilets for disabled ✖ (ex guide & service dogs) ▭

BALLINDALLOCH

The Glenlivet Distillery

Glenlivet AB37 9DB
☎ 01340 821720 ▤ 01340 821718
✉ betty.munro@chivas.com

Dir: 10m N of Tomintoul, off B9008

Guided tours of the whisky production facilities are available from the Glenlivet Visitor Centre, and the chance to see inside the vast bonded warehouses where the spirit matures. The new multimedia exhibition and interactive presentations communicate the unique history and traditions of Glenlivet Scotch Whisky.

Times: Open Apr-Oct, Mon-Sat 10-4, Sun 12.30-4.
Facilities: ℙ (no overnight parking) ☕ (licenced) ♿ Ground floor, Garden & Grounds accessible (cafeteria, lift to exhibition) toilets for disabled ✖ (ex guide dogs) ▭ (pre-booking preferred) ◀

MORAY

DUFFTOWN

Glenfiddich Distillery

AB55 4DH
☎ 01340 820373 🖷 01340 822083

Dir: N of town, off A941

Set close to Balvenie Castle, the distillery was founded in 1887 by William Grant and has stayed in the hands of the family ever since. Visitors can see the whisky-making process in its various stages, including bottling, and then sample the finished product.

Times: *Open all year Mon-Fri 9.30-4.30, also Etr-mid Oct, Sat 9.30-4.30, Sun 12-4.30. Closed Xmas & New Year
Facilities: P (only in designated areas) ♿ Ground floor, Garden & Grounds accessible (ramp access to production area & warehouse gallery) toilets for disabled (ex guide dogs) (must pre-book)

DUFFUS

Duffus Castle

☎ 01667 460232

Dir: 5m NW of Elgin on B9012 to Burghead

The original seat of the Moray family, this is one of the finest examples of a motte and bailey castle in Scotland, originally with wooden buildings. There are also the remains of a later, very fine, stone hall house and curtain wall.

Times: *Open at all reasonable times.
Facilities: P

ELGIN

Pluscarden Abbey

IV30 8UA
☎ 01343 890257 📄 01343 890258
✉ monks@pluscardenabbey.org

Dir: 6m SW on unclass road

The original monastery, founded by Alexander II in 1230, was burnt, probably by the Wolf of Badenoch who also destroyed Elgin Cathedral. It was restored in the 14th and 19th centuries, and reoccupied in 1948 by Benedictines from Prinknash. Once more a religious community, retreat facilities are available for men and women. All services (with Gregorian chant) are open to the public. Pluscarden Pentecost Lectures are held annually on the Tuesday, Wednesday and Thursday after Pentecost.

Times: Open all year, daily 4.45am-8.30pm
Facilities: 🅿 Ⓟ (100mtrs) ♿ Ground floor, Garden & Grounds accessible (induction loop, ramps to shop, garden partially accessible) toilets for disabled 🚗 (park in designated area only) 🔁

FOCHABERS

Baxters Highland Village

IV32 7LD
☎ 01343 820666 📄 01343 821790
✉ highland.village@Baxters.co.uk

Dir: 1m W of Fochabers on A96

The Baxters food firm started here over 130 years ago and now sells its products in over 60 countries. Visitors can see the shop where the story began, watch an audio-visual display, and visit five shops. See the great hall, audio-visual theatre and cooking theatre. A food tasting area is a new addition.

Times: *Open all year, Jan-Mar 10-5; Apr-Dec 9-5.30.
Facilities: 🅿 ✕ (licenced) ♿ Ground floor only accessible (parking facilities) toilets for disabled 🐕 (ex guide dogs) 🚗 (pre-booking required) 🔁

MORAY

FORRES

Falconer Museum

Tolbooth Street IV36 1PH
☎ 01309 673701 📄 01309 673701
✉ museums@moray.gov.uk

Dir: 11m W of Elgin, 26m E of Iverness

This museum was founded by bequests made by two brothers, Alexander and Hugh Falconer. Hugh was a distinguished scientist, friend of Darwin, recipient of many honours and Vice-President of the Royal Society. On display are fossil mammals collected by him, and items relating to his involvement in the study of anthropology. Other displays are on local wildlife, geology, archaeology and history. You can also see the Forres Quincentennial Time Capsule.

Times: *Open all year Apr-Oct, Mon-Sat 10-5; Nov-Mar, Mon-Thu 11-12.30 & 1-3.30. Closed Good Fri & May Day
Facilities: 🅿 🅿 (100yds) ♿ Ground floor only accessible (induction loop system) ✈ (ex guide dogs) 🚌 (prior booking preferred)

FORRES

Sueno's Stone

☎ 01667 460232

Dir: E end of Forres, off A96

Sueno's Stone is the most remarkable sculptured monument in Britain, probably a cenotaph, standing over 20 feet high and dating back to the end of the first millennium AD. On one side it is engraved with an image of fierce fighting, with dead and mutilated corpses. These days the stone is covered by a protective glass enclosure.

Times: *Open at all reasonable times.
Facilities: 🅿 🍴

ROTHES

Glen Grant Distillery

AB38 7BS
☎ 01340 832118 📠 01340 832104
✉ jennifer.robertson@chivas.com

Dir: On A941 Elgin-Rothes road

The Glen Grant Distillery was founded by the two Grant brothers in 1840, and is located in a sheltered glen. Visitors can discover the secrets of the distillery, including the delightful Victorian garden originally created by Major Grant, and now restored to its former glory, where you can enjoy a dram.

Times: *Open Apr-Oct, Mon-Sat 10-4, Sun 12.30-4.
Facilities: 🅿 & Ground floor, Garden & Grounds accessible (reception centre & still house) toilets for disabled ✗ (ex guide dogs) 🚍 (pre-booking advisable) ◀

SPEY BAY

The Moray Firth Wildlife Centre

IV32 7PJ
☎ 01343 820339 📠 01343 829109
✉ enquiries@mfwc.co.uk

Dir: off A96 onto B9014 at Fochabers, follow road approx 5m to village of Spey Bay. Turn L at Spey Bay Hotel and follow road for 500mtrs

This wildlife centre, owned and operated by the Whale and Dolphin Conservation Society, lies at the mouth of the River Spey and is housed in a former salmon fishing station, built in 1768. There is a free exhibition about the Moray Firth dolphins and the wildlife of Spey Bay. Visitors can browse through a well-stocked gift shop and enjoy refreshments in the cosy tea room.

Times: Open Apr-Oct 10.30-5. Check for winter opening times
Facilities: 🅿 🅿 (20mtrs) 🍽 & all parts accessible toilets for disabled ✗ (ex guide dogs & outside) 🚍 must pre-book ◀

TOMINTOUL

Tomintoul Museum

The Square AB37 9ET
☎ 01309 673701 ▤ 01309 673701
✉ museums@moray.gov.uk

Dir: On A939, 13m E of Grantown

Tomintoul is one of the highest villages in Britain and the museum is located in the village square. The exhibits feature reconstructions of a crofter's kitchen and smiddy, with other displays on the area's wildlife, the story of Tomintoul, the local skiing industry and Glenlivet. Incorporated into the museum are a Tourist Information Centre and a shop.

Times: *Open 25 Mar-May, Mon-Fri 9.30-12 & 2-4; Jun-Aug, Mon-Sat, 9.30-12 & 2-4.30; Sep, Mon-Sat, 9.30-12 & 2-4; 30 Sep-25 Oct, Mon-Fri, 9.30-12 & 2-4. Closed May Day & Good Fri.
Facilities: 🅿 🅿 (200mtrs) & All parts accessible (induction loop and sound commentaries) ✖ (ex guide dogs) 🚌 (pre-booking preferred)

IRVINE

Vennel Gallery

10 Glasgow Vennel KA12 0BD
☎ 01294 275059 ▤ 01294 275059
✉ vennel@north-ayrshire.gov.uk

The Vennel Gallery has a reputation for exciting and varied exhibitions, ranging from international to local artists. Behind the museum is the heckling shop where Robert Burns, Scotland's most famous poet, spent part of his youth learning the trade of flax dressing. In addition to the audio-visual programme on Burns, there is a reconstruction of his lodgings at No 4 Glasgow Vennel, Irvine.

Times: *Open all year Thu-Sun 10-1 & 2-5
Facilities: 🅿 (residential area) & Ground floor only accessible ✖ (ex guide dogs) 🚌

MILLPORT

Museum of the Cumbraes

Garrison House KA28 0DG
☎ 01475 531191 📠 01475 531191
📧 namuseum@north-ayrshire.gov.uk

Dir: Ferry to Millport, from Largs Cal-Mac Terminal. Bus meets each ferry

The Museum of the Cumbraes is a small institution which displays the history and life of Millport and the islands of Great and Wee Cumbrae. Exhibits focus on local schools, maritime trade and local industries. There is also a fine collection of local photographs.

Times: *Open Apr-Sep, Thu-Mon 10-1, 2-5.
Facilities: 🅿 🅿 (50mtrs, on street) ♿ all parts accessible ✖ (ex guide dogs) 🚌 (pre-booking preferred)

SALTCOATS

North Ayrshire Museum

Manse Street Kirkgate KA21 5AA
☎ 01294 464174 📠 01294 464174
📧 namuseum@north-ayrshire.gov.uk

The main museum for North Ayrshire is housed in an 18th-century former parish church. It features a rich variety of artefacts from the North Ayrshire area, including archaeological and social history material. There is an exhibit on the area's maritime heritage and a reconstruction of a traditional North Ayrshire cottage. A continuing programme of temporary exhibitions is also run.

Times: *Open all year, Mon-Sat (ex Sun & Wed) 10-1 & 2-5.
Facilities: 🅿 (100mtrs) ♿ all parts accessible toilets for disabled ✖ (ex guide dogs) 🚌 (advance booking, max 40)

MOTHERWELL

Motherwell Heritage Centre

High Rd ML1 3HU
☎ 01698 251000 📄 01698 268867
✉ museums@northlan.gov.uk

Dir: A723 for town centre. L at top of hill, after pedestrian crossing and just before railway bridge

An award winning audio-visual experience, 'Technopolis', traces the history of the area from Roman times to the rise of 19th-century industry and the post-industrial era. There is also a fine viewing tower, an exhibition gallery and family history research facilities. A mixed programme of community events and touring exhibitions occur throughout the year.

Times: Open Wed-Sat 10-5 (Thu 10-7), Sun 12-5. Closed Mon & Tue, ex BHs
Facilities: 🅿 🅿 50yds ₠ All parts accessible (lifts, audio info & Braille buttons) toilets for disabled ✖ (ex guide dogs) 🚌

BIRSAY

Earl's Palace

KW15 1PD
☎ 01856 721205

Dir: On A966

The gaunt remains of the residence of the 16th-century Earl of Orkney dominates the coastal village of Birsay. The palace, constructed round a courtyard, was once a very fine building, reflecting the royal pretensions of Earl Robert Stewart, the illegitimate son of James V.

Times: *Open at all reasonable times.
Facilities: 🍴

DOUNBY

Click Mill

☎ 01856 841815

Dir: 2.5m from Dounby on B905

The last surviving horizontal water mill in Orkney, of a type well represented in Shetland and Lewis, the Dounby click mill is kept in working condition. Visitors who come to explore the mill are advised to to wear sensible shoes.

Times: *Open at all reasonable times.
Facilities: ☷

FINSTOWN

Stones of Stenness Circle and Henge

☎ 01856 841815

Dir: 5m NE of Stromness on B9055

Dating back to the second millennium BC, the remains of this stone circle are near the Ring of Brogar - a splendid circle of upright stones surrounded by a ditch. According to tradition, if you walk (or are carried) three times round the Stones of Stenness you will be cured of disease.

Times: *Open at any reasonable time.
Facilities: 🅿 �̶ ☷

O R K N E Y

HARRAY

Corrigall Farm & Kirbuster Museum

KW17 2JR
☎ 01856 771411 📠 01856 874615

The museum consists of two Orkney farmhouses with outbuildings. Kirbuster (Birsay) has the last surviving example of a 'Firehoose' with its central hearth; Corrigall (Harray) represents an improved farmhouse and steading of the late 1800s.

Times: *Open Mar-Oct, Mon-Sat 10.30-1 & 2-5, Sun 2-7.
Facilities: 🅿 🅿 (at museum) ♿ all parts accessible ✖ (ex guide dogs) 🚻 🍴

KIRKWALL

Scapa Flow Visitor Centre & Museum

Hoy KW15 1DH
☎ 01856 791300 📠 01856 871560
✉ museum@orkney.gov.uk

Dir: On A964 to Houton, ferry crossing takes 45 mins, visitors centre 2 mins from ferry terminal

Also known as the Lyness Interpretation Centre, this fascinating museum is home to a large collection of military equipment used in the defence of the Orkneys during World War I and World War II. There are also guns salvaged from the German ships scuppered in World War II. Visitors arrive at the island after a short boat trip from the Orkney mainland.

Times: *Open all year: Mon-Fri 9-4.30 (mid May-Oct also Sat, Sun 10.30-3.30)
Facilities: 🅿 🍴 ♿ all parts accessible toilets for disabled ✖ (ex guide dogs) 🚻 🍴

KIRKWALL

The Orkney Museum

Broad St KW15 1DH
☎ 01856 873191 📠 01856 874616
✉ museum@orkney.gov.uk

Dir: Town centre

One of the finest vernacular town houses in Scotland, located opposite the 12th-century St Magnus Cathedral, this 16th-century building, known as Tankerness House, accommodates The Orkney Museum. Displays cover the past 5,000 years of Orkney history, including the islands' fascinating archaeology, refurbished Neolithic/Bronze Age galleries and exhibits on 'Life and Death in Viking Orkney', and 'Medieval Orkney'. Smuggling activities are also reflected, and the rise of the merchant lairds in the 16th and 17th centuries. There is also a programme of temporary exhibitions.

Times: *Open, Oct-Mar Mon-Sat, 10.30-12.30 & 1.30-5, Apr-Sep, 10.30-5 Mon-Sat. **Facilities:** 𝐏 (50yds) ♿ Ground floor only accessible ✖ (ex guide dogs) 🚌 🚢

STROMNESS

Pier Arts Centre

KW16 3AA
☎ 01856 850209 📠 01856 851462
✉ info@pierartscentre.com

The Pier Arts Centre is located in two historic buildings standing on a stone pier in Stromness Harbour. Local, Scottish and international contemporary art is shown alongside the permanent collection of 20th-century work. A £4.5 million refurbishment programme is being undertaken (2005-2006), including a gallery extension which will link the two existing buildings and create easy access for people with mobility difficulties.

Times: *Open all year, Tue-Sat 10.30-12.30 & 1.30-5. **Facilities:** 𝐏 (100yds) ♿ Ground floor only accessible ✖ (ex guide dogs) 🚌

ORKNEY

WESTRAY

Noltland Castle

☎ 01856 841815

Dir: 1m W of Pierowall village

The castle comprises a fine, ruined Z-plan tower, built between 1560 and 1573 but never completed. The tower is remarkable for its large number of gun loops and impressive staircase. The castle was never completed, being at the centre of political intrigue surrounding the battle for succession between supporters of Mary, Queen of Scots and her son James IV.

Times: *Open 11 Jun-Sep, daily 9.30-6.30.
Facilities: 👄

DUNKELD

The Ell Shop & Little Houses

The Cross PH8 0AN

☎ 01350 727460 ❸ dunkfeld@nts.org.uk

Dir: Off A9, 15m N of Perth

The National Trust owns two rows of 20 houses in Dunkeld, and has preserved their 17th/18th-century character. They are not open to the public, but there is a display and audio-visual show in the Information Centre. The Ell Shop, also owned by the National Trust, features the original 'ell' measure, just over a metre long, used for measuring cloth.

Times: *Open Ell Shop mid Mar-Sep, Mon-Sat, 10-5.30, Sun 12.30-5.30. Oct-mid Dec, Mon-Sat 10-4.30, Sun 12.30-4.30.
Facilities: ℙ (300yds) ♿ All parts accessible toilets for disabled 🚌 👄

MILNATHORT

Burleigh Castle

KY13 7XZ

Dir: 0.5m E of Milnathort on A911

The roofless but otherwise complete ruin of a tower house of about 1500, with a section of defensive barmkin wall and a remarkable corner tower with a square cap-house corbelled out. This castle, which overlooks Loch Leven, was built by the Balfour family and visited often by James IV. The Balfours of Burleigh lost the castle in the the mid 1700s because of the infamy of its then master. He fell in love with a young servant girl and was sent abroad to forget her. He vowed that if she ever married he would kill her husband. She married a schoolmaster from Inverkeithing, and true to his word the master of Burleigh returned and shot him dead.

Times: *Open summer only. Keys available locally, telephone 01786 45000.
Facilities: ☃

PERTH

Caithness Glass Factory & Visitor Centre

Inveralmond Industrial Est PH1 3TZ
☎ 01738 637373 📄 01738 492300
✉ visitor@caithnessglass.co.uk

Dir: On Perth Western Bypass, A9, at Inveralmond Roundabout

All aspects of paperweight-making can be seen from the purpose-built viewing galleries at this Caithness Glass factory. Visitors can now enter the glasshouse on a route which enables them to watch the glassmakers closely. There is also a factory shop, a best shop, children's play area and tourist information centre with internet access.

Times: *Open all year, Factory shop & restaurant, Mon-Sat 9-5, Sun 10-5 (Dec-Feb 12-5). Glassmaking Mon-Fri 9-4.30.
Facilities: 🅿 ✖ (licenced) ♿ All parts accessible (wheelchair available) toilets for disabled 🐕 (ex guide dogs) � 🚃

PERTH

Perth Museum & Art Gallery

78 George Street PH1 5LB
☎ 01738 632488 📠 01738 443505
✉ museum@pkc.gov.uk

Dir: In town centre

Visit Perth Museum and Art Gallery for a fascinating look into Perthshire throughout the ages. The impressive building was opened in 1935, but it incorporates the earlier building of the Literary and Antiquarian Society of Perth, which was erected 1822-24. Collections cover Perth silver, glass, art, natural history, archaeology and human history. The art gallery features local artists, local views and local portraits; Dutch and Flemish Old Masters; and artists associated with the area including Landseer, Millais and Beatrix Potter.

Times: *Open all year, Mon-Sat 10-5. Closed Xmas-New Year.
Facilities: ℗ (adjacent) ♿ Ground floor only accessible toilets for disabled ✈ (ex guide dogs) 🚌

PITLOCHRY

Edradour Distillery

PH16 5JP
☎ 01796 472095 📠 01796 472002

Dir: 2.5m E of Pitlochry on A924

It was in 1825 that a group of local farmers founded Edradour, naming it after the bubbling burn that runs through it. It is Scotland's smallest distillery and is virtually unchanged since Victorian times. Have a dram of whisky while watching an audio-visual in the malt barn and then take a guided tour through the distillery itself.

Times: Open Jan-Feb, Mon-Sat 10-5, Sun 12.4; Mar-Oct Mon-Sat 9.30-6, Sun 11.30-6; Nov-Dec, Mon-Sat 9.30-5, Sun 12-5. (Last tour 1hr before close, private tours arranged for a fee).
Facilities: ℗ ♿ Ground floor, Garden & Grounds accessible toilets for disabled ✈ (ex guide & hearing dogs) 🚌 (pre-booking required)

QUEEN'S VIEW

Queen's View Visitor Centre

PH16 5NR
☎ 01350 727284 🖹 01350 728635
✉ peter.fullarton@forestry.gsi.gov.uk

Dir: 7m W of Pitlochry on B8019

Queen Victoria admired the view on a visit here in 1866; it is possibly one of the most famous views in Scotland. The area, in the heart of the Tay Forest Park, has a variety of woodlands that visitors can walk or cycle in. A new exhibition and audio-visual display 'The Cradle of Scottish Forestry' tells the history of the people and the forests of highland Perthshire.

Times: *Open Apr-Oct, daily 10-6.
Facilities: 🅿 charged 🅿 (500mtrs) 🍴 ♿ all parts accessible toilets for disabled 🚍 🚍

PAISLEY

Coats Observatory

49 Oakshaw Street West PA1 2DE
☎ 0141 889 2013 🖹 0141 889 9240
✉ museums.els@renfrewshire.gov.uk

Dir: M8 J27, follow signs to town centre until Gordon St (A761). L onto Causeyside St, L onto New St then L onto High St

The Observatory, funded by Thomas Coats and designed by John Honeyman, was opened in 1883. It houses a five-inch telescope under the dome at the top. Weather recording activities have been carried out here continuously since 1884. There is also earthquake-measuring equipment and the Renfrewshire Astronomical Society holds regular meetings here.

Times: *Open all year, Tue-Sat 10-5, Sun 2-5. Last entry 15 minutes before closing.
Facilities: 🅿 (150yds) (meters/limited street parking) 🐕 (ex guide dogs) 🚍 max 40

PAISLEY

Paisley Museum & Art Galleries

High Street PA1 2BA
☎ 0141 889 3151 ▤ 0141 889 9240
✆ museums.els@renfrewshire

Dir: M8 J27 A741, rdbt 2nd exit A761-town centre. At traffic lights take L lane towards Kilbride. Onto Gordon St, R onto Causeyside St, L onto New St, L onto High St

Pride of place at the Paisley Museum & Art Galleries is given to a world-famous collection of Paisley shawls. Other collections illustrate local industrial and natural history, while the emphasis of the art gallery is on 19th-century Scottish artists and an important studio ceramics collection.

Times: *Open all year, Tue-Sat 10-5, Sun 2-5. BH 10-5.
Facilities: ℗ (330yds) ċ Ground floor only accessible (parking on site) toilets for disabled ✖ (ex guide dogs) ▭ max 80

KELSO

Kelso Abbey

☎ 0131 668 8800

Founded by David I in 1128 and probably the greatest of the four famous Border abbeys, Kelso became extremely wealthy and acquired extensive lands. In 1545 it served as a fortress when the town was attacked by the Earl of Hertford, but now only fragments of the once imposing abbey church give any clue to its long history.

Times: *Open at any reasonable time.
Facilities: ċ all parts accessible ▭ ♨

Halliwells House Museum

Halliwells Close Market Place TD7 4BC
☎ 01750 20096 📄 01750 23282
✉ museums@scotborders.gov.uk

Dir: Off A7 in town centre

A row of late 18th-century town cottages has been converted to create Halliwells House Museum. Displays recreate the building's former use as an ironmonger's shop and home, and tell the story of the Royal Burgh of Selkirk. The Robson Gallery hosts a programme of contemporary art and craft exhibitions.

Times: *Open Apr-Sep, Mon-Sat 10-5, Sun 10-12; Jul-Aug, Mon-Sat 10-5.30, Sun 10-12; Oct, Mon-Sat 10-4.
Facilities: 🅿 charged 🅿 ♿ All parts accessible (lift to first floor, large print, interpretation) toilets for disabled 🐕 (ex guide dogs) 🚌 (24hrs notice preferred) 🍴

Sir Walter Scott's Courtroom

Market Place TD7 4BT
☎ 01750 20096 📄 01750 23282
✉ museums@scotborders.gov.uk

Dir: On A7 in town centre

Built in 1803-4 as a sheriff court and town hall this is where the famous novelist, Sir Walter Scott dispensed justice when he was Sheriff of Selkirkshire from 1804-1832. Displays tell of Scott's time as Sheriff, and of his place as a novelist as well as those of his contemporaries, writer James Hogg and the explorer Mungo Park.

Times: *Open Apr-Sep, Mon-Fri 10-4, Sat 10-2; May-Aug also Sun 10-2; Oct, Mon-Sat 1-4.
Facilities: charged 🅿 (100mtrs) (30min on street, car park 50p for 2hrs) toilets for disabled 🐕 (ex guide dogs) 🚌 (pre-booking preferred) 🍴

LERWICK

Clickimin

ZE1 0QX
☎ 01466 793191

Dir: 1m SW of Lerwick on A970

These are the remains of a prehistoric settlement that was fortified at the beginning of the Iron Age with a stone-built fort. The site was occupied for over 1,000 years. The remains include a partially demolished broch (round tower) which still stands to a height of 17 feet.

Times: *Open at all reasonable times.
Facilities: ♨

LERWICK

Fort Charlotte

ZE1 0JN
☎ 01466 793191

Dir: In centre of Lerwick

A five-sided artillery fort with bastions projecting from each corner. The walls are high and massive. It was built in 1665 to protect the Sound of Bressay from the Dutch, but taken by them and burned in 1673. It was rebuilt in 1781 but has never seen action. It served as a garrison in the Napoleonic Wars, and later as a base for the naval reserve; it was the town jail and courthouse from 1837 to 1875, and then a custom house and coastguard station.

Times: *Open at all reasonable times. Key available locally.
Facilities: ♨

LERWICK

Shetland Museum

Lower Hillhead ZE1 0EL
☎ 01595 695057 ▯ 01595 696729
✉ shetland.museum@sic.shetland.gov.uk

The massive brass propeller blade outside the building is from the 17,000-ton liner 'Oceanic', wrecked off Foula in 1914. The archaeology gallery covers Neolithic burials, axe-making, Bronze-Age houses, Iron-Age farming and domestic life. There are also agricultural and social history displays, including peat-working, corn harvest, local businesses, medals, boot-making and Shetland weddings. Changing exhibitions of contemporary art are also shown.

Times: Open until 31 Mar, Wed-Sat 10-5. (Closed 31 Mar 2005 & new Museum opens early 2006)
Facilities: 🅿 ℗ (30yds) ♿ all parts accessible (lift, wheelchair available) toilets for disabled ✖ (ex guide dogs) 🚌 (pre-booking preferred) ▰

MOUSA ISLAND

Mousa Broch

☎ 01466 793191

Dir: Accessible by boat from Sandwick

This broch is the best-preserved example of an Iron Age drystone tower in Scotland. The tower is nearly complete and rises to a height of 40 feet. The outer and inner walls both contain staircases that may be climbed to the parapet. Storm petrels nest in its stone chambers.

Times: *Open at all reasonable time.
Facilities: ♟

SCALLOWAY

Scalloway Castle

ZE1 0TP
☎ 01466 793191

Dir: 6m from Lerwick on A970

These are the ruins of a castle designed on the medieval two-step plan. The castle was built in 1600 by Patrick Stewart, Earl of Orkney, in what was then the capital of Shetland, Scalloway. When the Earl, who was renowned for his cruelty, was executed in 1615, the castle fell into disuse.

Times: *Open at all reasonable time.
Facilities: 🅿 ⛾

HAMILTON

Chatelherault Country Park

Ferniegair ML3 7UE
☎ 01698 426213 🖹 01698 421532

Dir: 2.5km SE of Hamilton on A72 Hamilton-Larkhall/Lanark Clyde Valley tourist route

Designed as a hunting lodge by William Adam in 1732, Chatelherault is built of unusual pink sandstone and has been described as a gem of Scottish architecture. It is situated close to the motorway, and there is a visitor centre, shop and adventure playground. Look out for the herd of white Cadzow cattle.

Times: *Open all year, Mon-Sat 10-5, Sun 12-5. House closed all day Fri & Sat.
Facilities: 🅿 🅿(no overnight parking) 🍽 ♿ Ground floor, Garden & Grounds accessible (ramps, parking, large print guide) toilets for disabled ✈ (ex in grounds & guide dogs) 🚌 (prefer pre-booking) ◀

HAMILTON

Low Parks Museum

129 Muir Street ML3 6BJ
☎ 01698 328232 📄 01698 328412

Dir: Off M74 J6, by Asda Superstore

The museum tells the story of Hamilton and the Clyde Valley, created by linking the former District Museum and The Cameronians (Scottish Rifles) Museum. Housed in the town's oldest building, dating from 1696, the museum features a restored 18th-century assembly room and exhibitions on Hamilton Palace and The Covenanters.

Times: *Open late Mar-mid Oct, Sun-Thu 10.30-5; House 11-4 (Sep-Oct 11-3). Gardens & tearoom open during winter, please contact for opening times.
Facilities: 🅿 🅿(400yds) ♿ Ground floor, Garden & Grounds accessible ✈ (ex guide dogs) 🚌 (pre-booking preferred) 🍴

STIRLING

Mar's Wark

Broad Street FK8 1EE

A remarkable Scottish Renaissance mansion built by the Earl of Mar, Regent for James VI in 1570 and later used as the town workhouse. It is a two-storey building in a parallelogram shape, that was never completed (the Earl of Mar died in 1572) and now just the highly decorated and carved façade can be seen.

Times: *Open all reasonable times.
Facilities: 👹

CARLOWAY

Dun Carloway Broch

Dir: 1.5m S of Carloway on A858

Brochs are late-prehistoric circular stone towers, and their origins are mysterious, though they are thought to be a kind of residence that could be defended against attack. One of the best examples can be seen at Dun Carloway, where the tower still stands about 30 feet high. The broch is in a fabulous location overlooking Loch Roag on the west coast of Lewis.

Times: *Open at all reasonable times.
Facilities: 🅿 🚌 ♿

BRYNCELLI DDU

Bryn Celli Ddu Burial Chamber

☎ 29 2050 0200

Dir: 3m W of Menai Bridge off A4080

Bryn Celli Ddu, which translates as 'the mound in the dark grove', was excavated in 1865 and then again in 1925-1929. It is a prehistoric circular cairn covering a passage grave with a polygonal chamber, the best to be found in Wales. In the chamber is a free-standing pillar, the original of which is in the National Museum of Wales in Cardiff, but a copy has been left on site.

Times: *Open at all times.
Facilities: 🅿 🚌 ✢

HOLYHEAD

RSPB Nature Reserve
South Stack Cliffs

Plas Nico South Stack LL65 1YH
☎ 01407 764973 📄 01407 764973

Dir: A5 or A55 to Holyhead then follow brown heritage signs

High cliffs with caves and offshore stacks, backed by the maritime heathland of Holyhead Mountain, make this an ideal reserve for watching seabirds. Live video pictures of breeding seabirds are shown in the cliff-top information centre during the summer. Choughs, guillemots, razorbills, fulmars and puffins are among the species that may be seen.

Times: Open: Information Centre daily, Etr-Sep, 11-5. Reserve open daily at all times.
Facilities: 🅿 🚌 (pre-booking required)

LLANALLGO

Din Llugwy Ancient Village

Dir: 0.75m NW off A5025

The remains of a 4th-century village, Din Llugwy, can be seen here. There are two circular and seven rectangular buildings, still standing up to head height and encircled by a pentagonal stone wall some four to five feet thick.

Times: *Open at all times.
Facilities: 🚌 ♿

BRIDGEND

Newcastle

☎ 01656 659515

The small castle dates back to the 12th century. It is ruined, but a rectangular tower, a richly carved Norman gateway and massive curtain walls enclosing a polygonal courtyard can still be seen. It was built by the Marcher Lord Robert Fitzhamon, and first mentioned in 1106, and marks the western limit of Norman penetration into South Wales.

Times: *Open - accessible throughout the year. Key keeper arrangement.
Facilities: 🅿 🚍 ♿

COITY

Coity Castle

CF35 6BG
☎ 01656 652021

Dir: 2m NE of Bridgend, off A4061

This castle along with Newcastle Castle at Bridgend and Ogmore Castle, southwest of Bridgend, were established at the western limit of the early Norman penetration into South Wales. It is a 12th to 16th-century stronghold, with a hall, chapel and the remains of a square keep.

Times: *Open all year, at all times. Key keeper arrangement.
Facilities: 🅿 🚍 ♿

CARDIFF

National Museum & Gallery Cardiff

Cathays Park CF10 3NP
☎ 29 2039 7951 📠 029 2037 3219
✉ post@nmgw.ac.uk

Dir: In Civic Centre, 5 mins walk from city centre & 20 mins walk from bus and train station

This establishment is unique among British museums and galleries in its range of art and science displays. 'The Evolution of Wales' exhibition takes visitors on a spectacular 4,600-million-year journey, tracing the world from the beginning of time and the development of Wales. There are displays of Bronze-Age gold, early Christian monuments, Celtic treasures, silver, coins and medals, ceramics, fossils and minerals. A significant collection of French Impressionist paintings sits alongside the work of Welsh artists, past and present, in the elegant art galleries.

Times: Open all year, Tue-Sun 10-5. Closed Mon (ex BHs) & 24-26 Dec.
Facilities: 🅿 charged 🅿 (adjacent to museum) 🍽 ✗ (licenced) & all parts accessible (wheelchair available, Tel 029 2057 3509 for access guide) toilets for disabled 🐕 (ex guide dogs) 🚐 (pre-booking required) 🔳

ST FAGANS

Museum of Welsh Life

CF5 6XB
☎ 29 2057 3500 📠 029 2057 3490
✉ post@nmgw.ac.uk

Dir: 4m W of Cardiff on A4232

A stroll around the indoor galleries and 100 acres of beautiful grounds at this museum will give you a fascinating insight into how people in Wales have lived, worked and spent their leisure hours since Celtic times. You can see people practising the traditional means of earning a living, the animals they kept and at certain times of year, the ways in which they celebrated the seasons.

Times: Open all year daily, 10-5. Closed 24-26 Dec.
Facilities: 🅿 charged 🍽 ✗ (licenced) & Ground floor, Garden & Grounds accessible (wheelchairs available on a 'first come-first served' basis) toilets for disabled 🐕 (ex in grounds if on lead) 🚐 (pre-booking required) 🔳

ABERGWILI

Carmarthenshire County Museum

SA31 2JG

☎ 01267 228696 📠 01267 223830

✉ cdelaney@carmarthenshire.gov.uk

Dir: 2m E of Carmarthen, just off A40, at Abergwili rdbt

The museum is housed in the old palace of the Bishop of St David's, where the New Testament was first translated into Welsh in 1567. It offers a wide range of local subjects to explore, from geology and prehistory to butter making, Welsh furniture and folk art. Temporary exhibitions are also held. Visitors can see the bishops' private chapel and picnic in the seven acres of delightful grounds. The Bishop's Pond is a Site of Scientific Interest.

Times: Open all year, Mon-Sat 10-4.30. Closed Xmas-New Year
Facilities: 🅿 🅿 (100yds) 🍴 ♿ All parts accessible (lift) toilets for disabled 🐕 (ex guide dogs) 🚌 (advance booking prefered)

DRE-FACH FELINDRE

National Woollen Museum

SA44 5UP

☎ 01559 370929

Dir: 16m W of Carmarthen off A484, 4m E of Newcastle Emlyn

The National Woollen Museum has recently re-opened following a £2.6 million redevelopment programme. It is housed in the former Cambrian Mills and has a comprehensive display tracing the evolution of the woollen industry from its beginnings to the present day. Demonstrations of the fleece to fabric process are given on 19th-century textile machinery.

Times: Open Apr-Sep, daily 10-5; Oct-Mar, Tue-Sat 10-5.
Facilities: 🅿 🅿 🍴 ♿ Ground floor, Garden & Grounds accessible (wheelchair access to ground floor & ample seating) toilets for disabled 🐕 (ex guide dogs) 🚌 (prior notification essential) 🍵

DRYSLWYN

Dryslwyn Castle

☎ 29 2050 0200

Dir: On B4279

The ruined 13th-century castle was a stronghold of the native Welsh. It stands on a lofty mound, and played a significant part in the struggles between the English and the Welsh. It is gradually being uncovered by excavation.

Times: *Open - entrance by arrangement with Dryslwyn Farm.
Facilities: 🅿 🚃 ♿

KIDWELLY

Kidwelly Industrial Museum

Broadford SA17 4LW
☎ 01554 891078

Dir: Signed from Kidwelly bypass & town, stack visible from bypass

Two of the great industries of Wales are represented in this museum: tinplate and coal mining. The original buildings and machinery of the Kidwelly tinplate works, where tinplate was hand made, are now on display to the public. There is also an exhibition of coal mining with pit-head gear and a winding engine, while the more general history of the area is shown in a separate exhibition.

Times: Open Etr, Jun-Sep, BH wknds, Mon-Fri 10-5, Sat-Sun 12-5. Last admission 4. Other times by arrangement for parties only. Facilities: 🅿 ☕ ♿ Ground floor, Garden & Grounds accessible (ramps on entrances) toilets for disabled 🚃

LLANSTEFFAN

Llansteffan Castle

☎ 01267 241756

Dir: Off B4312

The ruins of this 11th to 13th-century stronghold stand majestically on the west side of the Towy estuary, backed by beautiful green rolling hill country. Visitors should park in the beach car park and walk up the pathway signposted to the castle.

Times: *Open - access throughout the year.

Facilities: � 🔄

CAPEL BANGOR

Rheidol Hydro Power Station & Visitor Centre

Cwm Rheidol SY23 3NF

☎ 01970 880667 📄 01970 880670

Dir: Off A44 at Capel Bangor

A guided tour of the hydro power station and fish farm can be taken here in the beautiful, secluded Rheidol Valley, just ten miles from Aberystwyth. There is a visitor centre, where you can learn all about the workings of a hydro electrical power station, a nature trail and scenic drive. You can also stop for refreshments in the café.

Times: *Open Apr-Oct, daily 10-4 for free tours of the Power Station, fish farm & visitor centre.

Facilities: 🅿 🅿 (300yds) 🍽 ⅙ Ground floor, Garden & Grounds accessible toilets for disabled � (pre-booking necessary)

CERRIGYDRUDION

Llyn Brenig Visitor Centre

LL21 9TT
☎ 01490 420463 📄 01490 420694
✉ llyn.brenig@dwrcymru.com

Dir: On B4501 between Denbigh & Cerrigydrudion

The 1,800-acre estate has a unique archaeological trail and a round-the-lake walk of 10 miles, which takes about four hours. A hide is available and disabled anglers are catered for with a specially adapted fishing boat. The sailing season runs from April till November. The centre has an exhibition on archaeology, history and conservation, and an audio-visual programme.

Times: *Open mid Mar-Oct, daily 9-5.
Facilities: 🅿 charged 🍴 (licenced) ♿ all parts accessible (boats for disabled & fishing open days) toilets for disabled 🐾 (ex guide dogs) 🚌 (pre-booking preferred)

LLANRWST

Gwydyr Uchaf Chapel

☎ 01492 640578

Dir: 0.5m SW off B5106

Built in the 17th century by Sir John Wynn of Gwydir Castle, the chapel is noted for its painted ceiling and wonderfully varied woodwork. The Gwydyr Uchaf Forest Park is a pleasant place for walking and picnicking, and the chapel is included on the route for the forest's 1.5 mile trail, Lady Mary's Walk.

Times: *Open any reasonable time.
Facilities: 🅿 ♿

TREFRIW

Trefriw Woollen Mills Ltd

LL27 0NQ
☎ 01492 640462 🖨 01492 641821
✆ info@t-w-m.co.uk

Dir: On B5106 in centre of Trefriw, 5m N of Betws-y-Coed

Established in 1859, the mill is situated beside the fast-flowing Afon Crafnant, which drives two hydro-electric turbines to power the looms. All the machinery of woollen manufacture can be seen here: blending, carding, spinning, dyeing, warping and weaving. In the Weaver's Garden, there are plants traditionally used in the textile industry, mainly for dyeing. Hand-spinning demonstrations are a feature.

Times: Mill open Etr-Oct, Mon-Fri 10-1 & 2-5. Weaving demonstrations & turbine house: open all year, Mon-Fri 10-1 & 2-5. Handspinning & weaver's garden Jun-Sep Tue-Thu Jul-Aug Mon-Fri 10-5
Facilities: Ⓟ (35yds) 🍽 ♿ Ground floor, Garden & Grounds accessible (access to shop, cafe, weaving & turbine house) ✖ (ex in grounds on lead) 🚌 (pre-booking preferred) 🎫

EWLOE

Ewloe Castle

Dir: 1m NW of village on B5125

Standing in Ewloe Wood are the remains of Ewloe Castle. It was a native Welsh castle, and Henry II was defeated nearby in 1157. Part of the Welsh Tower in the upper ward still stands to its original height, and there is a well in the lower ward. Remnants of walls and another tower can also be seen.

Times: *Open at all times.
Facilities: 🚌 ✚

FLINT

Flint Castle

CH6 5PH

☎ 1352 733078 **Dir:** NE side of Flint

The castle was started by Edward I in 1277 and overlooks the River Dee. It is exceptional for its great tower, or Donjon, which is separated by a moat. Other buildings would have stood in the inner bailey, of which parts of the walls and corner towers remain.

Times: *Open at all times.
Facilities: 🅿 🚌 ♿

HOLYWELL

Basingwerk Abbey

Greenfield Valley Heritage Pk Greenfield CH8 7GH

☎ 1352 714172 **Dir:** Just S of A458

The abbey was founded around 1131 by Ranulf de Gernon, Earl of Chester. The first stone church dates from the beginning of the 13th century. The last abbot surrendered the house to the crown in 1536. The abbey is close to the Heritage Park Visitor Centre and access to the museum and farm complex at Greenfield Valley.

Times: *Open all year, daily 9-6.
Facilities: 🅿 ✕ ♿ all parts accessible (disabled facilities in Heritage Park) toilets for disabled 🚌 ♿

CAERNARFON

Segontium Roman Museum

Beddgelert Road LL55 2LN
☎ 01286 675625 ▤ 01286 678416
✉ info@segontium.org.uk

Dir: On A4085 to Beddgelert approx 1m from Caernarfon

Segontium Roman Museum tells the story of the conquest and occupation of Wales by the Romans and displays the finds from the auxiliary fort of Segontium, one of the most famous in Britain. You can combine a visit to the museum with exploration of the site of the Roman Fort, which is in the care of Cadw: Welsh Historic Monuments. The exciting discoveries displayed at the museum vividly portray the daily life of the soldiers stationed in this remote outpost of the Roman Empire.

Times: *Open Tue-Sun 12.30-4. Closed Mon except BH
Facilities: ℙ ✖ (ex guide dogs) ☷ (pre-booking preferred) ◩

LLANBERIS

Welsh Slate Museum

Gilfach Ddu Padarn Country Park LL55 4TY
☎ 01286 870630 ▤ 01286 871906
✉ slate@nmgw.ac.uk

Dir: 0.25m off A4086. Museum within Padarn Country Park

Set among the towering quarries at Llanberis, the Welsh Slate Museum is a living, working site located in the original workshops of Dinorwig Quarry, which once employed 15,000 men and boys. You can see the foundry, smithy, workshops and mess room which make up the old quarry, and view original machinery, much of which is still in working order.

Times: Open Etr-Oct, daily 10-5; Nov-Etr, Sun-Fri 10-4.
Facilities: ℙ charged ℙ (800yds) ● ♿ all parts accessible (all parts accessible except patten loft) toilets for disabled ✖ (ex guide dogs) ☷ (pre-booking advisable) ◩

LLANFIHANGEL-Y-PENNANT

Castell-y-Bere

☎ 29 2050 0200

Dir: Off B4405

The castle was begun around 1221 by Prince Llewelyn ap Iorwerth of Gwynedd to guard the southern flank of his principality. It is typically Welsh in design with its D-shaped towers. Although it is a little off the beaten track, the castle lies in a spectacular setting, overshadowed by the Cader Idris range.

Times: *Open all reasonable times.
Facilities: 🚌 ♿

LLANGYBI

St Cybi's Well

☎ 01766 810047

Dir: Off B4354

Cybi was a 6th-century Cornish saint, known as a healer of the sick, and St Cybi's Well (or Ffynnon Gybi) has been famous for its curative properties through the centuries. The corbelled beehive vaulting inside the roofless stone structure is Irish in style and unique in Wales. The buildings comprise two well chambers, a cottage for the well's custodian and a latrine.

Times: *Open at all times.
Facilities: ♿ Ground floor only accessible 🚌 ♿

PENARTH FAWR

Penarth Fawr

☎ 01766 810880

Dir: 3.5m NE of Pwllheli off A497

The hall, buttery and screen are preserved in this stone-built hall house, which was constructed in the mid 15th century, restored in 1937, and has many fascinating architectural features. Stables next to the house have been converted to provide a gallery exhibiting locally made ceramics. Hand book binding is also undertaken here.

Times: *Open at all times.
Facilities: ㋕ Ground floor only accessible
🚌 ㋿

MERTHYR TYDFIL

Cyfarthfa Castle Museum & Art Gallery

Cyfarthfa Park CF47 8RE
☎ 01685 723112 🖨 01685 723112
🄴 museum@cyfarthfapark.freeserve.co.uk

Dir: Off A470, N towards Brecon, follow brown heritage signs

Set in wooded parkland beside a beautiful lake, this imposing gothic mansion now houses a superb museum and art gallery. Providing a glimpse into 3,000 years of history, the museum displays collections of fine art, social history and objects from around the world in a Regency setting.

Times: Open Apr-Sep: Mon-Sun 10-5.30; Oct-Mar, Tue-Fri 10-4, Sat-Sun 12-4. Closed between Xmas & New Year
Facilities: 🅿 🅿 (300yds) (restricted during some special events) 🍽 ㋕ all parts accessible (stair lift & wheelchair available) toilets for disabled 🐾 (ex guide dogs) 🚌 (pre-booking required)

CAERWENT

Caerwent Roman Town

☎ 29 2050 0200

Dir: Just off A48

Caerwent Roman Town is a 44-acre site where you can see a complete circuit of the 4th century town wall of 'Venta Silurum', together with excavated areas of houses, shops and a Romano-Celtic temple. Caerwent was the tribal capital of the Silures.

Times: *Open - access throughout the year.
Facilities: 🚌 ♿

GROSMONT

Grosmont Castle

☎ 01981 240301

Dir: On B4347

Grosmont is one of the 'trilateral' castles of Hubert de Burgh, along with Skenfrith and White Castle. It stands on a mound with a dry moat, and the considerable remains of its 13th-century great hall can still be seen. Three towers once guarded the curtain wall, and the western tower is well preserved.

Times: *Open - access throughout the year.
Facilities: ♿ Ground floor only accessible 🚌 ♿

LLANTHONY

Llanthony Priory

☎ 29 2050 0200

William de Lacey discovered the remains of a hermitage dedicated to St David. By 1108 a church had been consecrated on the site and just over a decade later the priory was complete. After the priory was brought to a state of siege in an uprising, Hugh de Lacey provided the funds for a new church, and it is this that makes the picturesque ruin seen today. Visitors can still make out the west towers, north nave arcade and south transept.

Times: *Open - access throughout the year.
Facilities: 🅿 ♿ Ground floor only accessible toilets for disabled 🚌 ✥

MONMOUTH

The Nelson Museum & Local History Centre

New Market Hall Priory Street NP25 3XA
☎ 01600 710630
✉ nelsonmuseum@monmouthshire.gov.uk

Dir: In town centre

Commemorative glass, china, silver, medals, books, models, prints and Admiral Nelson's own fighting sword feature here. The local history displays deal with Monmouth's past as a fortress market town, and include a section on the co-founder of the Rolls Royce company, Charles Stewart Rolls, who was also a pioneer balloonist, aviator and, of course, motorist.

Times: *Open all year, Mon-Sat 10-1 & 2-5; Sun 2-5. Closed Xmas & New Year.
Facilities: 🅿 (200yds) (small daily charge) ♿ Ground floor only accessible toilets for disabled ✖ (ex guide dogs) 🚌 (pre-booking necessary) 🚩

SKENFRITH

Skenfrith Castle

☎ 29 2050 0200

Dir: On B4521

Skenfrith is one of the 'trilateral' castles of Hubert de Burgh, along with Grosmount and White Castle, built to defend the Welsh Marches. Skenfrith, dating from the 13th-century, has a round keep set inside an imposing towered curtain wall.

Times: *Open - access throughout the year. Key keeper arrangement.
Facilities: 🅿 🚍 ⊕ ♨

CRYNANT

Cefn Coed Colliery Museum

SA10 8SN
☎ 01639 750556 📄 01639 750556

Dir: 1m S of Crynant, on A4109

The museum is on the site of a former working colliery, and tells the story of mining in the Dulais Valley. A steam-winding engine has been kept and is now operated by electricity, and there is also a simulated underground mining gallery, boilerhouse, compressor house, and exhibition area. Outdoor exhibits include a stationary colliery locomotive. Exhibitions relating to the coal mining industry are held on a regular basis.

Times: *Open daily, Apr-Oct 10.30-5; Nov-Mar, groups welcome by prior arrangement.
Facilities: 🅿 ♿ toilets for disabled 🚍

NEATH

Gnoll Estate Country Park

SA11 3BS

☎ 01639 635808 📄 01639 635694

Dir: Follow brown heritage signs from town centre

The extensively landscaped country park is based in 18th-century landscaped gardens, easily accessible from the centre of Neath, with lakes, cascades and a grotto. It offers tranquil woodland walks, picnic areas, stunning views, children's play areas, an adventure playground, a nine-hole golf course, and coarse fishing. A varied programme of events is scheduled along with school holiday activities.

Times: Open all year - Vistor centre, daily from 10. Closed 24 Dec-2 Jan

Facilities: 🅿 🅿(no designated coach parking) 🐾 ♿ Ground floor only accessible (wheelchair & scooter for hire, designated parking) toilets for disabled ✕ (ex guide dogs) 🚌 (advance notice required)

NEATH

Neath Abbey

SA10 7DW

☎ 01639 812387

Dir: 1m W off A465

These are the ruins of an abbey founded in 1130 by Richard de Grainville as a daughter house of Savigny in Normandy, but it was soon absorbed into the Cistercian order. The abbey was dissolved in 1539 and a few years later part of the cloister ranges were converted into a mansion house, which was occupied until the end of the 17th century. The abbey precinct was then turned into a copper smelting and casting workshop, the remnants of which industry were cleared away in the early 20th century.

Times: *Open at all times. Key keeper arrangement.

Facilities: 🅿 ♿ Ground floor only accessible 🚌 ⊕

CAERLEON

Roman Legionary Museum

High Street NP18 1AE
☎ 01633 423134 🖷 01633 422869
✉ roman@nmgw.ac.uk

Dir: Close to Newport, 20 min from M4, follow signs from Cardiff & Bristol

The museum illustrates the history of Roman Caerleon and the daily life of its garrison. On display are arms, armour and equipment, with a collection of engraved gemstones, a labyrinth mosaic and finds from the legionary base at Usk. Please telephone for details of children's holiday activities.

Times: Open all year:
Mon-Sat 10-5, Sun 2-5.
Facilities: 🅿 (100yds) ⚫ all parts accessible toilets for disabled ✖ (ex guide dogs) 🚌 (advance booking essential) ◼

LLANYCEFN

Penrhos Cottage

SA66 7XT
☎ 01437 760460 🖷 01437 760460

Dir: Near Maenclochog & Llanycefn, N of Haverfordwest

Local tradition has it that cottages built overnight on common land could be claimed by the builders, together with the ground a stone's throw away from the door. This thatched cottage is an example, built with help from friends and family; and it gives an insight into traditional Welsh country life.

Times: *Open mid May-Sep Mon-Fri, by appointment only. Tel: 01437 731328.
Facilities: 🅿 (roadside) ⚫ All parts accessible ✖ (ex in grounds or guide dogs) 🚌 (telephone to book)

LLAWHADEN

Llawhaden Castle

☎ 01437 541201

Dir: Off A40, 3m NW of Narberth

The castle was first built in the 12th century to protect the possessions of the wealthy and powerful bishops of St David's. The 13th and 14th-century remains of the bishops' hall, kitchen, bakehouse and other buildings can be seen, all surrounded by a deep moat. Following the Dissolution, the castle was abandoned and was subsequently quarried for building materials.

Times: *Open at all times. Key keeper arrangement.
Facilities: & Ground floor only accessible 🚌 ⊕

NEWPORT

Pentre Ifan Burial Chamber

☎ 029 2050 0200

Dir: 3m SE from B4329 or A487

Found to be part of a vanished long barrow when excavated in 1936 and 1937, the remains of the chamber at Pentre Ifan include the capstone, three uprights and a circular forecourt. It is probably the most popular megalithic site in Wales and according to local tradition fairies with red caps are sometimes to be seen here.

Times: *Open - access throughout the year.
Facilities: 🚌 ⊕

MONTGOMERY

Montgomery Castle

☎ 029 2050 0200

Montgomery Castle was initially an earth and timber structure guarding an important ford in the River Severn, Montgomery was considered a 'suitable spot for the erection of an impregnable castle' in the 1220s. Building and modifications continued until 1251-53, but the final conquest of Wales by Edward I meant the castle lost much of its role.

Times: *Open all year, any reasonable time.
Facilities: ⅃ all parts accessible ▄ ✦

SWANSEA

Glynn Vivian Art Gallery

Alexandra Road SA1 5DZ
☎ 01792 516900 ▤ 01792 516903
✉ glynn.vivian.gallery@swansea.gov.uk

Dir: M4 J42 along Fabian Way A483 up Wind St. L at train station opp library

The gallery shows a broad spectrum of visual arts form the original bequest of Richard Glynn Vivian, including Old Masters and an international collection of porcelain and Swansea china. The 20th century is also well represented with painting and sculpture by British and foreign artists, with the emphasis on Welsh artists.

Times: *Open all year, Tue-Sun & BH Mon 10-5. Closed 25-26 Dec & 1 Jan.
Facilities: ℗ (200 yds) ⅃ Ground floor, Garden & Grounds accessible toilets for disabled ✖ (ex guide dogs & hearing dogs) ▄ (subject to school/college visits) ▄

SWANSEA

Swansea Museum

Victoria Road Maritime Quarter SA1 1SN
☎ 01792 653763 🖷 01792 652585
✉ swansea.museum@swansea.gov.uk

Dir: M4 J42, on main road into city centre

This is the oldest museum in Wales, showing the history of Swansea from the earliest times until today. The museum has a tram shed and, in the summer months, there are floating boats to explore. A continuous programme of temporary exhibitions and events is run all year round.

Times: *Open all year, Tue-Sun 10-5 (last admission 4.45). Closed Mon except BH Mon, 25-26 Dec & 1 Jan.
Facilities: ℗ (50yds) (charged) & Ground floor only accessible toilets for disabled ✈ (ex guide dogs) ⛟ (prior notification preferred) ⛟

BLAENAVON

Big Pit National Mining Museum of Wales

NP4 9XP
☎ 01495 790311 🖷 01495 792618
✉ bigpit@nmgw.ac.uk

Dir: M4 J25/26, follow signs on A4042 & A4043 to Pontypool & Blaenavon. Signed off A465

For the authentic underground experience, Big Pit is the UK's leading mining museum. It is a real colliery and was the place of work for hundreds of men, women and children for over 200 years. Go 300 feet down for a guided tour of the mine with a real miner and experience life on the coal face. Visit colliery buildings and learn about modern mining from interactive exhibits.

Times: *Open Mid Feb-End Nov, daily 9.30-5, telephone to confirm
Facilities: ℗ 🍽 (licenced) & all parts accessible (underground tours by prior arrangement) toilets for disabled ⛟ (pre-booking required)

OGMORE

Ogmore Castle

☎ 01656 653435

Dir: 2.5m SW of Bridgend, on B4524

This castle, along with Coity Castle and Newcastle Castle at Bridgend, were established at the western limit of the early Norman penetration into South Wales. It is located on the River Ogmore, and the west wall stands 40 feet high. A hooded fireplace is preserved in the 12th century, three-storey keep and a dry moat surrounds the inner ward.

Times: *Open - access throughout the year. Key keeper arrangement.
Facilities: 🅿 ♿ Ground floor only accessible 🚌 ♿

ST HILARY

Old Beaupre Castle

☎ 01446 773034

Dir: 1m SW, off A48

Old Beaupre Castle is a ruined manor house dating from about 1300, rebuilt during the 16th century, with work begun by Sir Rice Mansel, continued by William Bassett and finished by his son Richard. Its most notable features are an Italianate gatehouse and porch. The porch is an unusual three-storeyed structure and displays the Bassett arms.

Times: *Open - access throughout the year. Key keeper arrangement.
Facilities: 🅿 🚌 ♿

Botanic Gardens

3 College Park BT7 1LP
☎ 28 9032 4902 ▤ 028 9032 4902
✉ maxwellr@belfastcity.gov.uk

Dir: From City Hall, Bedford St then Dublin road for Botanic Avenue

The Botanic Gardens, which opened in 1828, are among of the most popular parks in Belfast. A particular highlight is the beautiful glass-domed Victorian Palm House, built between 1839 and 1852 and restored between 1975 and 1983. This palm house pre-dates the one in Kew Gardens and is one of the earliest curved glass and iron structures in the world. Another feature is the Tropical Ravine - stand on a balcony to get a wonderful view through a steamy ravine full of exotic plants.

Times: *Open Palm House Tropical Ravine: Apr-Sep 10-12, 1-5; Oct-Mar 10-12, 1-4. Sat, Sun & BHs 1-5 (Summer), 1-4 (Winter).
Facilities: ℙ (street) ♿ Ground floor, Garden & Grounds accessible 🚌

Giant's Ring

☎ 28 9023 5000 ▤ 028 9031 0288

Dir: 0.75m S of Shaws Bridge

The Giant's Ring is a circular, Bronze-age enclosure nearly 200 feet in diameter, similar in style to Stonehenge, with a stone chambered grave in the centre and bordered by banks 20 feet wide and 12 feet high. Very little is known for sure about this site, except that it was used for ritual burial.

Times: *Open all times.
Facilities: ℙ

BELFAST

Ulster Museum

National Museums of N.Ireland Botanic Gardens BT9 5AB
☎ 28 9038 3000 ▤ 028 9038 3003

Dir: M1/M2 to Balmoral exit

Both a national museum and an art gallery, the Ulster Museum has some 8,000 square metres of galleries. The collections are Irish and international in origin and cover archaeology and ethnography, art, botany and zoology, geology and local history, including industrial archaeology. An annual programme of changing temporary exhibitions and events takes place.

Times: Open all year, Mon-Fri 10-5, Sat 1-5, Sun 2-5. Tel for details of Xmas closures.
Facilities: ℙ (100yds on street) (Clearway 8-9.30 & 4.30-6) ➋ ⅚ all parts accessible (all galleries except one. Loop system, wheelchair lifts) toilets for disabled ✕ (ex guide dogs) ➡ (pre-booking preferred) ◀

LISBURN

Irish Linen Centre & Lisburn Museum

Market Square BT28 1AG
☎ 28 9266 3377 ▤ 028 9267 2624
✉ irishlinencentre@lisburn.gov.uk

Dir: Signed both in and outside town centre

The centre tells the story of the Irish linen industry past and present. The recreation of individual factory scenes brings the past to life and a series of imaginative hands-on activities describes the linen manufacturing processes. The museum is also dedicated to local history in Lisburn and the Lagan Valley. A range of temporary exhibitions is also shown.

Times: *Open all year, Mon-Sat, 9.30-5.
Facilities: ℙ (200mtrs) (limited for disabled and coaches) ➋ ⅚ All parts accessible (lift, induction loop, staff trained in sign language) toilets for disabled ✕ (ex guide dogs) ➡ (advance booking preferred) ◀

TEMPLEPATRICK

Templetown Mausoleum

BT39

Dir: In Castle Upton graveyard on A6, Belfast-Antrim road

Situated in the graveyard of Castle Upton, this family mausoleum is in the shape of a triumphal arch and was designed by Robert Adam. It was built in 1789 by Hon Sarah Upton in memory of the Rt Hon Arthur Upton and features classical urns, leafy swags and circular reliefs. Castle Upton, located close by, is privately owned and not open to the public.

Times: *Open daily during daylight hours.
Facilities: 🅿 🅿 200 yds 🎴

ARMAGH

Armagh County Museum

The Mall East BT61 9BE
☎ 028 3752 3070 🖷 028 3752 2631
🖂 acm.um@nics.gov.uk

Dir: In city centre

The museum is housed in a distinctive building, a 19th-century former schoolhouse, close to the centre if the city. The building also accommodates a library and an art gallery, as well as a collection of local folkcrafts and natural history. The museum's collections reflect the lives of the people of Armagh at home and at work. Special events are planned thoughout the year.

Times: Open all year, Mon-Fri 10-5, Sat 10-1 & 2-5.
Facilities: 🅿 🅿 (500yds) ♿ all parts accessible (entrance, ramp & lift for disabled) toilets for disabled 🐾 (ex guide dogs) 🚌 🚃

CAMLOUGH

Killevy Churches

☎ 028 9023 5000 ▤ 028 9031 0288

Dir: 3m S lower eastern slopes of Slieve Gullion

The ruins of the two churches (10th and 13th century) stand back to back at the foot of Slieve Gullion, sharing a common wall but with no way through from one to the other. The churches stand on the site of an important nunnery founded by St Monenna in the 5th century. A huge granite slab in the graveyard supposedly marks the founder's grave. A holy well can be reached by climbing the path north of the graveyard. The nunnery was in use until the Dissolution in 1542.

Times: *Open all year.
Facilities: よ all parts accessible ⇔

ARDGLASS

Jordan's Castle

☎ 028 9054 6552

Although Ardglass is an important fishing port today, it was once the busiest seaport in Northern Ireland. Between the 14th and 15th centuries a ring of tower houses and fortified warehouses was built to protect the port. Jordan's Castle, a late 15th-century, four-storey tower house situated in the centre of town, is one of these. Besieged in the early 1600s and held for three years, the castle was bought, repaired and filled with bygones by a Belfast solicitor in the early part of this century.

Times: *Open Jul-Aug; Tue, Fri & Sat 10-1, Wed-Thu, 2-6. Other times on request.
Facilities: toilets for disabled ⇔

BALLYWALTER

Grey Abbey

☎ 028 9054 6552

Dir: On E edge of village

Founded in 1193 by Affreca, daughter of the King of the Isle of Man, these extensive ruins of a Cistercian abbey, sitting in lovely sheltered parkland, are among the best preserved in Northern Ireland. The chancel, with its tall lancet windows, magnificent west doorway and an effigy tomb - believed to be Affreca's - in the north wall, are particularly interesting. The abbey was burned down in 1572, and then re-used as a parish church. There are many 17th and 18th-century memorials to be seen in the church ruins, which occupy a pleasant garden setting. The abbey now has a beautiful medieval herb garden, with over 50 varieties of plants, and a visitors' centre.

Times: *Open Apr-Sep; Tue-Sat 10-7, Sun 2-7; Oct-Mar, wknds, Sat 10-4, Sun 2-4.
Facilities: P & all parts accessible toilets for disabled 🚌

CASTLEWELLAN

Drumena Cashel

☎ 028 9023 5000 📄 028 9031 0288

Dir: 2.25m SW

There are many stone ring forts in Northern Ireland, but few so well preserved as Drumena Cashel. Dating back to early Christian times, the fort is 30 metres in diameter and has an 11-metre accessible underground stone-built passage, probably used both as a refuge and for storage. There are also the remains of some beehive huts.

Times: *Open all times
Facilities: P 🚌

Down County Museum

The Mall BT30 6AH
☎ 028 4461 5218 ▤ 028 4461 5590
✉ museum@downdc.gov.uk

Dir: On entry to town follow brown signs to museum

The museum is located in the restored buildings of the 18th-century county gaol, where the regime was tough, the cells crowded, and prisoners subsisted on a diet of potatoes, oatmeal, bread and water. The stories of some of the prisoners, who were transported to Australia, are told through a diorama in the restored cells. The museum also has displays on the history of County Down. Temporary exhibits and special events are a regular feature, and there is also a tea-room and shop.

Times: *Open all year, Mon-Fri 10-5, wknds 1-5
Facilities: ℙ (100yds) ➲ & Ground floor only accessible (wheelchair available, handling boxes on application) toilets for disabled ✷ (ex guide dogs) ➾ (advance booking for guided tours) ➽

Loughinisland Churches

☎ 028 9023 5000 ▤ 028 9031 0288

Dir: 4m W

This remarkable group of three ancient churches stands on an island in the lough, accessible by a causeway. The middle church is the oldest, probably dating back to the 13th century, with a draw-bar hole to secure the door. The large north church was built in the 15th century, possibly to replace the middle church and continued in use until 1720. The smallest and most recent church is the south (MacCartan's) church.

Times: *Open all times
Facilities: ℙ & all parts accessible

HILLSBOROUGH

Hillsborough Fort

☎ 028 9268 3285 🖷 028 9031 0288

On a site that dates back to early Christian times, the existing fort was built in 1650 by Colonel Arthur Hill to command a view of the road from Dublin to Carrickfergus. The building was ornamented in the 18th century. It is set in the lovely Hillsborough Forest Park, which has a lake and way-marked routes providing a number of pleasant walks through the forest.

Times: *Open all year; Apr-Sep, Tue-Sat 10-7, Sun 2-7; Oct-Mar, Tue-Fri 10-4, Sat 10-4, Sun 2-4.,
Facilities: 🅿 ♿ Garden & Grounds only accessible

KILLINCHY

Sketrick Castle

☎ 028 9023 5000 🖷 028 9031 0288

Dir: 3m E on W tip of Sketrick Islands

Sketrick Castle is a badly ruined tall tower house, probably dating from the 15th century. It is located on the west of Sketrick island in Strangford Lough. A raised footpath from the mainland is nearly dry at low tide. The ground floor rooms of the castle include a boat bay and prison. An underground passage leads from the northeast of the bawn to a freshwater spring.

Times: *Open at all times.
Facilities: 🅿 ♿ all parts accessible 🚌

NEWCASTLE

Dundrum Castle

☎ 028 9054 6518

Dir: 4m N

This medieval castle, one of the finest in Ireland, was built in 1777 by John De Courcy in a strategic position overlooking Dundrum Bay, a location that offers visitors fine views over the sea and to the Mourne Mountains. The castle was captured by King John in 1210 and was badly damaged by Cromwellian troops in 1652. Still an impressive ruin, it shows a massive round keep with walls 16 metres high and two metres thick, surrounded by a curtain wall, and a gatehouse which dates from the 13th century.

Times: *Open Apr-Sep, Tue-Sat 10-7, Sun 2-7; Oct-Mar, wknds, Sat 10-4, Sun 2-4.
Facilities: ◘ க Garden & Grounds only accessible toilets for disabled ━

NEWTOWNARDS

Scrabo Tower

Scrabo Country Park 203A Scrabo Road BT23 4SJ
☎ 028 9181 1491 ▤ 028 9182 0695

Dir: 1m W

The 135-foot high Scrabo Tower, one of Northern Ireland's best-known landmarks, dominates the landscape of North Down and is also the centre of a country park around the slopes of Scrabo Hill. The tower has a fascinating series of interpretative diplays about the surrounding countryside, and the viewing platform boasts spectacular views over Strangford Lough and County Down. The park provides walks through fine beech and hazel woodlands, and the unique sandstone quarries show evidence of volcanic activity and are breeding sites for peregrine falcons.

Times: *Open end Mar-mid Sep, Sat-Thu 10.30-6.
Facilities: ◘ toilets for disabled ━

CO FERMANAGH

DERRYGONNELLY

Tully Castle

☎ 028 9054 6552

Dir: 3m N, on W shore of Lower Lough Erne

These are the extensive ruins of a Scottish-style stronghouse with an enclosing bawn overlooking Lough Erne. Built by Sir John Hume in the early 1600s, the castle was destroyed, and most of the occupants slaughtered, by the Maguires in the 1641 Rising. There is a re-creation of a 17th-century garden in the bawn.

Times: *Open Jul & Aug, Wed-Sun, 10-6.
Facilities: 🅿 & Ground floor, Garden & Grounds accessible 🚌

ENNISKILLEN

Monea Castle

☎ 028 9023 5000 📄 028 9031 0288

Dir: 6m NW

A fine example of a plantation castle still with much of its enclosing bawn wall intact, Monea Castle was built around 1618 by the Reverend Malcolm Hamilton, Rector of Devenish. The Scottish design reflects the origin of the builder, and of particular interest is the castle's stone corbelling - the Scottish method of giving additional support to turrets.

Times: *Open at any reasonable time.
Facilities: 🅿 & all parts accessible 🚌

COLERAINE

Mount Sandel

☎ 028 9023 0560 🖹 028 9031 0288

Dir: 1.25m SSE

This 200-foot oval mound overlooking the River Bann is believed to have been fortified in the Iron Age. Nearby is the earliest known inhabited place in Ireland, where post holes and hearths of wooden dwellings, and flint implements dating back to 6,650 BC have been found. The fort was a stronghold of de Courcy in the late 12th century and was re-fortified for artillery in the 17th century.

Times: *Open at all times.
Facilities: 🅿 ♿ all parts accessible 🚌

DUNGIVEN

Banagher Church

☎ 028 9023 5000 🖹 028 9031 0288

Dir: 2m SW

This church was founded by St Muiredach O'Heney in 1100 and altered in later centuries. Today impressive ruins remain. The nave is the oldest part and the square-headed lintelled west door is particularly notable. Just outside, the perfect miniature stone house, complete with pitched roof and the sculpted figures of a saint at the doorway, is believed to be the tomb of St Muiredach. The saint was said to have endowed his large family with the power of bringing good luck. All they had to do was to sprinkle whoever or whatever needed luck with sand taken from the base of the saint's tomb.

Times: *Open at all times.
Facilities: 🅿 ♿ all parts accessible 🚌

DUNGIVEN

Dungiven Priory

☎ 028 9023 5000 📄 028 9031 0288

Dir: SE of town overlooking River Roe

Up until the 17th century, Dungiven was the stronghold of the O'Cahan chiefs and the Augustinian priory, of which extensive ruins remain, was founded by the O'Cahans around 1150. The church, which was altered many times in later centuries, contains one of Northern Ireland's finest medieval tombs. It is the tomb of Cooey na Gall O'Cahan who died in 1385. His sculpted effigy, dressed in Irish armour, lies under a stonework canopy. Below are six kilted warriors.

Times: *Open Church at all times, chancel only when caretaker available. Check at house at end of lane.
Facilities: 🅿 ♿ all parts accessible 🚐

LIMAVADY

Rough Fort

☎ 028 7084 8728 📄 028 7084 8728
🌐 downhillcastle@nationaltrust.org.uk

Dir: 1m W off A2

The Rough Fort is one of the best examples of an earthwork ring fort in Ireland, dating back around 1,000 years. It is an early Christian rath - a fortified farmstead - which is a significant feature of the landscape, in a picturesque location surrounded by pine and beech trees.

Times: *Open at all times.
Facilities: 🐾

City Walls

☎ 028 9023 5000 📄 028 9031 0288

The walls at Londonderry are the finest and most complete city walls to be found in Ireland. The walls date back to the 17th century and stand at 20-25 feet high and are mounted with ancient canon. The walled city is a conservation area with many fine buildings. Visitors can walk round the city ramparts - a circuit of one mile.

Times: *Open all times.
Facilities: 🅿 charged ♿ all parts accessible ⛟

Foyle Valley Railway Museum

Foyle Road BT48 6SQ
☎ 028 7126 5234 📄 028 7137 7633

A collection of relics from the four railway companies which served Londonderry are displayed at the Foyle Valley Railway Heritage Centre. Steam locomotives, diesel railcars and all the paraphernalia of a station can be seen and the Railway Gallery tells the story of the railways. Travel in the historic County Donegal railcars for a trip to the historic mill.

Times: *Open all year, Apr-Sep Mon-Sat 10-5, Sun 2-5; Oct-Mar Mon-Sat 10-4.
Facilities: 🅿 ♿ Ground floor only accessible toilets for disabled ⛟

CO LONDONDERRY/CO TYRONE

MAGHERA

Maghera Church

☎ 028 9023 5000 🖃 028 9031 0288

Dir: E approach to the town

Maghera Church is on the site of an important 6th-century monastery founded by St Lurach, which later became a bishop's see and finally a parish church. The much-altered church has a magnificently decorated 12th-century west door, and a cross-carved stone to the west of the church is supposed to be the grave of the founder.

Times: *Key from Leisure Centre.
Facilities: 🅿 ♿ all parts accessible 🚗

ARDBOE

Ardboe Cross

☎ 028 9023 5000 🖃 028 9031 0288

Dir: Off B73

Situated at Ardboe Point, on the western shore of Lough Neagh, is the best example of a high cross to be found in Northern Ireland. Marking the site of an ancient monastery, the cross has 22 sculpted panels, many recognisably biblical, including Adam and Eve and the Last Judgement. It stands over 18 feet high and dates back to the 10th century. It is still the rallying place of the annual Lammas, but praying at the cross and washing in the lake has been replaced by traditional music-making, singing and selling of local produce. The tradition of 'cross reading' or interpreting the pictures on the cross, is an honour passed from generation to generation among the men of the village.

Times: *Open at all times.
Facilities: 🅿 ♿ all parts accessible 🚗

BEAGHMORE

Beaghmore Stone Circles and Alignments

☎ 028 9023 5000 🖹 028 9031 0288

Discovered in the 1930s, these impressive, ritualistic stones have been dated back to the early Bronze Age, or maybe even the Neolithic Age. There are three pairs of stone circles, one single circle, stone rows or alignments and cairns, which range in height from one to four feet. This is an area littered with historic monuments, many discovered by people cutting turf.

Times: *Open at all times.
Facilities: 🅿 ♿ all parts accessible

BENBURB

Benburb Castle

☎ 028 9023 5000 🖹 028 9031 0288

The castle ruins - three towers and massive walls - are dramatically placed on a cliff-edge 120 feet above the River Blackwater. The northwest tower is newly restored and has dizzy cliff-edge views. The castle, built by Sir Richard Wingfield around 1615, is actually situated in the grounds of the Servite Priory. There are attractive walks down to the river.

Times: *Castle grounds open at all times. Special arrangements, made in advance, necessary for access to flanker tower.
Facilities: 🅿 ♿ Ground floor, Garden & Grounds accessible 🚍

CASTLECAULFIELD

Castle Caulfield

☎ 028 9023 5000 🖷 028 9031 0288

Sir Toby Caulfield, an Oxfordshire knight and ancestor of the Earls of Charlemont, built this manor house in 1619 on the site of an ancient fort. It was badly burnt in 1641, repaired and lived in by the Caulfield/Charlemont family until 1670. It boasts the rare distinction of having had Saint Oliver Plunkett and John Wesley preach in its grounds. Some fragments of the castle are re-used in the fine, large 17th-century parish church.

Times: *Open at all times.
Facilities: P & all parts accessible 🚍

COOKSTOWN

Tullaghoge Fort

☎ 028 9023 5000 🖷 028 9031 0288

Dir: 2m S

This large hilltop earthwork, planted with trees, was once the headquarters of the O'Hagans, Chief Justices of the old kingdom of Tyrone. Between the 12th and 16th centuries the O'Neill Chiefs of Ulster were also crowned here - the King Elect was seated on a stone inauguration chair, new sandals were placed on his feet and he was then anointed and crowned. The last such ceremony was held here in the 1590s; in 1600 the stone throne was destroyed by order of Lord Mountjoy.

Times: *Open at all times.
Facilities: P 🚍

MOUNTJOY

Mountjoy Castle

Magheralamfield
☎ 028 9023 5000 📄 028 9031 0288

Dir: 3m SE, off B161

These are the ruins of an early 17th-century brick and stone fort, with four rectangular towers, overlooking Lough Neagh. The fort was built for Lord Deputy Mountjoy during his campaign against Hugh O'Neill, Earl of Tyrone. It was captured and re-captured by the Irish and English during the 17th century and was also used by the armies of James II and William III.

Times: *Open at all times.
Facilities: 🅿 🚍

NEWTOWNSTEWART

Harry Avery's Castle

☎ 028 9023 5000 📄 028 9031 0288

Dir: 0.75m SW

The hilltop ruins of a Gaelic stone castle, built around the 14th century by one of the O'Neill chiefs, are the remains of the oldest surviving Irish-built castle in the north. Only the great twin towers of the gatehouse are left. A new stairway enables the public to gain access to one of these.

Times: *Open at all times.

CO TYRONE

CARRIGTWOHILL

Fota Arboretum & Gardens

Fota Estate
☎ 021 4812728 📄 021 4812728

Dir: 14km from Cork on Cobh road

Fota Arboretum contains an extensive collection of trees and shrubs extending over an area of approx 27 acres and includes features such as an ornamental pond and Italian walled gardens. The collection includes many tender plants that could not be grown at inland locations, with many examples of exotic plants from the Southern Hemisphere.

Times: *Open 1st wknd Apr-Oct, daily, Mon-Sat 9-6 & Sun 11-6; Nov-Mar, daily, Mon-Sat 9-5, Sun 11-5. Closed Xmas.
Facilities: 🅿 charged & Ground floor, Garden & Grounds accessible toilets for disabled 🚐

BALLYSHANNON

The Water Wheels

Abbey Assaroe
☎ 071 9851580

Dir: Cross Abbey River on Rossnowlagh Rd, next turning L & follow signs

Abbey Assaroe was founded by Cistercian Monks from Boyle Abbey in the late 12th century, who excelled in water engineering and canalised the river to turn water wheels for mechanical power. There are two restored 12th-century mills; one is used as a coffee shop and restaurant, and the other houses a small museum related to the history of the Cistercians. Some interesting walks can be taken in the vicinity.

Times: *Open May-Oct, daily 10.30-6.30
Facilities: 🅿 🅿 (200mtrs) (narrow road) 🍴 ✕ (licenced) & All parts accessible toilets for disabled 🚐 40/50 people

ARDARA

Ardara Heritage Centre

The Diamond
☎ 074 9541704 📄 074 9541381

The Heritage Centre offers information about this fabulous region of mountain passes, forests, lakes and historical landmarks. It is an area rich in folklore and archaeology, as well as a cultural centre for traditional music. Ardara is the heart of Ireland's manufacture of handwoven tweed, handmade knitwear and hand loomed woollens, and there are many craft and factory shops as well as exhibitions within the heritage centre.

Times: *Open Apr-Sep, 10-6.
Facilities: 🅿 🅿 (100 yards) 🍽 ✕ 🚻 Ground floor only accessible toilets for disabled ✕ (ex guide dogs) 🚼

DUBLIN

National Gallery of Ireland

Merrion Square
☎ 01 6615133 📄 01 6615372
✉ artgall@eircom.net

Dir: 5 mins walk from Pearse Station

The gallery, founded in 1854 by an Act of Parliament, houses the national collections of Irish art and European Old Masters from the 14th to the 20th centuries, including work by Caravaggio, Poussin, El Greco, Roderic O'Conor, and the Yeats'. A feature of the gallery is a display of 50 portraits of Irish men and women who have made a particular contribution to their country, socially, politically or culturally, including 'Image of Bono' by Louis le Brocquy.

Times: *Open all year, Mon-Sat 10-5.30 (Thu 10-8.30), Sun 2-5. Closed 24-26 Dec & Good Fri.
Facilities: 🅿 (5 mins walk) (meter parking, 2hrs max) ✕ (licenced) 🚻 all parts accessible (Braille/audio tours, lifts, ramps, parking bay) toilets for disabled 🚼 (must be supervised)

DUBLIN

National Library of Ireland

Kildare Street
☎ 01 6030200 📄 01 6766690

The National Library of Wales was founded in 1877 and is based on collections from The Royal Dublin Society. It holds an estimated five million items, including collections of printed books, manuscripts, prints and drawings, photos, maps, newspapers, mircofilms and ephemera. The library's research facilities are open to all those with genuine research needs. A genealogy service is also available, and there is a regular programme of exhibitions open to the public.

Times: *Open all year, Mon-Wed 10-9, Thu-Fri 10-5 & Sat 10-1. Closed Sun, BHs, Good Fri & 23 Dec-2 Jan.
Facilities: & Ground floor, Garden & Grounds accessible toilets for disabled ✕ (ex guide dogs)

DUBLIN

National Photographic Archive

Meeting House Square Temple Bar
☎ 01 6030200 📄 01 6777451
✉ photoarchive@nli.ie

Dir: Opposite The Gallery of Photography

The National Photographic Archive, which is part of the National Library of Ireland, was opened in 1998 in an award-winning building in the Temple Bar area of Dublin. The archive holds an unrivalled collection of photographic images relating to Irish history, topography and cultural and social life. The collection is especially rich in late 19th and early 20th century topographical views and studio portraits, but also includes photographs taken during the Rebellion of 1916 and the subsequent War of Independence and Civil War, as well as other historic events.

Times: *Open all year, Mon-Fri 10-5. (Closed BH's, Good Fri & 23 Dec-2 Jan).
Facilities: & all parts accessible toilets for disabled ✕ (ex guide dogs) 🚗 (prior notice required) 🔷

The Chester Beatty Library

The Clock Tower Building Dublin Castle
☎ 01 4070750 📄 01 4070760
✆ info@cbl.ie

Dir: 10 mins walk from Trinity College, up Dame St towards Christ Church Cathedral

The contents of this fascinating gallery were bequeathed to Ireland by its first honorary citizen, American mining engineer and collector, Sir Alfred Chester Beatty (1875-1968). The collection includes manuscripts, prints, icons, miniatures and objets d'art of great importance from 2700 BC to the present day. See illuminated copies of the Qur'an and the Bible, Egyptian papyrus texts and Buddhist paintings.

Times: *Open all year, May-Sep, Mon-Fri 10-5; Oct-Apr, Tue-Fri 10-5, Sat 11-5, Sun 1-5. Closed BHs.
Facilities: P (5mins walk) ● ✕ & all parts accessible toilets for disabled ✖ (ex guide dogs) ● (must contact in advance)

Howth Castle Rhododendron Gardens

Howth
☎ 01 8322624 & 📄 01 8392405
✆ sales@deerpark.iol.ie

Dir: 9m NE of city centre, by coast road to Howth. Before Howth follow signs for Deer Park Hotel

Howth Castle, on the northern boundary of Dublin Bay, is justly famous for its gardens and especially for its rhododendron walk. The walk is open all year, but is at its best in May and June. There are lovely views north to the Mourne Mountains and to the west of Dublin Bay.

Times: *Open all year, daily 8am-dusk. Closed 25 Dec.
Facilities: P & (steep hills unsuitable, ramped entrance) toilets for disabled ✖ (ex guide dogs) ● ●

DUBLIN

Hugh Lane Municipal Gallery of Modern Art

Charlemont House Parnell Square
☎ 01 8741903 📄 01 8722182
✉ info@hughlane.ie

Situated in Charlemont House, a fine Georgian building, the gallery's exhibits include one of the most extensive collections of 20th-century Irish art. A superb range of international and Irish paintings, sculpture, works on paper and stained glass is also on show. There are public lectures every Sunday and regular concerts (at noon on Sundays) throughout the year.

Times: *Open all year, Tue-Thu 9.30-6, Fri-Sat 9.30-5, Sun 11-5. Late night opening Thu until 8, Apr-Aug only. Closed Mon, Good Fri & 24-25 Dec.
Facilities: ℙ (100mtrs) (meter parking) 🍽 ♿ all parts accessible (ramp & reserved parking) toilets for disabled 🐾 (ex guide dogs) 🚗

DUBLIN

Irish Museum of Modern Art

Royal Hospital Military Road Kilmainham
☎ 01 6129900 📄 01 6129999
✉ info@imma.ie

Dir: 3.5km from city centre, just off N7 opposite Heuston Station

Housed in the Royal Hospital Kilmainham, an impressive 17th-century building, the Irish Museum of Modern Art is Ireland's leading national institution for the collection and presentation of modern and contemporary art. The museum presents a wide variety of art and artists' ideas in a dynamic programme of exhibitions, which regularly includes bodies of work from the museum's own collection – its award-winning Education and Community Department and the Studio and National Programmes.

Times: Open all year Tue-Sat 10-5.30, Sun & BHs 12-5.30. Closed Mon & 24-26 Dec.
Facilities: ℙ ℙ (100yds) (parking in allocated C/P only) 🍽 (licenced) ♿ All parts accessible toilets for disabled 🐾 (ex guide dogs) 🚗

National Botanic Gardens

Glasnevin
☎ 01 8374388 📄 01 8360080

Dir: On Botanic Road, between N1 and N2

Ireland's premier Botanic Gardens, cover a total area of 19.5 hectares (48 acres), part of which is the natural flood plain of the River Tolka. The gardens contain a large plant collection, which includes approximately 20,000 species and cultivated varieties. There are four ranges of glasshouses including the recently restored Curvilinear Range. Notable features include herbaceous borders, the rose garden, rockery, alpine yard, arboretum, extensive shrub collections and wall plants.

Times: *Open all year, Gardens: Summer Mon-Sat 9-6, Sun 11-6; Winter Mon-Sat 10-4.30, Sun 11-4.30. (Closed 25 Dec). Glasshouses: Summer Mon-Wed & Fri 9-5, Thu 9-3.15, Sat 9-5.45, Sun 2-5.45; Winter, Mon-Wed, Fri & Sat 10-4.15, Thu 10-3.15, Sun 2-4.15.
Facilities: 🅿 charged 🅿 ☕ & all parts accessible toilets for disabled ✖ (ex guide dogs)

Natural History Museum

Merrion Street
☎ 01 6777444 📄 01 6777828
📧 education.nmi@indigo.ie

Dir: In city centre

The Natural History Museum, which is part of The National Museum of Ireland, is a zoological museum containing diverse collections of world wildlife. The Irish Room, on the ground floor, is devoted largely to Irish mammals, sea creatures and insects. It includes the extinct giant Irish deer and the skeleton of a basking shark. The World Collection has as the centre-piece the skeleton of a 60-foot whale suspended from the roof. Other displays include the Giant Panda and a Pygmy Hippopotamus.

Times: *Open all year, Tue-Sat 10-5, Sun 2-5. Closed Mon, Xmas day & Good Fri
Facilities: 🅿 (parking meters wkdays) ⛟

CO DUBLIN

SKERRIES

Skerries Mills

☎ 01 8495208 📠 01 8495213
📧 skerriesmills@indigo.ie

Dir: Signed off M1

Skerries Mills is a collection of restored mills, including a watermill, a five-sail and a four-sail windmill, all in working order. The site dates from the 16th century and was originally part of a monastic establishment. It came into private ownership in 1538, and a bakery has been there since 1840. Nature lovers will enjoy the millpond and nearby wetlands.

Times: Open Apr-Sep, daily 10.30-5.30; 2 Jan-Mar & Oct-19 Dec, daily 10.30-4.30. Closed Good Fri
Facilities: 🅿 ♿ toilets for disabled 🚆 🚆

GALWAY

Royal Tara China Visitor Centre

Tara Hall Mervue
☎ 91 705602 📠 091 757574
📧 mkilroy@royal-tara.com

Dir: N6 from Tourist Office. At rdbt take 2nd L & at lights turn R

Royal Tara China Visitor Centre, located minutes from Galway City Centre, operates from a 17th-century house set in five acres of grounds. Here you can see craftspeople at work on the internationally renowned hand-made china. There are seven guided tours a day between 9.30am and 3.30pm, Monday to Friday, with an audio visual presentation on Saturday and Sunday. The tours enable visitors to see the full process of china production (groups should book ahead). Five factory showrooms display an extensive collection of Royal Tara giftware and tableware.

Times: Open all year, Mon-Sat 9-6, Sun 10-5
Facilities: 🅿 ♿ All parts accessible (all facilities accessible for disabled) toilets for disabled ✈ (ex guide dogs) 🚆 🚆

ROUNDSTONE

Roundstone Music, Crafts & Fashion

Craft Centre
☎ 95 35875 📄 095 35980
✉ bodhran@iol.ie

Dir: N59 from Galway to Clifden. After approx 50m turn L at Roundstone sign, 7m to village. Attraction at top of village

The Roundstone Music Craft and Fashion shop is located within the walls of an old Franciscan Monastery. Here you can see Ireland's oldest craft, the making of the Bodhran drum. Regular talks and demonstrations are also given. The first River Dance stage drums were made here and are still on display in the 'Craftsman's Craftshop'. There is an outdoor picnic area alongside the bell tower in a beautiful location by the water, where the dolphins swim up to the wall in summer.

Times: Open Apr-Oct 9.30-6, Jul-Sep 9-7, Winter 6 days 9.30-6.
Facilities: P P (50yds) 🍽 (licenced) & all parts accessible toilets for disabled ✕ (ex guide dogs) 🚌

MONAGHAN

Monaghan County Museum

1-2 Hill Street
☎ 47 82928 📄 047 71189
✉ comuseum@monghancoco.ie

Dir: Near town centre, opposite market house exhibition galleries

This award winning museum was first opened in 1974 and was originally housed in the Courthouse in the centre of town. Following a fire which gutted the building the collection was moved to temporary accommodation at Saint Macartan's College. The museum was officially re-opened in 1990 in its current location, a conversion of two large town houses at 1-2 Hill Street. The museum's collection includes exhibits of local archaeology, history, arts and crafts, and throughout the year various special exhibitions take place.

Times: *Open Tue-Fri 10-1 & 2-5 Sat 11-1 & 2-5. Closed Sun & Mon
Facilities: P (near town centre) (restricted on-street parking) & Ground floor only accessible ✕ (ex guide dogs) 🚌 (pre-booking required)

CASHEL

Brú Ború Heritage Centre

☎ 62 61122 🖹 062 62700
✉ bruboru@comhaltas.com

Dir: Below Rock of Cashel in town

At the foot of the Rock of Cashel, a 4th-century stone fort, this heritage centre is dedicated to the study and celebration of native Irish music, song, dance, story telling, theatre and Celtic studies. There's the Folk Theatre where three performances are held daily in the summer, and in the evening, banquets evoke the Court of Brian Ború, 11th-century High King of Ireland, with songs, poems and sagas, promoted by Comhaltas Ceoltóirí Éireann. There is also a subterranean, 'Sounds of History', experience.

Times: *Open Jan-May & Oct-Dec, Mon-Fri 9-5; Jun-Sep Tue-Sat 9-11, Sun-Mon 9-5.
Facilities: 🅿 charged 🍽 ✕ ♿ all parts accessible (wheelchair bay in theatre) toilets for disabled 🐕 (ex guide dogs) 🚼

WEXFORD

Wexford Wildfowl Reserve

North Slob
☎ 53 23129 🖹 053 24785

Dir: 8km NE from Wexford

Wexford Wildfowl Reserve is a natural haven for birds in its coastal location on the coast at its closest point to Britain and the Continent, and is of international importance for Greenland white-fronted geese, brent geese, Bewick's swans and wigeon. It is a superb place for birdwatching and visitors have use of several hides, including a tower hide. The visitor centre has recently been revamped and features an attractive interpretive display.

Times: *Open all year, Etr-Sep, daily 9-6; Oct-Etr, daily 10-5. Closed 25 Dec. Other hours by arrangement.
Facilities: 🅿 ♿ Ground floor, Garden & Grounds accessible toilets for disabled 🐕 (ex guide dogs) 🚼 (pre-booking essential)